How to Use This Book

Look at this information through the lens of *your* context.

The best way to manage greywater depends on your goals, climate, soil, etc. So, we've tried to make it easy to take different paths through this book, including skipping or skimming advice that doesn't apply to you.

Sections that apply only to certain goals or conditions start with a note describing who they apply to and suggesting where to skip to if it's not you.

- ❖ **Most houses are suitable for a Laundry to Landscape system**, some for a Branched Drain as well; all the other systems combined apply in ¼ of projects.
- ❖ **If you just want a simple system**—You can skip most of the book, reading only the sections marked "greywater basics," thusly. (Skip to p. 2 now if you like.)
- ❖ **If you are in a big hurry**—Skip to the System Selection Chart, p. 52. If one of the simple systems will work for you, read about that system in Chapter 7 and you may be done. If not, then go back to Chapter 2, and take it from there.
- ❖ **For new construction or remodeling**—Permits will be a factor, and you will require our *Builder's Greywater Guide* as well (see inside back cover). That book is also recommended if you are a tradesperson, regulator, or academic.
- ❖ **Outside the US**—Parts and rules may be different. For village conditions, see p. 137.
- ❖ **For a complex or difficult installation**—We suggest you read the book straight through.

Of course, we'd love for you to read every word regardless, and you'll wind up with a well-rounded greywater education if you do. Good luck with your project!

Continue p. 2

Cover Photo Key

Branched Drain greywater system in city of Santa Barbara, California (Real World Example #1).

Snowbound greywater greenhouse with winter greens in Massachusetts.

Greywater-irrigated lawn in million-dollar landscape.

Testing soil percolation rate.

Bathhouse and greywater-nurtured oasis.

Mexican village women turning greywater into fruit and shade.

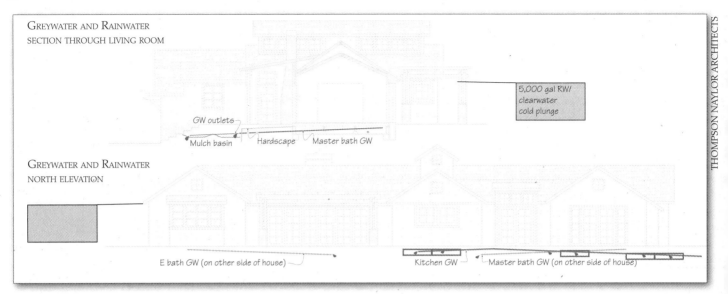

GREYWATER AND RAINWATER
SECTION THROUGH LIVING ROOM

5,000 gal RW/
clearwater
cold plunge

GW outlets

Mulch basin   Hardscape   Master bath GW

GREYWATER AND RAINWATER
NORTH ELEVATION

E bath GW (on other side of house)   Kitchen GW   Master bath GW (on other side of house)

THOMPSON NAYLOR ARCHITECTS

A drawing that shows elevation relationships is a great design aid. This one shows how elevations of greywater outlets, infiltration chambers, and a gravity-flow rainwater tank could work on a flat lot.

Acknowledgments

The average word or image in this book has been weighed by a dozen editors, a dozen times each! Thanks to Ted Adams, Michael Andrews, Sharin Kurstin, and Andrea Lara for their plumbing guidance; Larry Farwell, Val Little, Mimi Stewart, Melissa McDonald, Paul Paryski, Laura Allen, Brad Lancaster, and Alison Jordan for their work legalizing greywater systems; Robert Kourik for his pioneering dissemination of greywater information; the numerous greywater system suppliers and users who shared their experiences and ideas, including Karen Ferguson at Geoflow, Steve Bilson at ReWater, Harold Ball and Sandra Huffstutter at Orenco, Barbara Wishengrad at Sweetwater, Fred Hunter at Dreamscape, Laura Allen at Greywater Action, and Michael Ogden at Natural Systems International; Gayla Groom, Kate Herman, Michael G. Smith, and Christina Sava for tireless editing persistence; Parker Abercrombie, Joseph Marshall, Kaj Hoffman, and Maya Shoemaker for graphics and layout work; Michelle Howard and Amanda Sarkis for book production, marketing, and office magic; and Lynn Shoemaker for guidance and support of all kinds.

Skye, 13 year old graphics wizard.

Photo, Drawing Credits

Cover photos: main photo—Kaj Hoffman; greenhouse photo—Clivus; back cover Oasis Team photo—Chris Henrey. All photos not otherwise credited are by Art Ludwig. Drawings not otherwise credited are Art/Parker collaborations.

Legal Disclaimer

About Our Eco-Logical Book Design

Our books evolve in response to goals like those that shape our other designs: How can we improve our readers' success? How can we deliver more, better information with fewer trees cut and less cost?

There may seem to be as much information in our books as in others that are two or three times as big...because there is! A lot of thought goes into designing our books to conserve resources. This book uses 90% less virgin pulp than it would with industry standard specs. The inside pages are **100% post-consumer (PC),** chlorine-free recycled paper. (We're still working on the cover stock.) Recycled paper uses 64% less energy, 50% less water, and 100% less trees. It creates 74% less air pollution and five times more jobs than paper from virgin pulp. Additional savings come from making the layout paper-efficient. ("Recycled," usually 20–30% PC, is more common than 100% PC because the latter costs 30% more, even though it saves a great deal of external costs.)

Published by:
Oasis Design
Santa Barbara, CA

oasisdesign.net/greywater
Check our website for more info and updates.

Cost figures are 2015 US dollars unless otherwise noted.

ISBN 978-0-9643433-3-7 20th revision, 6th edition
Copyright © 1991–2023, Art Ludwig.
All rights reserved. Honor System for Use of Oasis Design Innovations and Content: oasisdesign.net/about/fairuse

What This Book Is About

Create an Oasis with Greywater describes how to choose, build, and use 20 types of residential greywater reuse systems in just about any context: urban, rural, or village. It explains how you can put together a simple greywater system in an afternoon for under $50. It also includes information for taking your greywater reuse to the next level: integrating it with water efficiency, rainwater use, and food production. This book includes:

❖ how to clarify your goals, and how various greywater system options can serve you
❖ the same Site Assessment Form and procedures I use for my design consulting
❖ common mistakes and how to avoid them
❖ greywater plumbing principles and procedures in detail
❖ information on soils and plants, tools and parts
❖ several of our own original design innovations to improve greywater systems' longevity, simplify maintenance, and reduce environmental impacts
❖ real life examples of greywater designs for a wide range of contexts

This book offers underlying design principles as well as design specifics. If you run into a situation not specifically covered, you'll likely be able to use these general principles to figure it out yourself.

Most of the world's aquifers are being pumped faster than replenished, and all reservoirs are slowly diminishing in capacity as they fill with sediment. At the same time, natural surface waters and groundwaters are being degraded by the wastewater continually dumped into them. Greywater reuse enables you personally to do more with the same amount of water and to increase your water security. At the same time, your greywater reuse reduces the problems of supply and pollution for everyone.

Any greywater system will realize some benefits. Obtaining *all* the potential benefits is trickier than it seems. Many pitfalls await the unwary. In the average installation, this book will pay for itself many times over in savings on construction, maintenance, and errors avoided.

Most of the information otherwise available on greywater comes from vendors. Oasis Design doesn't sell greywater systems, so you don't have to worry that we're steering you toward stuff you don't need. Rather, we make our living by providing accurate information to help people have a higher quality of life with lower environmental impact.

Wishing you the best of luck with your projects,

Art Ludwig

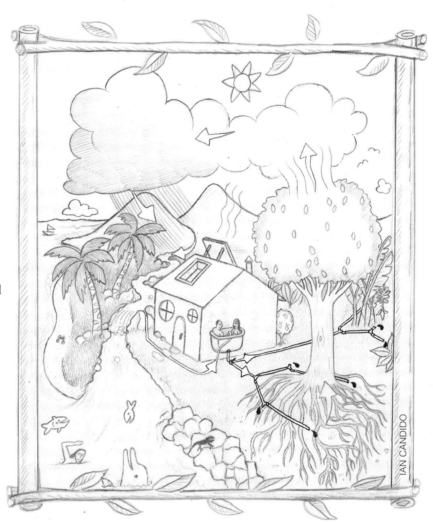

Humans enjoying responsible stewardship of their part of the water cycle.

Contents

What Do C, I, and R Mean?

C: Collection plumbing
I: Irrigation piping
R: Receiving landscape

These are the parts that together make a complete greywater system.

Diversion setup for simple, high-performance Laundry to Landscape system (p. 58).

Figures and Tables

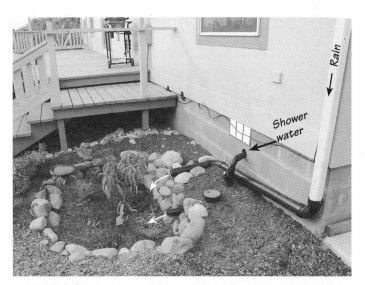

Mulch-filled greywater/rainwater basin nourishes a peach tree in Arizona.

The downspout extension is for rain. The pipe exiting the foundation is shower greywater, which splits between this and another basin via a Branched Drain (outlet in rock work). The tree is planted on an island in the middle to keep the root crown dry. (In all but the driest climates, rainwater should be movable and divertable away from the greywater basins to avoid overflow or saturation.)

Introduction

On Christmas Eve of the year I turned 16, my present to the family was to move into a decaying tack room in the lower reaches of our backyard. The facilities consisted of a lone garden faucet outside. If I could deal with a lack of plumbing while backpacking, I reasoned, I could deal with this. The ecocidal adult establishment thought it needed all that overengineered infrastructure, but I surely didn't.

To my family's delight, I maintained an independent household based on the faucet and later improvements (wood-heated outdoor bathtub, etc.). In fact, my systems became so refined I didn't leave until I had a wife and a two year old daughter, 14 years later.

During a break in my backyard stay, I bicycled around the world for three years, studying myriad philosophies of wastewater management. Later, I studied ecological design at UC Berkeley. My thesis was that *every house should be surrounded by an oasis of biological productivity nourished by the flow of nutrients and water from the home.* Most elements added to water in the home are nutritious for plants; if the small amount of toxins in cleaners could be eliminated, washwater could nurture an edible landscape sustainably.

However, I found that cleaners bio*compatible* with plants or soil were not available. But through my research, I learned enough, and befriended enough experts, to assemble a team to create the world's first plant and soil biocompatible cleaners.

Meanwhile, my hometown of Santa Barbara, in an advanced stage of drying up and blowing away due to prolonged drought, became the first locale in the nation to legalize greywater use for irrigation. Consequently, I took a six-year side trip to develop, produce, and market Oasis Biocompatible Cleaners, launched in Santa Barbara on Earth Day, 1990.

The amount of time that my staff and I spent answering questions about greywater plumbing became untenable, so I wrote the first edition of this book. I sold the cleaner business in 1996 and have been innovating, consulting, writing, and helping develop policy since then. The Oasis greywater books evolved from an incidental to the main part of our business today. Oasis Design has walked central, neutral ground between warring factions during sweeping changes in the emergent greywater industry. Our customers entrust us with their darkest greywater secrets, system manufacturers keep us abreast of their offerings, academics appreciate our research, and, as we have become the world's greywater "information central," regulators seek us out for help writing plumbing codes.

People have schlepped greywater around in buckets since time immemorial. However, the modern generation of systems, which attempt automated, efficient delivery, have been in use only a few decades. Legal requirements favor engineering overkill, while the simple and economical methods—the ones that people actually use—remain technically illegal. Happily, starting with visionary jurisdictions such as Arizona, followed by several more states, there is a strong trend toward rational regulation.[4] Still, most government agencies and contractors know little about practical greywater systems. And, in jurisdictions where practical systems remain illegal, they can't help you anyway. This information void leaves hundreds of thousands of do-it-yourselfers to "reinvent the wheel" with little useful guidance.

Oasis Design's books have filled this void since 1991. This edition of *Create an Oasis*—the world's most popular greywater book*—incorporates all this collective wisdom, several of my original designs, and experiences from major droughts and changing climate in one comprehensive design and installation manual. (Our *Builder's Greywater Guide,* which covers permits, professional installation, and greywater science, remains separate.) With nine times the information as in the first edition, this book presents guiding principles for breaking new ground, as well as an expanded range of proven designs and practices, legal and not yet legal, ancient and experimental. The aim is to help you design not just for drought, but also for flood, fire, food production, economic resilience, and climate safety.

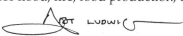

Art Ludwig
San Jose Creek, Santa Barbara, California

Greywater reuse follows the same principles that make wild rivers clean, even though they drain many square miles of dirt, worms, and feces. Beneficial bacteria break down nasties into water-soluble plant food, and the plants eat it, leaving pure water. The author is shown here deeply absorbed in his tireless study of this fascinating process.

---

*This book is frequently the #1 landscape book on Amazon. It and our Water Storage *book have been taking turns as the #1 plumbing book. They have been near the top of these lists since it first occurred to us to check in 2007.*

Chapter 1: Greywater Basics

First, let's get your feet wet (so to speak)—what is greywater, what can you do with it, why, how, and some greywater lingo.

What Is Greywater?

Any wastewater generated in the home, except water from toilets, is called greywater. Dish, shower, sink, and laundry greywater comprise 50–80% of residential "wastewater." Greywater may be reused for other purposes, especially landscape irrigation.

Toilet-flush water is called blackwater. A few systems that can safely recycle toilet water are included in this book.

Contaminated or difficult-to-handle greywater, such as solids-laden kitchen sink water or water used to launder diapers, I call "dark greywater"; most US regulators consider these blackwater. However, the level of pathogens in even the darkest greywater is a small fraction of that in blackwater.[1]

Wastewater without added solids, such as warmup water from the hot water faucet, reverse osmosis purifier drain water, or refrigerator compressor drip, is called clearwater.

Reclaimed water is highly treated mixed municipal greywater plus blackwater, usually piped to large-volume users such as golf courses via a separate distribution system. There are ecological reservations about this practice, which is outside the scope of this book.

"Any wastewater not generated from toilet flushing" is the official greywater definition commonly used in Europe and Australia.

—Water Environment Research Foundation[41]

What Can You Do with Greywater?

Conventional plumbing systems dispose of greywater via septic tanks or sewers. The many drawbacks of this practice include overloading treatment systems, contaminating natural waters with poorly treated effluent, and high ecological/economic cost.[2]

Instead, you can reuse this water. The most common reuse of greywater is for irrigation—the focus of this book. It can also be cascaded to toilet flushing or laundry. Even a greywater-only dispersal system has less negative impact than septic/sewer dispersal, because the beneficial bacteria and roots in the topsoil are better than anything else at treating water.

Why Use Greywater?

It is said that there is no such thing as "waste," just misplaced resources. Greywater systems turn "wastewater" and its nutrients into useful resources. Why irrigate with drinking water when most plants thrive on used water containing small bits of compost?

Unlike many ecological stopgap measures, greywater use is part of the fundamental solution to many ecological problems. It will probably remain an essential feature of ecological houses in the distant future. The benefits of greywater recycling include:

❖ **Reduced use of freshwater**—Greywater can replace freshwater for some uses. This saves money and increases the effective water supply, especially in regions where irrigation is needed. Residential water use, on average, is almost evenly split between indoors and outdoors. Most water used indoors can be reused outdoors for irrigation, achieving the same result with less water diverted from nature.

❖ **Less strain on septic tanks or treatment plants**—Greywater, which comprises the majority of the wastewater stream, contains vastly fewer pathogens than blackwater and 90% less nitrogen (a nutrient that is a problematic water pollutant). Reducing a septic system's flow by getting greywater out greatly extends its service life and capacity. For municipal treatment systems, decreased flow means higher treatment effectiveness and lower costs.

❖ **More effective purification**—Greywater is purified to a spectacularly high degree in the upper, most biologically active region of the soil. This protects the quality of natural surface and groundwaters. Topsoil is a purification engine many times more powerful than engineered treatment plants, or even septic systems, which discharge wastewater into the subsoil, below most of the treatment capacity.[3]

❖ **Feasibility for sites unsuitable for a septic tank**—For sites with slow soil percolation or other problems, a greywater system can partially or completely substitute for a costly, over-engineered septic system. (In extreme cases this can enable otherwise undevelopable lots to be built on—a double-edged sword environmentally.)

Greywater Lingo, Measurements

Words with squiggly underline you'll find defined in the text and cross-referenced in the Index. Where a figure does a good job of illustrating a term it's flagged with squiggly underline there, too.

Unfamiliar measurement? Metric user? See Appendix H: Measurements and Conversions.

❖ **Reduced use of energy and chemicals**—This is due to reduced pumping and treatment of freshwater and wastewater. If you provide your own water or electricity, you'll benefit directly from lessening this burden. Also, turning washwater into fruit definitely encourages you to dump less toxins down the drain.

❖ **Groundwater recharge**—Greywater application in excess of plant needs recharges aquifers. Abundant groundwater keeps springs flowing between rains.

❖ **Plant growth**—Greywater can support a flourishing landscape where irrigation water might otherwise not be available.

❖ **Reclamation of nutrients**—Loss of nutrients through wastewater dispersal in rivers or oceans is a subtle but highly significant form of erosion. Reclaiming otherwise wasted nutrients in greywater helps to maintain the land's fertility.[2,3]

❖ **Increased awareness of, and sensitivity to, natural cycles**—The greywater user, by having a reason to pay more attention to seasonal progression, water circulation between Earth and sky, and plants' needs, benefits intangibly but greatly by participating directly in the wise husbandry of vital global nutrient and water cycles.

❖ **Just because**—Greywater is fairly harmless and great fun to experiment with. Moreover, life with alternative waste treatment is less expensive and more interesting.

When Not to Use Greywater

There are a number of possible reasons *not* to use greywater, or to use it only at certain times:

❖ **Insufficient space**—In some situations, neighbors are too close, or the yard too small or nonexistent. (However, even a tiny suburban lot with lots of people may be able to process greywater. There is also indoor greywater reuse. The latter is mostly outside of the scope of this book, but see Appendix F and <u>oasisdesign.net/greywater/indoors</u>.)

❖ **Inaccessible drainpipes**—If all plumbing is entombed under a concrete slab, accessing most of the greywater won't be economical (but you can almost always get at the laundry water, and a combined wastewater reuse system may work).

❖ **Unsuitable soil**—Soil that is either extremely permeable or impermeable may preclude the use of a greywater system, or at least require special adaptations.

❖ **Unsuitable climate**—In very wet climates, where using greywater for irrigation is of little benefit, better ways to dispose of it may be available. In very cold climates, freezing may prevent the use of a greywater system for part of the year (but see Appendix C).

❖ **Legality concerns and/or permit hassles**—In much of the industrialized world, the legality of greywater systems is a "grey" area. There is movement toward a less paranoid, more realistic official attitude, concurrent with increased experience and improved systems, not to mention water shortages and pollution problems. For example, all of the systems described here are legal in several states including Arizona, New Mexico, and Texas.[4] In the rest of the US, the trend is toward allowing the most practical greywater systems. Authorities generally turn a blind eye toward greywater use even where illegal. The State of California, for example, once published a pamphlet that explained the illegality of greywater use but then explained how to do it—and get a tax credit for it![6]

❖ **Health concerns**—In many areas, the rationale for keeping greywater illegal is supposed concern for public health. In practice, the health threat from greywater has proven insignificant. There isn't a single documented instance of a person in the US becoming ill from greywater. A quantitative field test by the Department of Water Reclamation in Los Angeles found that greywatered soil did teem with pathogens—but so did the tap water–irrigated control soil. The study's conclusion: don't eat dirt, with or without greywater.[5] (Health concerns are considered on p. 18, and in detail in the *Builder's Greywater Guide*.)

❖ **Poor cost-benefit ratio**—In some situations, especially when legal requirements mandate a complex system for only a small flow of water, the economic and ecological costs may outweigh the benefits. This is common with professionally installed systems, which are generally much more expensive than owner-installed ones.

❖ **Inconvenience**—So far, many greywater systems are more expensive or require considerably more user involvement than well-functioning septic or sewer systems.

❖ **Lowered return flows**—In the Southwest, in particular, the rule is: the more wastewater a city dumps in a river, the more it can take out. Greywater reuse for irrigation reduces re-

The competition: A seawater desalination plant provides some of the world's most costly, climate-unsafe freshwater.

An activated sludge sewage treatment plant dumps water and nutrients in the ocean after energy- and chemical-intensive treatment.

turn flows, but it also reduces the amount of freshwater needed for irrigation, sewage treatment, and pumping. No doubt a complete accounting would find direct greywater reuse to be more pro than con for the water/ecology balance.

❖ **Insufficient combined wastewater flow**—In the unlikely scenario that everyone reused *all* greywater, the reduced flow through municipal sewers designed for higher flow could be insufficient to move toilet solids through.

❖ **Inappropriate development**—Greywater systems and composting toilets are sometimes pursued by developers whose only interest is developing property that is unbuildable due to soil in which a septic system isn't allowed.

Elements of a Greywater System

What a greywater system does is collect greywater, then divide and distribute the flow among planted areas. Most of the systems described here are variations on this basic functionality, even those systems designed primarily to get rid of greywater rather than extract value from it. An *optimized* greywater system tunes fixture flow rates, user habits, plant selection and location, and stormwater management all together for the site and soil conditions. The "hardware" that accomplishes this generally consists of:

1. **greywater source(s)**—e.g., washing machine, shower, bathtub, and/or sinks
2. **collection plumbing**—pipes that transport greywater from the house to one or more points just outside the house
3. **surge tank, filter, and pump**—optional elements that add cost/complexity but can make the irrigation piping's job easier, especially for large flows
4. **irrigation piping**—plumbing that transports greywater through the yard and divides it among plants; this includes <u>outlet chamber</u> options: <u>outlet shields</u>, <u>mulch shields</u>, and <u>subsoil infiltration chambers</u> (Figure 9.8)
5. **receiving landscape**—soil, roots, plants, and mulch basins that contain, cover, purify, and use the greywater
6. **people** those who design, make, and maintain the system, generate the greywater, tend the garden, and eat the fruits—a critical, but often overlooked, component of the overall system.

The drawing below shows a few simple greywater systems with parts labeled. Check it out, then roll up your sleeves, sharpen your pencil, and proceed to Chapter 2.

Greywater Facts and Figures

❖ *7% of US homes reuse greywater.*

❖ *13% of California and Arizona households use greywater for landscape irrigation, with laundry water the most utilized source (66%).*

❖ *Greywater constitutes about 50% of total household wastewater generated—that's 65 gal/day/ person (gpd/person).*

❖ *An average (2.6-person) household has 90 gpd of greywater available for outside use, not including the kitchen sink.*

❖ *A homeowner with a 2,500-ft² house on a ¼ acre lot could irrigate about half a climate-appropriate yard with greywater.*

❖ *In Arizona, a two-year study on the landscape and plants irrigated with greywater in residential areas revealed that, except for a slight increase in boron, no salts had accumulated in either the plants or the surrounding soil.*

—Water Environment Research Foundation[41]

FIGURE 1.1: ELEMENTS OF GREYWATER SYSTEMS
(KEY IS LIST ABOVE)

System types:

LANDSCAPE DIRECT (BATHING GARDEN)

DRAIN TO MULCH BASIN

LAUNDRY TO LANDSCAPE
(SINGLE OUTLET, GARDEN HOSE VERSION)

Chapter 2: Goals and Context

If you just want to start building a simple system, you can skip ahead to the System Selection Chart, p. 51. However, even the simplest system will turn out better if you read straight through…

This book covers the territory of just about every possible greywater system. Here is the general path to the right system for you, around which this book is organized:

❖ get clear on your goals and assumptions
❖ assess your context
❖ choose the most appropriate greywater irrigation system for your context
❖ make fixtures more efficient and design connections to rainwater harvesting, landscape, etc.
❖ design the greywater collection plumbing (if needed)
❖ build the system from top to bottom, following the flow from fixtures to receiving landscape
❖ use it, maintain it, troubleshoot it

In this chapter, you'll get clear on your goals and assumptions, and then assess your context—in other words, what you want, and where you are.

Get Clear on Your Goals

Unless you are totally shooting from the hip, I strongly suggest you photocopy or clip out the **Site Assessment Form** *(Appendix A) and fill it with your goals and site data as you proceed through this chapter. There's an example of site assessment info on the next page.*

This form is a great way to organize your thoughts. It's the same form I use when designing a system for a client. (You can download an editable, printable version from our website, oasisdesign.net/design/consult/checklist.)

The foundation of ecological design is getting clear on your goals and context. These affect every aspect of the design in a major way. In conventional construction, this step often doesn't exist, because it doesn't need to; conventions and codes are understood to guide the project. In ecological design, you're inventing a new system rather than fitting into an existing one. It is useful and necessary to reexamine your assumptions each time. Start by asking:

❖ **What is your guiding philosophy and aesthetic?**—Is the project in an exclusive gated subdivision, or a cottage in a hippie commune?
❖ **How are you willing to change your lifestyle?**—Lifestyle change is far and away the best way to conserve resources. For example, if you decide you don't really need long, high-flow showers and a vast ornamental lawn, that decision will save most of the water and energy right off the bat. Then you can install a simpler, cheaper greywater system for the water you're still using. If you can choose between reducing and reusing, reducing is the priority. (For more on this topic, see our booklet *Principles of Ecological Design.*[15])
❖ **What perfection standard are you working to?**—Do you want aesthetics, efficiency, etc. to be 70, 90, 95, or 98% perfect? This is a cultural and personal preference. Each standard has its charm—and cost. Each jump to the next highest of these standards roughly *doubles* the amount of money, time, and materials required for the job, and the negative environmental impact as well. Perfection standard is a huge variable but is rarely discussed explicitly.
❖ **Are you trying to reuse your greywater, or just get rid of it safely?**—Responsible dispersal and reuse are both beneficial. In either case, don't forget to explore conservation first.
❖ **How much effort do you want to put into increasing reuse efficiency?**—It is quite a bit more effort to ensure that greywater use will actually lower your freshwater use.
❖ **What are your other greywater system goals?**—Improve sanitation? Reduce pollution? Save a failing septic? Save money? Feel good? Make a demonstration? (Ideally, demonstrations should justify themselves without resort to the theory that inspiring other people to "do the right thing" makes up for waste in the demonstration itself.)
❖ **Do you want a particular economic payback time?**—Greywater system economics are best when you save septic pumping/replacement, for do-it-yourself systems, and in drought.
❖ **What are your landscape goals?**—Beauty? Food production? Erosion control? Slope stabilization? Firebreak? Privacy screen? Outdoor living oasis?

Give it some thought, and write your goals down. If you're working with other people, include them in the discussion.

Assess Your Context

Now we'll turn to your specific context: site, greywater sources, irrigation need, percolation rate, climate, etc.

Greywater Systems Are Very Context Dependent

The one general principle in greywater system design: *There are no general principles.* Greywater systems are very context dependent. That is, a small change in your context can mean drastic change in your system selection and design. Your particular path through this territory (and this book) depends on your context. This book is organized around the following path:

A carefully considered and optimized, do-it-yourself, residential, retrofit system for gravity-flow irrigation, not too ritzy, built without a permit, in a moderate climate, with a plumber involved in the collection plumbing, and a septic or sewer backup.

Multiple side trips or shortcuts from this path may apply to you—on the next page we'll see which ones.

Does Greywater Matter?

Viewed narrowly, greywater systems don't look that important. A low-flow showerhead can save water with less effort. A septic system can treat greywater almost as well.

But when you look at the whole picture—how everything connects—the keystone importance of greywater is revealed.

Ecological systems design is all about context, and integration between systems. Ecological systems—rainwater harvesting, runoff management, passive solar, composting toilets, edible landscaping—all of these are more context sensitive than their counterparts in conventional practice. That's most of what makes them more ecological.

And greywater systems are more context sensitive than any other man-made ecological system, and more connected to more other systems.

Get the greywater just right, and you've got most of the whole package right, and that's what matters.

Many people and organizations instinctively recognize that greywater is the ideal test case for the transition to a new way of regulating and building appropriate to a mature civilization.

The US Green Building Council; the City of Santa Barbara, California; Oregon ReCode, and SLO Green Build are among those organizations which independently chose to launch their programs of regulatory reform with greywater standards.

Site Assessment Example

(This is the site assessment for Real World Example #1, Chapter 12.)

Greywater system goals: Irrigate large garden without excessive water use, dispose of water safely, reduce ocean pollution, and provide demonstration for State of California greywater study.

Landscape goals: Beauty, food production, privacy screen, outdoor living.

Perfection standard: Moderately high. The house and yard could be in *Sunset Magazine*...on the rustic end.

Location: City of Santa Barbara, latitude 34°, altitude 150' *(45 m)*, ¼ acre lot *(1,000 m²)*, 1950s suburb.

Water system: City water meter with tiered rates that climb steeply with water use. City water deliveries were down 45% in a prior drought.

Rainwater and runoff: All absorbed onsite due to thick mulch layer, basins, and moderate slope. There is no surface water nearby. Groundwater is 50' *(15 m)* down.

Existing wastewater treatment facilities: Sewer, which ultimately dumps in the ocean.

Water users: 3 average, 20 peak, 1 minimum.

Landscape and irrigation: Native vegetation was coastal scrub. The whole lot is gardened intensively with a mix of fruit trees, vegetables, and flowers, all underlain with thick wood chip mulch. The garden is low water use for how extensive, beautiful, and productive it is.

Slope: 2% to the NE, away from the house. The whole yard is below the water sources.

Soil and groundwater: Soil is rich and loamy, gardened organically for 50 years, excellent perk, and easy to dig. Biocompatible cleaners used exclusively.

Climate: Rainfall = 4–44" / year, 18" / year average, max evapotranspiration = 1½" / week[m] between November and March, regularly 6 months with zero rainfall, few to no killing frosts.

Forces of nature: Severe recurring drought.

Site map, system elevations: See Example #1, p. 121.

People: The owners did most of the work on the system, with help from a plumber on the collection plumbing and yours truly on the irrigation piping. Owners are enthusiastic gardeners and conservers of water. Original users were very keen on maintaining the system, the current owners less so.

Regulatory climate: Permitted under California greywater code as part of a State study.

Economics: The owners didn't care too much about the economic payback time. The sewer plant savings don't accrue to them, only the savings on water. These will pay back the cost of the system in 10–20 years (half that if you don't count added costs from measuring the water and complying with unnecessary legal requirements). As a participant in a landmark study, this site had significant political and scientific value.

System used: Branched Drain to sub-mulch emitters.

---

[m]**Metric:** *10–110 cm/year, 45 cm/year average, 4 cm/wk evapotranspiration*

Side Trips and Shortcuts That May Apply to You

Check this section to identify which kind of greywater user you are, so you'll know when I'm talking to your situation—and when to skim or skip ahead. Also, most sections start with an indication of whom they apply to.

Quick and Easy *(a shortcut compared to carefully considered and optimized)*

Greywater systems can be made with a great deal of care to optimize the outcome; or, they can be slapped together without much thought or trouble—as the vast majority are. Greywater work is pretty forgiving; no matter how it gets done, you'll realize a portion of the possible benefits. Either approach (or anything between) is valid. If you just want to slap together a quick, super-simple system and don't care whether it is 50 or 90% perfect, you can skim or skip most of this book, focusing on Chapter 7: Simple Greywater Systems.

Dispersal Only *(a shortcut compared to reuse for irrigation)*

If your system is for dispersal only (for example, to take the load off a septic system), then the information on optimizing irrigation efficiency will only concern you inasmuch as it helps you spread greywater over a wide area and avoid overloading the soil with water.

Multiunit, Institutional, Industrial, High Flow *(a longer journey than residential)*

Residential systems have two defining characteristics: the same people who generate the greywater inhabit the landscape it waters, and the flow is low. Rules are different for high-flow (multiunit, institutional, and industrial) systems. They usually require filtration and pumps, as well as professional installation.

The principles described in this book are relevant at any scale. A few of the systems described can be scaled up to serve 100 or so people (see System Selection Chart, "Suitable for large flows" column). For more information on medium-sized systems, see our *Builder's Greywater Guide*.[6] Giant centralized systems are beyond the scope of our publications.[7]

New Construction *(can take less or more time than a retrofit, and yield more benefit)*

If your system is to be retrofit to an existing building, you're pretty much stuck working with what you've got. But if it's for new construction, you have the opportunity to make everything better integrated—a much more challenging and potentially rewarding task. You have to coordinate the efforts of the architect, plumber, engineer, and landscaper, even if you are all these people yourself (see Figure 3.1).

Greywater use is best incorporated during the design phase. **Like passive solar, greywater is a primary design consideration**. It affects the location of the house and every other water feature. The higher the greywater sources above the irrigated area, the better. The more accessible the drainpipes, the better.

Elevation relationships between water features are critical and are difficult to change once the house is built. Don't let your plumber squander <u>fall</u> (the vertical height between parts of the system)—make sure the pipes come out as high as possible (see Squander No Fall, p. 22).

Although legality is virtually never an issue for retrofits, it is virtually always an issue for permitted new construction or remodeling.

Permitted *(a longer, more exasperating path that may not go where you want)*

You usually must permit a system when it is part of permitted new construction or remodeling (unless your system is in Arizona or one of the several other states that exempt simple greywater systems from permitting[4]—then you're home free).

If permits are involved, you'll need to deal with impractical requirements. To get through this maze, use our *Builder's Greywater Guide*, written expressly for folks dealing with permits. You may choose to arrange plumbing conventionally first, to pass inspection, and then add greywater plumbing later. If you keep blackwater and greywater lines separate, installing a greywater system later is easy. Arranging things to pass inspection, and plumbing drain lines to work in septic/sewer as well as greywater modes, requires the services of an especially skilled, cooperative plumber.

Most reasonable greywater systems, including all versions of the Branched Drain and Laundry to Landscape, are allowed in Arizona, New Mexico, and Texas. Rules in other states are so maddening and unreasonable that the vast majority of greywater users subject to them only get a permit if they absolutely must. Thus, restrictive codes cause amateurs to install systems themselves rather than hire professionals, achieving the opposite of the codes' intended effect (see oasisdesign.net/greywater/law).

Professionally Installed *(in some ways a longer journey than do-it-yourself, but then you have help)*

If you want a professionally produced, turnkey system, the first hurdle is to find a professional greywater installer (see oasisdesign.net/greywater/references.htm). Thanks to codes, professional installers are rare and mostly new, with their experience starting from the adoption of the first realistic codes in Arizona in 2001. The second hurdle is that professionals tend to make the process more complicated, and certainly more expensive. If you want to do as little work as possible yourself, the most efficient approach is to act as a contractor and hire specialists to help with the tasks in Figure 3.1, using this book to help you check their work. The more you can do yourself, the better—except the collection plumbing.

Do-It-Yourself Collection Plumbing *(a false shortcut compared to professional collection plumbing installation)*

Remember the "no general principles" principle? Whereas most greywater work is better the more of it you do yourself, collection plumbing generally turns out better the *less* of it you do yourself. Reading Chapter 4: Greywater Collection Plumbing will set you up either way.

Pumped *(a longer, more convoluted journey than gravity flow)*

You're best off not pumping unless you have new construction, high flows, or nowhere to go but uphill—see Appendix E. Despite salesmens' claims, you may be better off with no greywater system than with a pumped system. Hopefully this will change.

Extremely Cold, Wet, Dry, Etc. *(more involved than a moderate-climate journey)*

For extreme cold, read Appendix C. For extreme wet, see What to Do with Greywater When Plants Don't Need It, Chapter 5. A variety of other extremes is covered in Chapter 12: Real World Examples.

Very Low- or No-Perk Soil *(more extensive and expensive than the high-perk path)*

If your greywater loading rate is high and your soil infiltrates water slowly (low perk), you may end up with standing water. If the soil space doesn't get air at least once every 24 hours, it may become anaerobic and smelly. If spreading the greywater more evenly over a wider area can't prevent this condition, consider a Constructed Wetland, or an unlined bog with wetland plants, or a Solar Greywater Greenhouse, Chapter 8.

No Plants or Soil *(a totally different path)*

If the system is only for indoor reuse—for example, flushing toilets with greywater—and involves no plants or soil, purification will be entirely artificial. Such systems are not economical or ecological on a residential scale, so we don't cover them. However, we list suppliers at oasisdesign.net/greywater/references.htm and some novel systems at oasisdesign.net/greywater/indoors.

Failing Leachfield *(a strong incentive to get moving!)*

A failing septic leachfield[8] may be revived by reducing or eliminating the flow of greywater through it. The first priority is to divert the laundry water, as lint tends to pass through the tank and *papier-mâché* the leachfield surface shut. Then divert the rest of the greywater. Savings on septic tank pumping and leachfield replacement pay off many a greywater system. All you have to do is get the greywater out of the septic—no optimization or complication is necessary.

High Water Table *(a more involved journey)*

If you have a high water table, exceedingly fast perk, and a well in close proximity, see Constructed Wetlands and Solar Greywater Greenhouse, Chapter 8. For a high water table alone, mulch basins may still be the best option.

No Septic/Sewer *(simpler than greywater with septic/sewer backup)*

If radical simplicity draws you to the greywater system/composting toilet lifestyle, see Radical Plumbing, Chapter 4. This has huge ecological and economic advantages.

System in Nonindustrialized World *(a simpler, different path)*

The hardware available in nonindustrialized countries is different, and it may be more practical to custom-make items such as 3-way valves than to buy them. Solutions that are labor intensive in use are more practical. See Radical Plumbing, Chapter 4, and Appendix D.

Now that you've got an idea of which kind of greywater user you are, it will be easier to recognize what applies to you and what doesn't as you press onward.

If you feel overwhelmed with information, remember that you can lower the bar quite a lot—just make a quick and easy system—and things will still turn out okay. (Even the worst greywater disasters don't amount to much. You can get in a lot more trouble with woodstoves, electrical work, blackwater systems, roofing, or any number of other do-it-yourself projects.)

Assess Your Site

Continue p. 18

You can skim this if you don't care about optimizing your system.

Filling out the Site Assessment Form (Appendix A) facilitates understanding. A site map is a great aid for designing a system. A map with a scale of ⅛" = 1' *(1:100)* with 1' *(25 cm)* contours is ideal. If such a map is not available, make a sketch showing the house, boundaries, irrigated areas, natural water features, utility lines, routes of plumbing under the house, etc.—all the features listed on the Site Assessment Form. You'll want a few copies of your site map, or tracing paper to lay over it. There are examples of site maps on p. i, 13, 40, 123, and 126.

Assess Your Water Resources

The first question for any human habitation is, "Where does the water come from?" Ideally, for minimum impact and long-term sustainability, **rain should be the primary water source, followed by greywater, gravity-flow spring or creek water, then well or municipal water.**[9] Wherever the water source, note its characteristics and limitations on the Site Assessment Form. On the site plan, note downspout locations with average gallons per year (gpy) and volume for a peak rain event like 1" in 1 hr (see inside front cover, numbers in blue). Also note greywater average and surge volumes (purple numbers). Note locations and amounts of runoff and "run-on" (water flowing onto the property), and water storage.[10]

Evaluate Conservation Options

If you aim to live ecologically, thoroughly explore conservation options before turning to reuse. Because of the unavoidable inefficiencies inherent in reuse, **the gain from reducing consumption with water-conserving fixtures is always greater than that from reusing the water.**

Assess Existing Wastewater Treatment Facilities

The state, capacity, and location of other wastewater treatment systems influence greywater system design. Locate these on your site map and describe them in the Site Assessment Form. If you're on septic, you'll easily pay for your greywater system by septic savings. If you're on sewer, you won't benefit directly from lower treatment plant loading, but your community and receiving waters will.

Assess Your Greywater Sources

For any system, do at least a rough reality check to make sure the greywater output and irrigation/treatment capacity are in the same ballpark.

It is commonly assumed that however much greywater there is and however much irrigation is needed, they'll magically match up. Even if you don't want to reuse the greywater, it's good to have an idea of how much you've got in order to know whether your dispersal/treatment area is big enough. For most purposes, you can take the home's population and multiply it by an approximate daily use figure, as follows:

Homes without water-conserving fixtures generate about 55 gpd/

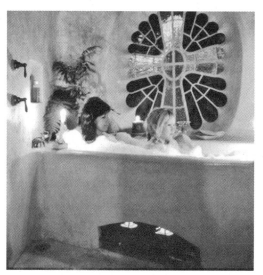

First, reduce water use with efficient fixtures. *In this "forever hot" bathtub in Mexico, water is heated from below by gas burners. The sides of the tub are insulated. There is no need to add more water just to heat the tub. Also, such a tub can be filled with solar preheated water, then brought to temperature, which is more efficient—and potentially eliminates the need for any other water heater.*

TABLE 2.1: GREYWATER SOURCES, QUALITIES, AND QUANTITIES

Source *Ease of replumbing* ⇨	Quality *Ways to improve quality*	Quantity *Ways to conserve* (See also graphs on inside back cover)	*Metric Quantity*
Sources with their own pumps			
Washing machine *Easiest collection plumbing. Getting washer lint out of septic leachlines greatly extends their life.*	**Good.** Medium concentration of soaps, lint. Diapers can dramatically increase pathogen level. *Can be improved to* **excellent** *by using biocompatible cleaners.*	**Large:** 30–50 gal / load, **10-25 gal for HE washer.** 2½ loads / week / person. *105 gpw/person average.*	*400 Lpw/person average*
Automatic dishwasher *May be easily replumbed by a do-it-yourselfer.*	**Bad.** High solids, depending on pre-rinsing. High salt and pH from automatic dishwashing compounds preclude irrigation use in dry climates or clay soils; alternative cleaners don't clean well.	**Small:** 5–10 gal / load. *7 gpw/person average.*	*20–40 L/load*
Gravity-flow sources			
Shower *Professional collection plumbing recommended. May be impossible with slab foundation.*	**Excellent.** Minimal concentration of soap and shampoo is of little concern. Contains pump-snarling hair. *Use the least amount of soap and shampoo necessary. Use liquid soap to reduce sodium.*	**Large:** 20 gpd / person for high flow, **10 gpd for low-flow.** 70–100 gpw/person.	*76 Lpd/person, 38 Lpd/person, 260–380 Lpw/person*
Tub *Requires professional replumbing. May be impossible with slab foundation, unless on exterior wall.*	**Excellent.** Same desirable qualities as shower, only more so.	**Variable:** 40 gal / adult bath, **25 gal/low bath.** *Use is highly variable.*	*150 L/adult, 95 L/kid*
Bathroom sink *Requires professional replumbing.*	**Good.** Concentration of soap, shaving cream, and toothpaste can be high. *Use liquid soap. Exercise discretion in choice and quantity of other products.*	**Small:** 1–5 gpd / person. *7–35 gpw/person.* **Turn down stopcock under sink to minimum flow.**	*4–20 Lpd/person, 26–130 Lpw/person*
Kitchen sink *Professional collection plumbing recommended.*	**Good** but **problematic** in delicate systems. High in nutrients, but also in solids, grease, and soap. *Despite low pathogens, many authorities consider kitchen sink water to be blackwater not worth reuse. I like it, due to its nutrient value. It can be a design problem for systems, but is not a problem in soil. One workaround is to plumb only the rinse side of a double sink to the greywater system. Meat eaters can add a grease trap.*	**Medium:** 5–15 gpd / person. 35–105 gpw/person. **Use two bins for dishwashing. Dedicated utensils for each person reduce water required for sanitation.**	*20–55 Lpd/person*
Reverse osmosis water purifier drain water *May be easily replumbed by a do-it-yourselfer.*	**Excellent.** "Clearwater" with no suspended solids. Contains 25% more of the same dissolved solids as tap water.	**Medium:** 3–5 gal / gal drinking water used. 13–21 gpw/person. **Adjust bladder tank pressure.**	*50–80 Lpw/person*
Water softener backwash *May be easily replumbed by a do-it-yourselfer.*	**Very bad.** Water softener backwash is extremely high in salt, harmful for plants. *Even with potassium[s1] instead of sodium, it is still too concentrated for plants. (Use for toilet flushing?)*	**Small:** 5% of indoor water use. *Get rid of softener.*	
Softened water	**Poor.** Softened water contains salt (sodium chloride), harmful for plants. *Potassium chloride[s1] can be used instead, raising its quality to* **okay.** *Better to get rid of the water softener.*	**All greywater** if softener is in use. *Get rid of softener.*	
Toilet water *Requires professional replumbing. May be impossible with slab foundation. Combined wastewater may be diverted after septic.*	**Very bad.** High pathogens, suspended solids, and salt. Toilet water is blackwater, inappropriate for reuse in an ordinary greywater system. *In a system designed to address the solids and health issues, toilet water is* **good** *(see System Selection Chart).*	**Medium:** 5–8 gpd / person low-flow, three times that for high flow. 60–135 gpw/person. **Use compost or UHE toilet.**	*20–30 Lpd/person, 230–510 Lpw/person*

Notes: Leaks can add 5% or more to water use. Good strainers on drains can dramatically reduce solids.

person of non-toilet wastewater. Efficient fixtures cut this daily output to 40 gpd/person, or enough to water four mature fruit trees or a dozen shrubs in an average climate.[11] Extreme conservation habits can cut production to 5 gpd. Households that haul water by hand generate 5–10 gpd of greywater.[m]

To estimate the flow from a single fixture or a subset of fixtures (such as a washing machine, or a shower and bathroom sink), or to do a more detailed analysis, use Table 2.1 and the worksheet in the Site Assessment Form.

You can also use Table 2.1 to get a more precise idea of the total amount of greywater generated. However, even if you have an engineering mind, let go of the possibility of a truly precision-engineered system. Greywater volume and irrigation demand vary independently over such a huge range that we can only approximate a match between available greywater and irrigation need. Getting numbers to ±50% is reasonable.

On your site map, note where the greywater sources are, with average surge volumes, and (if they are not combined) how much of the total flow comes from each set of sources (Table 2.2). Group fixtures that share a common drain into subtotals (for example, the bathroom sink, tub, and shower often share a drain). Note where their plumbing goes. Consider whether it is appropriate to move any greywater sources (such as a washing machine), add an outdoor shower, move trees, or take any other action to improve the fit of water sources to irrigation need. The places where greywater is generated should ideally be high on the property, so you can irrigate more area by gravity.

Note variations in the population of water users on the Site Assessment Form. If everyone goes away in the dry season for an extended time, this obviously affects the system's design; you won't want to set up water-loving plants to be irrigated by greywater only.

Units: gpd, gpw, gpy, or gpdc?

I use all these units. Gallons per day (gpd) and gpd/capita (gpdc) are in common use. But some greywater sources are used less than once per day, evapotranspiration changes daily, and soil stores irrigation moisture easily for a week. Thus, gallons per week (gpw) is a useful greywater design unit. For calculating water efficiency overall, I use gallons per year (gpy) or gallons per dry season.[mm]

TABLE 2.2: EXAMPLE OF WASTEWATER AMOUNTS

Washer: 5 loads/wk × 32 gal/load	=	160 gpw	*600 Lpw*
Reverse osmosis water purifier drain water (clearwater): ½ gpdc × 4 gal rejected/gal used × 4 people × 7 days	=	56 gpw	*210 Lpw*
Kitchen sink: 3 gpd/person × 4 people × 7 days	=	84 gpw	*320 Lpw*
Shower: 1 shower/day/person × 8 min × 2 gpm × 4 people × 7 days	=	448 gpw	*1,700 Lpw*
Bathroom sink: 2 gpd/person × 4 people × 7 days	=	56 gpw	*210 Lpw*
Tub: 2 baths/wk × 30 gal	=	60 gpw	*230 Lpw*
Reusable subtotal	=	864 gpw	*3,270 Lpw*
Toilet: 3 flushes/day/person × 1.6 gal/flush × 4 people × 7 days	=	126 gpw	*477 Lpw*
Total indoor water use	=	990 gpw	*3,747 Lpw*

Call it 1,000 gal for two adults with two kids; this is 35 gpd/person indoors, below the 50 gpd/person average for households with piped-in water, and above the 10 gpd/person average for households without.

Check the Slopes and Elevations

This step is crucial for collection plumbing and gravity-powered greywater distribution, especially Branched Drain systems, where slopes must be accurately measured. For Greywater Furrow Irrigation, gauging slope mostly by eye seems to work. For pumped systems, elevations aren't so critical.

Check the slope from beginning to end of the intended system. You need to establish that there is enough fall to get from the greywater sources to destination plants with a constant downhill slope (generally ¼" per foot, or 2%). In the landscape the pipes should ideally still be at surface level, and in no case more than 1' below ground. For proper flow, drainpipes must inexorably get lower with distance from the source, and also with the negotiation of

Help! Too Many Numbers!

Don't worry if you get them or not. The vast majority of greywater systems are made without any calculations at all — and most still work.

Relax. If you get even a vague sense of the relationships from these pages you'll be way ahead of the curve.

---

[m]**Metric:** *Without conservation, 210 L/person/day; efficient fixtures, 150 L/person/day; extreme conservation, 20 L/person/day; hand carried, 20–40 L/person/day.*

[mm]**Metric:** *Cubic meters are the unit of choice: vastly superior. I could knock off work an hour earlier each day having done a better job measuring and calculating all lengths, areas, and volumes in meters instead of inches, feet, square feet, acres, gallons, inches per square foot, cubic feet, and acre feet—aiii!*

each obstacle, change of pipe size, etc.—and the pipe elevation can't ever go back up again. Fall is almost always a limiting factor for collection plumbing and gravity irrigation piping (see Squander No Fall, Chapter 4).

If you're fortunate enough to have a 1' *(25 cm)* contour map of your site, use it to check elevations. (Contours are lines showing land surface at the same elevation. For an example, see Figure 12.1.) If you don't have such a map, measure the elevations where the system is going to be installed. You can do this with a $700 transit, but a $5 water level works well enough (see Appendix B: Measuring Elevation and Slope).

Note these elevations on your site map, then determine which greywater sources can water which plants. Remember that you actually need a bit more than 2% slope from end to end, to allow for obstacles and other "fall eaters." It is often very helpful to make a drawing showing the system elevations in section view.

Check the Soil Perk

You should have at least an idea of the perk rate for any system. Quantitative measurement is necessary if a lot of greywater is going into a small area, or the perk appears to be low, or the soil is clayey.

The rate at which water absorbs into the soil—the percolation or <u>perk rate</u>—is an important variable in greywater system design. High clay content generally means slow perk, which can get dramatically slower if you add salt-laden water. Rock can have slow or no perk. High loading and slow perk can lead to standing water and noxious smells.

Very fast perk in gravel, for example, can lead to groundwater contamination from septics. This is unlikely from greywater if there is mulch and a network of plant roots.

Fissured limestone (Florida) and lava tubes (Hawaii) can be problematic for septics, as they form natural pipes that enable wastewater to bypass soil purification and flow directly into the groundwater at warp speed. Routing greywater to mulch basins with roots mitigates this problem.

It is vital to know about the perk where the greywater is going before committing to a design. I once embarrassed myself by building a system for a neighbor, based on my knowledge that the soil around here is very free-draining. Well, the *soil* is free-draining, but where I dug the infiltration basin turned out to be *subsoil* from the house's excavation, and it hardly drained at all.

If you're putting a small amount of greywater in a big area, the only perk issue would be a really, really slow perk rate. If you have enough experience with your soil—digging holes to various depths, perhaps filling them with water, observing how water absorbs into the ground—to know it perks reasonably fast, you don't need a perk test.

But if you are applying a large amount of greywater, or have a small area, or are applying greywater subsurface, a perk test is critical. Based on the result, you might change the size of the system by a factor of 4 or more, or even decide that a greywater system is infeasible.

A professional (read: expensive) perk test is required for designing septic leachfields. These tests are usually done with a truck-mounted borer to a depth that is irrelevant to greywater systems. If you already have one of these tests in hand and it shows that the perk rate is okay several feet down, it is surely fine at greywater depth. But an easy, shallow, do-it-yourself perk test gives you more relevant information (see sidebar).

How to Measure Perk

Dig holes to greywater discharge depth (usually 12", *30 cm*), in the locations you wish to discharge it. Fill the hole from a hose. Now turn the hose down until the flow just maintains this water level in the hole, usually somewhere between drips and a steady trickle. Leave it like this until the soil around the hole is saturated, possibly overnight. Place a stake into the bottom firmly. Mark reference elevations on the stake and fill the hole with water two to four times, measuring each time how far the water drops in a given number of minutes. When it drops at the same rate a couple of times in a row, that's your saturated perk rate (dry soil perks much faster—saturated perk is what matters for sizing the system). Convert the numbers to perk rate in min/in or cm (3" in 60 min is 20 min/in, for example), then see Table 2.3 to see how much area you need to treat that much water.

If it takes hours for the water to drop at all, or if the water vanishes as fast as you can fill the hole, or if the holes fill with water by themselves, you've got a problem! If the perk is super slow, consider a Constructed Wetland. If it is super fast, add compost, mulch, and plants that will develop a dense network of roots to help purify greywater on its rapid journey through the topsoil.

Assess Your Treatment/Dispersal Area

Skip to the next section if you want to irrigate.

If you only want to get rid of greywater, you can assess prospective treatment areas on your site map by indicating how much greywater they can handle. In this case, the only concern is to not overload the soil or sensitive plants (see Table 2.3). Bigger areas with higher perk rate, and more wind and sun, can take more water. Don't apply too much water near the foundation of the house.[12]

These rates are several times the amount needed for irrigation. Dispersal rate—the <u>Long-Term Acceptance Rate</u> (LTAR, p. 47)—is limited by soil perk rather than plant transpiration. The majority of the treated water ends up percolating down to groundwater rather than transpiring to the sky.

Assess Your Irrigation Need

Skip this section if you only want to dispose of greywater.

Note the vegetation types and the size of irrigated areas and trees on your site map. Indicate plants that like wetter conditions by different colors or shades. Or, you can make a list of irrigated areas and how much water they want—both options are shown in Table 2.4.

Again, if your aim is to live ecologically, first explore the option of removing nonproductive plants before looking at greywatering them.

Estimating irrigation demand is an inexact science. Getting within a factor of two of the real irrigation demand is a reasonable goal. As a rough rule of thumb, figure that **your plants need about ½ gpw of water for each square foot of plant** *(20 L/week/m²)*.

Double this figure for desert, and halve it for a cool, humid climate (see Table 2.5). You can also double or halve this figure again for plants that use more or less water. For trees, use the same formula (or calculate the area under the canopy and multiply it by the gallons per square foot per week*). This rule of thumb does not account for variations in evapotranspiration (ET) rate by season, climate, plant type, seasonal loss of leaves, rainfall, or irrigation efficiency. It does, however, land you more or less where you'd end up if you *did* consider all those things. If you crave more precision, have extreme conditions, or have a bigger than residential-sized area to irrigate, it may make sense to try a more rigorous analysis, which is covered in our *Builder's Greywater Guide,*[6] Evapotranspiration Formula.

TABLE 2.3: DISPERSAL LOADING RATES

Soil infiltration rate, min/in	Loading rate gpd/ft²	Area needed ft²/gpd	Soil infiltration rate, min/cm	Loading rate m³/day/m²	Area needed m²/m³/day	
0–30	2.5	0.4	*0–12*	*0.1*	*10*	CLIVUS MULTRUM
30–45	1.5	0.7	*12-18*	*.06*	*20*	
45–60	1.0	1.0	*18-24*	*.04*	*25*	
60–120	0.5	2.0	*24-47*	*.02*	*50*	

These rates are conservative, especially for Mulch Basins. Can be up to 3–5 gpd/ft² for greywater, up to 10 for secondary treated effluent.

TABLE 2.4: EXAMPLE OF IRRIGATION NEEDS ASSESSMENT

	Irrigation need	
	(gpw)	*(Lpw)*
533 ft² Fruiting Hedge	320	*1,200*
7 Small Fruit Trees	100	*380*
4' x 20' Wildflower Bed	10	*40*
Small Water Garden	30	*110*
5 Large Fruit Trees	575	*2,180*
Greywaterable Subtotal	**1,035**	*3,910*

	Irrigation need	
	(gpw)	*(Lpw)*
Herb Garden	50	*190*
3 Veggie Beds	80	*300*
15' x 20' Lawn	180	*680*
Non-Greywaterable Subtotal⁺	**310**	*1,170*
Grand Total	**1,345**	*5,080*

⁺*Due to hardware limitations of the chosen greywater systems (can't water turf) and health concerns (inadvisable to greywater veggies).*

This yard belongs to four people. This is 48 gpd/person outdoors, slightly below average. These numbers are generated with the ½ gpw/ft² shortcut. Use 3' (1 m) as the smallest diameter for newly planted trees—they like extra water.

---

*To get the area, take half the diameter of the tree canopy, square it, and multiply it by 3.14: $a = \pi r^2$.

Evapotranspiration (ET) = evaporation from plants plus transpiration through plant leaves. ET increases with temperature, low humidity, and especially wind. These are peak values; generally you want the greywater to cover less (see Choose the Proportion of Irrigation to Meet with Greywater, Chapter 5).

TABLE 2.5: PEAK EVAPOTRANSPIRATION (ET) VALUES BY CLIMATE

	in/wk	*mm/wk*
Cool humid	0.7–1.0	*18–25*
Cool dry	1.0–1.4	*25–35*
Warm humid	1.0–1.4	*25–35*
Warm dry	1.4–1.8	*35–46*
Hot humid	1.4–2.0	*35–50*
Hot dry	2.0–3.2	*50–81*

Cool = under 70°F average midsummer high
Warm = 70°–90°F average midsummer high
Hot = over 90°F average midsummer high
Humid = over 50% average midsummer relative humidity
Dry = under 50% average midsummer relative humidity
Metric: 70°F = 21°C; 90°F = 32°C

TABLE 2.6: SAMPLE GREYWATER PRODUCTION/IRRIGATION NEED REALITY CHECK
(FOR REAL WORLD EXAMPLE #2)

(Bold numbers are inputs from water bill; the others are calculated.)

Greywater production reality check	gallons			*cubic meters*			
	day	week	month	*day*	*week*	*month*	
Total wastewater calculated	89	**622**	2,674	*0.33*	**2.34**	*10.05*	
Check: Average consumption on wet season water bills	100	698	**3,000**	*0.37*	*2.62*	**11.28**	This checks out; wastewater should be close to but less than wet season water bills.
Check: Wastewater/person	25	174		*0.09*	*0.66*		This is pretty conservative (half of US average) but entirely plausible for a green household with low-flow fixtures.
Greywater	78	544		*0.29*	*2.04*		
Greywater/person (4 people)	19	136		*0.07*	*0.51*		
Check: % that is greywater		87%			*87%*		High but plausible. The toilet at this site is low flow, and "if it's yellow let it mellow, if it's brown flush it down" philosophy prevails.
Irrigation need reality check							
Average consumption on dry season water bills		2,093	**9,000**		*7.87*	*33.84*	
Check: Difference between wet/dry season bills (presumed to be irrigation)		1,395	6,000		*5.25*	*22.56*	US average is 50% of water use outdoors, so ⅔ during irrigation season is reasonable.
Check: Irrigation as a % of dry season use		67%			*67%*		
Calculated consumption of area to be greywatered		482			*1.81*		
Check: Greywatered area % of total irrigation consumption		35%			*35%*		This looks reasonable, comparing the total irrigated area on the site map for this system with the greywatered area.

Greywater Sources and Irrigation Need Reality Check

Look over your past water bills or meter records. Your total water consumption for the months when irrigation was not needed should be a good approximation of your *year-round* indoor consumption (greywater and toilet water). Subtract this from your water consumption during months when irrigation was needed, and the number you get should be your irrigation use. These numbers should jibe with your irrigation estimates (see Table 2.6). Leakage and outdoor use other than irrigation (car washing, swimming pool) may account for the difference. If not, jiggle your irrigation estimates up or down by a "fudge factor" to match your actual use records. We'll revisit irrigation in Chapter 5.

Assess the Climate and Forces of Nature

Take stock of the climate parameters in the Site Assessment Form. Note any forces of nature such as flooding, drought, fire, and high wind, which may affect the design of the system or landscape.

Assess the Regulatory and Social Climate

As mentioned previously, it is much easier to make a practical greywater system if you aren't in a situation where impractical greywater systems are legally mandated. Will your neighbors let you get away with a system that doesn't have a permit?

Appraise the People Part of the System

People are a key part of any greywater system. Who is going to design, build, use, and maintain it? How interested and dedicated are they? If a dedicated person is responsible for maintenance, the system can be more demanding and delicate and still work. If there is no skilled person to build or maintain it, the system must be simple. If the system is public, public parts will have to be idiotproof.

Cost-Benefit Analysis

Say your septic tank is failing and you can defer its replacement indefinitely by diverting all your greywater from it. Or, you know in your gut that it is wrong to send wastewater past your parched plants to pollute the river or ocean, while using electricity to pump freshwater out of a sensitive ecosystem miles away to slake their thirst, when you could water them with a simple, cheap greywater system instead.

In these cases, as in most, precision analysis is not needed. That's good, because accurate cost-benefit analysis is complicated. For starters, it requires accurate assessment of irrigation need in each season.

Simple systems can pay for themselves in water savings alone. This is more likely if water costs are high, if the system is designed to maximize reuse efficiency, and if you do the work yourself.

In new construction, complex, contractor-installed systems can pay for themselves in water savings alone with as little as 100 gpd *(0.5 m³/day)* of greywater, if well-designed, and especially if *all* costs and savings are included. Often, many costs and benefits are externalized. Individuals typically don't directly experience a cost savings from sending less water to the sewer, for example. Simplified cost-benefit analysis (see Table 2.7 for an example) does not consider lost interest, inflation, or detailed analysis of actual irrigation efficiency. If you have a compelling reason, you can take all these things and more into account.[13]

A Note on Lawns

Turf accounts for the bulk of the irrigation need in the typical landscape, hence lawn greywatering is a popular violation of commonsense greywater safety rules.

The only acceptable ways to irrigate lawns with greywater are via Automated Sand Filtration to Subsurface Emitters or Advanced Treatment System to Subsurface Drip (Chapter 8)—well beyond what most folks are likely to install. We suggest replacing most of your turf with something else and replacing what's left with a water-conserving grass such as a Tall Fescue variety. Water this with the freshwater you save from using greywater elsewhere, or just let your lawn go dormant when there's not enough rain to sustain it. (See also Error: Greywatering Lawns, Chapter 11.)

Greywatered lawn (color image on cover) One side is irrigated with greywater via subsurface drip, the other with potable water. It's absolutely impossible to tell the difference. This system would be perfect for, say, a high school with dozens of showers and acres of turf.

Lawn Statistics

- *Top crop in US; 4x more area, 4x more water than #2 crop*
- *30–60% of residential water use*
- *38 million lawnmowers produce 5% of total US emissions*
- *More gas spilled each year by garden equipment than Exxon Valdez spill*
- *Lawnmowers cause 100,000 emergency room visits/yr*
- *3 million tons of fertilizer/yr, 41% include ingredients banned/restricted in other countries*
- *More than 30,000 tons of synthetic pesticides/yr; 10:1 ratio of pesticide use per acre by average homeowner vs average farmer*

Revisit Your Goals

As you go through the design and installation of your greywater system, keep one eye on your previously identified goals. If new information or realizations outdate them, change them. For example, if you want a deeply ecological lifestyle but also want a perfect, classy system without suffering any cost or inconvenience, you may realize that these desires are in conflict; to make the transition from fantasy to reality, you'll have to let go of something. If you're working with a team, be sure to let the others know how the goals have changed.

TABLE 2.7: SAMPLE SIMPLIFIED COST-BENEFIT ANALYSIS
(FOR REAL WORLD EXAMPLE #2)

Savings	Value
Leachfield replacement deferred forever	**$8,000**
Longer interval between septic pumping for 20 yrs	**$1,000**
Theoretical freshwater saved per yr	40,000 gal (150 m³)
× reality factor (rainy season, system inefficiencies)	50%
Cost per gal (Santa Barbara average)	$0.01
Value of water saved per yr	$100
Value of water saved 20 yrs	**$2,000**
Total savings per year	**$550**
Savings over 20-yr system life (not counting value of owner labor)	$11,000
Savings over 20-yr system life (counting cost of owner labor, or paying someone else to do it)	*$5,995*
Costs	
Cost of parts	$600
20 hrs laborer @ $8/hr	$300
5 hrs plumber (collection plumbing) @ $50/hr	*$375*
Total out of pocket	**$1,275**
53 hrs owner labor inside & outside valued @ $15/hr	$1,325
Labor	
Grand total	**$2,600**
Net savings	
Payback yrs (not counting owner labor)	2.3
Payback yrs (counting cost of owner labor)	4.7
Return on investment (counting cost of owner labor)	21%

By comparison to this Branched Drain, an Automated Sand Filtration to Subsurface Emitters system easily costs $5,000 in parts and labor. In addition to requiring substantial electricity and ongoing service, major parts require replacement after a few to several years.

Chapter 3: Design for Your Context

Now that you've loaded up your Site Assessment Form, site map, and brain with information, it is time to put it to work. (If your brain is *over*loaded, consider skimming ahead to the next page, where the greywater basics track picks up again.) In this chapter, you're going to learn how to integrate your greywater system with the landscape and other systems, address health considerations, and best match your greywater sources with your irrigation/dispersal area.

Integrate Greywater with Other Systems

This section applies if you care about optimizing everything. It doesn't apply if you just want to get rid of greywater.

Greywater systems, even more than other aspects of natural building, benefit from a systems approach to design. This is because they connect to so many other systems (Figure 3.1).

Sometimes when a greywater system is a retrofit, there is less you can do about how it "fits in." In other cases—such as new construction on raw land—you can design a greywater system and all the other systems together. When you do this, you gain *economies of wholeness.* For example, a house can catch rainwater from its roof, heat it with the sun, provide supple-

FIGURE 3.1: INTEGRATED DESIGN WORK FLOW
FOR INDOOR EFFICIENCY, STORMWATER, GREYWATER, LANDSCAPING,
ARCHITECTURE, ENERGY EFFICIENCY, AND CLIMATE

Landscape Architect/Landscaper
- Locate appropriate plants to create microclimates (sunny/warm and shady/cool), outdoor living spaces, RW/GW* irrigation, provide food, privacy, and fire safety
- Manage rooftop RW and landscape stormwater, eliminate runoff, and infiltrate run-on
- Adjust landscape elevations and micro-grading (basins, swales)
- Install plants and distribution plumbing so each GW zone has a corresponding irrigation zone, which can be turned off independently to actualize water savings
- Install GW and RW distribution plumbing and plants at same time
- Amend soil, add mulch
- Define seasonal tasks and irrigation modes

Architect/Engineer
- Design water supply
- Site house uphill from irrigated area (as basic as facing building south for solar)
- Raise floors so GW plumbing can exit at grade
- Make plumbing accessible, e.g., in a crawl space, or on exterior walls
- Spec efficient fixtures, in workable locations for GW
- If cold, include passive solar greenhouse
- Coordinate roof RW plan and downspout locations with landscaper for infiltration, and cistern location
- Design excreta management system

Users
- Exercise water-wise habits
- Manage materials: reuse compost, excreta, mulch, fuel wood
- Select biocompatible cleaners, divert GW when using something toxic
- Adjust seasonally
- Maintenance, gardening

Elevations, distribution plumbing, RW, GW basins, plants, amendments

Indoor efficiency, house reuse-ready for GW and RW

Use, maintenance

Greywater/Systems Designer
- Assess goals, context, and resources
- Tune fixture flow rates, user habits, plant selection and location, and stormwater management together with GW reuse plumbing, in light of soil and other conditions
- Decide early: "lump" or "split" collection plumbing

Owner
- Clearly articulate goals
- Back up GW system designer with architect, plumber, contractor, etc.

Construction

Contractor
- Ensure that plumbing to GW specs is facilitated by masonry and carpentry

Gutter Installer
- Route downspouts to irrigation/infiltration areas
- Design gutters and downspouts for filtration, and for pressure if necessary
- Connect to cistern (if any)

Rainwater

Plumber
- Plumb as high as possible, conserving fall to get outlets in proper position/height (can take twice as much time but is essential to enable irrigation close to house—adjust your bid)
- Plumbing GW lines separately until outside house is a good way to go, especially if under slab; vents may be combined
- Install diverter valve(s) downstream from traps, vents to switch between garden and septic/sewer
- Route RW to laundry, toilet plumbing (if applicable)

GW collection plumbing

Compliance

Regulators/Inspectors
- Rise above role of policing for cheating on minimum standards, fulfill potential as advocate/resource for builders who are investing effort to build to highest environmental standard
- Ensure that systems are well designed and well built, using familiar systems' performance as an indicator of unfamiliar systems' quality

Note: On most projects individuals fill multiple roles.

RW= rainwater, GW= greywater.

Cont. from p. 9

Health Considerations

In practice, the health risk of greywater use has proven minimal to nonexistent. It is, after all, the water you just bathed in, or the residue from clothes you wore not long ago. Despite all sorts of grievous misuse (brought on in part by lack of useful regulatory guidance), there has not been a single documented case of greywater-transmitted illness in the US. Nonetheless, greywater may contain infectious organisms. It's poor form to construct pathways for infecting people, and totally unnecessary. Keep this in mind when designing and using a system.

All greywater safety guidelines stem from these two principles:

1. *Greywater must pass slowly through healthy topsoil for natural purification to occur.*

2. *Design your greywater system so no greywater-to-human contact occurs before purification.*

Here are examples of possible health-related greywater problems and solutions:

❖ *Direct contact or consumption—Solutions: Carefully avoid cross-connections (accidental connections between freshwater and greywater plumbing). Label greywater plumbing, including garden hoses. Use gloves and goggles when cleaning greywater filters. Wash your hands after greywater contact.*

❖ *Microorganisms on plants—Direct application to foliage can leave untreated microorganisms on surfaces. Solution: Don't apply greywater to lawns, or to fruits and vegetables that are eaten raw (e.g., strawberries, lettuce, or carrots). Greywatering fruit trees is acceptable.*

❖ *Pathogen overload—Greywater systems are safest when reusing water that is fairly clean initially. Solutions: Greywater should not contain water used to launder soiled diapers or generated by anyone with an infectious disease. In both cases, greywater should be diverted to the septic tank or sewer. Also, don't store greywater; use it within 24 hours, before bacteria multiply.*

❖ *System overload—If you are having a party and 50 people are going to use a system designed for two, consider diverting greywater to the sewer.*

❖ *Breathing of microorganisms—Droplets from sprinklers can evaporate to leave harmful microorganisms suspended in the air ("aerosols"), where people may breathe them. Solution: Don't broadcast greywater with sprinklers.*

❖ *Chemical contamination—Biological purification does not usually remove industrial toxins. Toxins will either be absorbed by plants or pollute groundwater. Many household cleaners are unsuitable for introduction into a biological system. Solutions: Divert greywater that contains chemicals so they poison the sewer or septic instead. Better yet, don't buy products that you wouldn't want in your greywater system.*

❖ *Contamination of surface water—Greywater needs to percolate through the soil, or else it might flow partially treated into creeks or other waterways. Solutions: Discharge greywater into a mulch-filled basin or subsoil to contain it and slow its movement toward surface waters or groundwater. Ensure that the greywater soaks into soil, and that the soil can aerate between waterings. Greywater that is confined within mulch basins at least 50' (15 m) from a creek or lake is not a problem.*

❖ *Contamination of groundwater or well—It is all but impossible to contaminate groundwater with a greywater system, as the treatment capacity of the topsoil is so enormous. Over 90% of plant roots and beneficial microorganisms are in the top few feet of soil. Most septic leachfields provide adequate treatment of far more hazardous effluent despite discharging below the majority of the soil's treatment capacity. However, if you have a poorly sealed well, greywater running over the surface could potentially pour into it. Solution: The CPC/UPC greywater codes, which are just crude adaptations of septic tank codes, call for 100' of separation between location of greywater application and a well, same as a septic. Probably half of this is sufficient.*

Six Factors for Good Natural Purification of Water or Wastewater

Observe enough engineered and natural water systems...and you realize we'd best do it as much like nature as possible. Here's a guide:

1. *Plenty of contact time—The longer the water is in contact with beneficial bacteria and plant roots, the better. To increase contact time, reduce flow and/or increase area.*

2. *Plenty of microsurface—The more microsurface with beneficial bacteria growing on it, and the more plant roots, the better. Loamy soil has thousands of times more surface area than gravel.*

3. *Moisture, oxygen, and nutrient levels which support growth/survival of roots and bacteria—If the system is totally dry long enough for the bacteria and roots to die, then gets spike loading, then is dry again, the treatment won't be as good. If the soil is saturated (no air) for more than 24 hours, the dissolved oxygen will be consumed.*

4. *Apply wastewater as close to the surface as possible, without causing an unsanitary condition—The top of the soil has a purification capacity thousands of times greater than 3' (1 m) down, because 90% of the life is within a foot of the surface.*

5. *Appropriate plants—You don't have to worry about bacteria; if the conditions are right, one will turn into trillions. However, it is generally helpful to actively manage plants to ensure there are the right number of the right kind. Evergreen plants are active all year. If you expect constant water-saturated conditions, use wetland plants, which pump oxygen out their roots.*

6. *Warmth—The warmer it is, the better the treatment. The rule of thumb is that for each additional 50°F (10°C) you get twice the treatment.*

mental heat from burning yard trimmings, use the water in super-efficient fixtures, and then irrigate trees with this water. These trees, if carefully selected and positioned, purify the water before it recharges the groundwater, and provide shade from heat, shelter from cold wind, privacy from neighbors, delicious fruit, habitat, and beauty.

Coordinate with Others

If a team is to install the greywater and related systems, and you want an optimal outcome, it will be necessary to coordinate everyone's efforts.

If you're doing all the work yourself, you'll still need to coordinate, but it will be easier with all the specialists under your one hat.

General Landscape Design Points

Here's the short version of my checklist (there's more on these points in Chapter 5):

❖ **100% rainwater and runoff infiltration**—Form landscapes with basins, swales, mulch, and rich, loamy soil so that *all the rain that falls on the property soaks in*. Or more: landscapes can absorb run-on from surrounding surfaces (as long as this won't create a landslide). This yields benefits including flood control, reduced irrigation need, and improved quality and quantity of natural surface waters. (Our book *Water Storage*[10] covers storage of water in soil, groundwater, and seasonal ponds.)

❖ **Rainwater/runoff flushing**—Particularly in places with clay soil or low rainfall, directing rainwater into the system in a controlled way flushes harmful salts out of the soil.

❖ **Irrigation near the house**—In most cases, though you don't want to wet your actual foundation, you want the greywater to irrigate plants right around your home, so you can eat the fruit before the birds do, and live in the oasis thus created, not way uphill from it. This usually means *watching elevations really carefully*.

❖ **Microclimate modification, outdoor living spaces**—Plants can dramatically improve the climate, indoors and out. I design landscapes with an outdoor living space that's sunny and warm and another that's shady and cool, both easily accessible from the house. Identify places that naturally have these attributes, then accentuate them by shading or reflecting sun, screening wind, and irrigating. (Transpiration provides outdoor air conditioning.)

❖ **Edible vs inedible landscaping**—My philosophy is to only water things I can eat—and a few things of overpowering beauty. If a nonedible plant is required, I pick one that will grow without irrigation.

❖ **Privacy plantings**—If you like privacy, hedges are a green, economical, and beautiful way to achieve it. Greywatering hedges makes sense, especially when landscape space is tight or later construction might tear up a system in the middle of the property.

Rainwater is used here to refer to clear rain direct from the sky or rooftop. Rainwater, suface runoff, and run-on are collectively referred to here as stormwater.

Connect Stormwater and Greywater with Irrigation or Dispersal Area

On your site map, review the gallons of greywater available per week from each group of fixtures, and where their drain plumbing goes. Do the same with stormwater from the roof, hardscape, runoff, and run-on.

Then look at the areas you've shaded on this map to indicate where irrigation is needed, or where the greywater could go for treatment/dispersal.

Now consider which greywater sources could be routed to which areas. For irrigating, you're generally looking for plants that are close to the house and, with a gravity system, reachable by a continuously downhill pipe run.

Lump or Separate the Greywater Flow?

This material applies to everyone.

The first design decision is whether to go with one combined line, or to separate the flows first by not combining them. This decision determines the layout of the collection plumbing in the house and, once done, is not easy to change. How do you decide?

Separate Flows

If you want a very simple system and/or reuse efficiency isn't critical, separate flows are for you.

The benefits of not combining flows are: simpler plumbing, less fall required (because the pipes don't have to go so far, first to join all together, then back to their own plants), and the ability to take advantage of the unique flow characteristics of individual fixture sets. Examples: An upstairs bathroom might be able to water a part of the garden that is too high to reach otherwise. If you tried to get the greywater up there after the flows were combined, it would bubble up the downstairs shower drain instead. Or, a washing machine can supply a higher part of the landscape by using its own pump to raise the water.

Separate flows reliably ensure some degree of irrigation reuse. No matter what, the water comes out in multiple outlets—for example, one spot watered by dishwashing, another by clothes washing, yet another by bathing.

Separate flows may be preferable to combined flows if:

- ❖ **You don't care about reuse efficiency.**
- ❖ **The house is large and sprawling.**
- ❖ **Rerouting plumbing from one side of the house to the other is difficult or impossible**— E.g., with slab-on-grade construction.
- ❖ **The house is more than one story and portions of the yard are above the ground floor**—If the greywater from the upper floor(s) is plumbed separately, it can gravity flow to more of the yard.
- ❖ **You have very little fall between sources and plants**—If the lot is flat, separate flows may be your only option. There may not be enough fall to join flows and get them to plants.

(Figures 9.1, 9.4a, 9.4d, 12.1, and 12.3 show systems with separate flows.)

Combined Flows

If you care about reuse efficiency, combined flows are more likely your route.

The advantage of combining greywater flows in the collection plumbing before splitting is that variations in flow from different fixtures average out. This greatly simplifies supplemental freshwater irrigation. This is especially true if some fixture sets have highly variable use, for example a guest bathroom.

Combined flows work out better if:

- ❖ **Your goal is high reuse efficiency for irrigation**—Especially if your plants will rely exclusively on greywater, management of combined flows is easier.
- ❖ **Your system requires filtration or pumping**—To avoid the need for multiple pumps and filters.
- ❖ **You want to be able to switch between multiple irrigation zones**—See below.

(Figures 9.4b and 9.4c show examples of flows combined before being split.)

Sketch your lumped and separated plumbing alternatives on your site map, and see how they look. Separated flows will generally look easier on paper and be easier to build. The *management* is trickier, as described above. Once the combined or separate decision is made, you can design the collection plumbing.

Multiple Greywater Zones

Greywater comes out many times a day, as it is generated. The only drying-out periods are when everyone is asleep or on vacation—and not even then if there is a leak. Having more than one irrigation zone, and the ability to alternate greywater between zones with valves or to reroute greywater into the sewer or septic system, is advantageous in some situations, to:

- ❖ **maintain aerobic conditions in irrigation zones**
- ❖ **divert greywater to dispersal**—when irrigation is not needed
- ❖ **divert greywater to dispersal**—or spread it more widely, when a steep slope could get oversaturated and slide
- ❖ **fit available greywater more closely to irrigation needs**

In one system (see Real World Example #1), the homeowners observed that their citrus trees did well with continued watering for two to three weeks without a drying-out period.

However, their stone fruit trees seemed stressed by the long irrigation periods.

Particularly with *low-perk soil* and/or sensitive plants, it would be good to make provision for drying-out periods between watering. Designing the greywater system to provide only a portion of the plants' water needs helps solve this problem (see Table 5.1). Another solution is to switch from one zone to another with a diverter valve or valves. Also, greywater can water two zones when it is sufficient to meet all plants' needs, then only water one or the other when it can't meet the needs in both. The obvious problem is remembering to switch the valve. An automatic controller is great for sending a few days' greywater to one zone, then another. These cost a few hundred dollars plus installation. Unless the greywater is pressurized, the valves themselves cost a few hundred dollars each, as well.

Provide for Maintenance and Troubleshooting

I'm a believer in making every part of the system findable, accessible, maintainable, replaceable, and flexible. Specifics on this important point will be discussed throughout.

Practice Optimal, Integrated Design

Here's a general recipe for the practice of optimal, integrated, ecological systems design:

❖ **Get a global, yet detailed view of your context**—Ecological design is based on a wide-angle view of the world, with high resolution zoom and x-ray vision to relevant details, clear as to scale, rooted in the past, and fast-forwardable into the future.
❖ **Get clear on goals.**
❖ **Inventory issues.**
❖ **Inventory resources.**
❖ **Do what makes sense in your context**—Creatively use resources to resolve issues.
❖ **Refine and repeat**—Have fun doing it…

For much more on this topic, see *Principles of Ecological Design*.[15]

Relate Well with the Natural Water Cycle

Here's a very brief overview of principles for plumbing your home properly into the global nutrient and water cycles:

❖ **Leave as much of the work as possible to nature**—The more humans intervene, the more likely the overall system will get thrown out of whack.
❖ **Work on solving several problems with one design**—Include integrated as well as specialist perspectives. More can be gained from improving connections between systems than from improving systems.
❖ **Divert a small amount of water.**
❖ **Divert just after natural purification**—If water from springs, rainwater harvesting, or wells is diverted after natural purification and before it is contaminated, little or no additional treatment is needed.
❖ **Divert from an elevation above the use point**—Or as little below it as possible, so less energy is needed for pumping. You can also save energy by using ultra-low-pressure plumbing.
❖ **Use water efficiently**—REDUCE comes before reuse in the hierarchy of ecological materials management. Always consider efficient fixtures before looking to reuse water from them.
❖ **Cascade**—Sequence uses so water cascades from those uses which require the cleanest water to those which tolerate the dirtiest.
❖ **Use super-efficient fixtures**—E.g., wood-burning bathtub, eco-luxury bathing chamber.
❖ **Add used water and nutrients back into the water cycle at large just before natural purification**—Greywater systems, composting toilets, Green Septic systems, compost, mulch...
❖ **Absorb all stormwater**—Permeable surfaces, vegetation cover, mulch, basins, and swales.
❖ **Rigorously confine incompatible materials (motor oil, solvents) to their own industrial cycles**—Add to water only a moderate quantity of substances which biodegrade into plant nutrients or nontoxins, and nothing else.

Chapter 4: Greywater Collection Plumbing

If you are only going after washer water, you can skip down to Collecting Laundry (Pressurized) Greywater...and skip the plumber as well. Otherwise, I suggest you read this whole chapter to sharpen your plumbing wherewithal. If you are building a very simple, unpermitted dwelling, and want to save as much money and resources as possible, consider Radical Plumbing (described at the end).

Collection plumbing takes the greywater from various generation points in the house to a point or points just outside. From there, irrigation piping takes the greywater to plants. For gravity-flow collection plumbing, codes provide useful guidance, and the services of a plumber are helpful. (For irrigation piping in the landscape, CPC/UPC-style codes and a plumber are counterproductive.)

Select and design your irrigation system before you start sawing under your house. Collection plumbing does vary a great deal depending on whether it is for gravity sources, appliances with their own pump (washer or dishwasher), or a greywater-only (Radical Plumbing) system. This chapter presents general plumbing principles and then looks at each of these three contexts.

Surge tanks (used to absorb surges in flow), filters, pumps, and disinfection (if any) go between the collection and irrigation piping.

General Greywater Plumbing Principles

For all greywater users, it is helpful to understand some plumbing principles and terms, 1) so you understand how greywater violates the laws of physics that govern freshwater, and 2) so you can communicate unique greywater considerations to your plumber. (Drawings in this section define useful plumbing terms. Definitions are flagged with <u>squiggly underline</u>. Table 9.2 shows parts with pictures.)

There isn't a well-developed code for some of the strange things greywater plumbers have to do, so understanding general principles[14] will help navigate this *terra incognita*.

When to Get Professional Help

Help from a plumber is recommended for collection plumbing.

It is said that "plumbers safeguard the health of the nation." This is not an exaggeration. Don't let the senselessness of some greywater codes delude you into thinking that *all* plumbing codes are for weenies. The place where codes lose credibility is in the garden, where greywater can be treated better and more ecologically than anywhere else. Under the house, use a plumber and deviate from code only when you know what you're doing, or your plumbing may burble and clog.

Squander No Fall

"<u>Fall</u>" is the vertical distance between greywater source and destination. Every trap, pipe run, joint, valve, etc. uses up fall in order to keep the water flowing downhill. Proper slope is the #1 driver of collection plumbing design and installation (and Branched Drain irrigation piping as well). For 90% of greywater installations, fall is a **critical, system-limiting factor to be conserved religiously**.

Tests with clear pipe have shown that unpressurized, crud-laden water flows best in pipes that are either vertical or that slope ¼" per foot (2%). At this slope the solids and the water move at the same speed. With shallower slope, water won't flow well. At steeper slope, especially over long pipe runs, the water tends to get ahead of the solids and leave them behind. If the next water down the pipe doesn't scour them off, the solids build up and clog the pipe (however, field accounts of this problem are rare with greywater systems). Most people get away with a bit more slope, and even (horrors!) a bit less, if the length is short. Be sure there is cleanout access

---

Collection Plumbing and Inspections

Use a skilled plumber for the house plumbing when the system is to be inspected. The typical inspector's eyes glaze over in the yard and they don't say much, perhaps not wishing to reveal ignorance. Then, they hold your feet to the fire on the inside plumbing where they really know how to apply the code, zapping you on the slightest deviation.

Warn your plumber and use this phenomenon to your advantage. Time and again it has been noted that if the standard plumbing is impeccable, inspectors assume the novel part is done to the same high standard and wave it through. Conversely, if the collection plumbing is flaky, they'll assume you did the irrigation piping wrong, too.

nearby. Going uphill is out of the question, for any distance. Crud will surely settle in the bottom of any U-shaped section and block the flow (except in traps, where the vertical drop just before the trap blasts the crud through; see Figure 4.1).

You've got to really watch your plumber because it is extra work to fanatically conserve fall, and they will probably be reluctant to do it.

Fall conservation may be a point of contention with your plumber as it can quadruple the design and installation effort. Septic tanks and sewer lines are typically *much* deeper underground than greywater lines, and their destination is unlikely to change. Therefore, plumbers are accustomed to conserving no more fall than is necessary to make it to the sewer/septic line, which is not much. Extra fall conservation tends to be viewed as a major waste of effort.

Greywater collection plumbing differs from conventional septic/sewer collection plumbing in two important respects. First, the destinations are generally much higher. Second, it is highly likely that as plants grow and die and new ones are added over the long life of the collection plumbing, you will want to send the greywater somewhere else at a slightly higher elevation.

Achieving proper slope often involves considerable heroics. I often chip through concrete, replumb far upstream, or do whatever else is necessary to get the right slope. I had to replumb the entire underneath of the house in Real World Example #1 to gain half a foot of elevation in the greywater pipes. Systems that require a surge tank require more fall.

Explain to your plumber clearly what you need and the logic behind it. Ask that they make every connection and pipe run as high as possible.

Build for Future Flexibility

This is important for all systems.

At every opportunity, leave flexibility to reconfigure the system in the future. Where possible, leave *enough pipe* between fittings so they can be sawn apart and reconfigured without throwing the whole assembly away. This may conflict with conserving fall at times, but do it whenever you can afford the fall. Your plumber will understand this issue. Expensive, complicated components such as valves and dipper boxes (Figure 9.5) should be installed with no-hub connectors (removable couplings), or silicone sealer instead of ABS glue. (Silicone should be allowed to dry 24 hours before use.) Outdoors, connections can be friction fit (that is, without glue). This enables these valuable components to be easily serviced, reused, reconfigured, or replaced.

Divert Greywater Downstream from Traps and Vents

This issue is specific to greywater collection plumbing. Once in the yard, traps are not needed, and venting is usually not an issue (any necessary venting is usually accomplished back through the house plumbing).

Vents and traps are unlikely to be a point of contention with your plumber. Running greywater separately from toilet water is unusual, but plumbers can do a great job on traps and vents with their existing knowledge base.

One of the features that distinguish modern plumbing from earlier, cholera-epidemic-era efforts is the vented P-trap, so named because it looks like a P on its side. The P-trap, by virtue of the small pocket of water it always holds, blocks noxious gases and pernicious filth in the sewer/septic from escaping up through the pipe into the house (Figure 4.1).

Careful distance, elevation, and size relationships must be maintained to prevent unforeseen P-trap failure. For instance, the P-trap must be vented just downstream to break the vacuum created behind a flow of water that would otherwise siphon the little pocket of water right out of it. (The S-traps in some older homes are unvented and can suffer this problem, which can be alleviated by making the S-trap a larger-sized pipe.) The vent must be within the critical distance, so the drainpipe can't siphon the water out of the trap.

Venting for greywater can be totally separate from the toilet vent.

> ### Note on Surge Tank Collection Plumbing
>
> *Plumbing to the surge tank for a pumped, centralized system can be done with less conservation of fall. However, these systems have not proven durable so far. If you decide in five years that you need a gravity-powered system, this collection plumbing will be useless if the outlet is too low.*

FIGURE 4.1: P-TRAP AND CRITICAL DISTANCE

Air in to break siphon / Sewer gas out

Vent allows sewer gas to escape and breaks siphon to prevent water from being sucked out of trap

Critical distance 3½' (1 m) for 1½" pipe, 5' (1.5 m) for 2" pipe (maximums: any more, and trap water could siphon)

Vertical drop blasts solids through trap

P-trap keeps sewer gas and bugs out of house

Trap weir (spill point)

¼"/ft fall (2%) = optimal pipe slope

Waste line to septic/sewer

Or, code allows you to tie into the toilet vent 12" *(30 cm)* above the spill point of the highest fixture served by the vent (see Figure 4.3). This eliminates the possibility of blackwater backing up through the vent into the greywater system. (In some areas you may be allowed to use auto-vents, a delicate kind of vent with a valve that lets air in but not out. These can go inside the house.)

Traps and vents are optional if you cut all ties to the septic/sewer and do Radical Plumbing.

Provide Cleanouts and Inspection Access

This is important for all systems.

Keep ease of service in mind. You don't want to build *anything* that cannot be inspected or serviced—especially plumbing that could last the life of your house.

Code calls for a cleanout, a port where you can run a plumber's snake into the pipe to clear it, every 135° of cumulative bend (a 90° plus a 45°, for example). Snaking down the pipe (with the flow) is preferable to snaking uphill. However, either direction works. Plumbers incorporate cleanouts in the collection plumbing as a matter of course (remember to add them to Branched Drain irrigation piping).

The face of some 3-way valves is removable,[s2] providing cleanout access in all three directions (care must be taken to not wreck the inside sealing surfaces of the valve with the snake). A dipper distribution box (p. 92) provides excellent access to every pipe connected to it, without worry of wrecking a seal.

Take plug out to clear clogs with a plumbing snake.

A cleanout right after the line exits the house is handy. Locate this by a rain downspout and you have a perfect setup for periodic flushing of salts as well as snaking. Don't hook the downspout into it permanently. That is illegal, and may overload the system at some point.

Design for Easy Maintenance and Troubleshooting

This is important for all systems.

A well-designed system provides auditory and visual signs of its distress. Slow drains or water running loose in the yard are *not* catastrophic failures. Water overflowing into the house, greywater siphoning into the potable water supply, or a $500 pump burning out *are*. An inaudible pump is likely to burn out when it strains, unheard, against a clogged irrigation line for days. With a system that overflows silently and cleanly into the sewer when the filter clogs, weeks' worth of greywater may be wasted each time the filter clogs, before it occurs to anyone to check it.

Greywater systems may require regular filter cleaning or other troubleshooting. Table 4.1 is geared to the Drum with Effluent Pump system, but the principle of thinking "what will happen if..." is valid for all system types. Design your system so it provides you with the proper cues—noticeable, but not catastrophic—when it needs attention. Incorporate an easily

TABLE 4.1: FAILURE MODES FOR FILTER AND PUMP SYSTEMS

Failure mode	Design feature	What will happen
Primary filter clogs (before surge tank; occurs normally with use)	No overflow (preferred)	Drains will run slowly, then not at all, letting you know it's time to clean filter. Disgusting water may back up into lower fixtures such as baths and showers.
	Overflow	Water will flow out overflow; *if you can hear it,* you'll know it's time to clean filter.
Secondary filter clogs (downstream of surge tank)	Pressure relief (preferred)	Water will be pumped out of pressure relief until you unclog filter.
	No pressure relief	Pump will work against clogged filter until you notice or it dies. *Note: most submersible pumps can operate against blocked line for a long time without damage, as long as they are submerged.*
Pump failure	N/A	Same as clogged primary filter, above.
Irrigation lines or emitters blocked	N/A	Same as clogged secondary filter, above.
Check valve held open by hair (see Figure 4.3)	N/A	Water may leak downhill from irrigation lines back into surge tank, causing pump to cycle on over and over.
Surge capacity exceeded before filter	No collection line overflow	Lower-elevation fixtures overflow.
Surge capacity exceeded in tank	No surge tank overflow	Lower-elevation fixtures overflow.
Irrigation area saturated	No dispersal alternative	Possibility of waterlogging, greywater runoff.

switchable bypass to the septic/sewer for when your system needs maintenance or you don't want to use greywater. In addition to a manual bypass, you want an overflow that splashes conspicuously but harmlessly outside if the system is non-operational (a more health-department-friendly option is an alarm that sounds when water overflows to the regular drain).

Collecting Laundry (Pressurized) Greywater

You can skip this if you are not diverting laundry water in its own separate system.

Washer pumps can be used to move greywater long distances horizontally and short distances vertically. The appeal is that you don't have to buy any additional hardware, surge tank, or filter. Both collection and irrigation piping are vastly simpler, cheaper, more ecological, and more flexible. Unless you have a centralized system to pressurize all greywater, it's worth it to plumb laundry greywater separately. For washing machines, collection plumbing can be as simple as shoving the outlet hose through a window or a hole drilled in the wall to irrigation piping just outside. For details, see Laundry to Landscape, Chapter 7.

In rare instances, using the washer pump to distribute greywater can result in premature pump failure. The washer can be vented of pressure through an air gap and treated as a gravity-driven source—this is how it's conventionally plumbed. The advantage is that the load on the pump is the same minimal load the appliance was designed for. The disadvantage: the collection and irrigation piping are way more costly.

Collecting Gravity-Flow Greywater

Read this closely if you are cutting into your plumbing or building a new house.

To collect water from gravity-driven greywater sources such as sinks, tub, and shower, major replumbing is necessary.

Greywater collection plumbing may be fairly straightforward if drainpipes are easily accessed, or impossible if they are entombed under a concrete slab foundation. In any case, using a **professional plumber to plan and execute collection plumbing is highly recommended.** Without the correct fall, venting, and traps, the system may not drain satisfactorily over time. In some areas, it is illegal to modify your own plumbing for these reasons.*

Collection plumbing is a good place to stick to code. An intelligent plumber unfamiliar with greywater can successfully ensure that the collection plumbing's fitting-by-fitting detail is done correctly. However, for the vast majority of plumbers, it is *critical* to guide them on the overall design and check frequently to be sure that they do a good job at the points where greywater plumbing diverges from conventional practice. Otherwise you will probably have to redo something. If you do want to tackle this yourself, refer to a plumbing book and the irrigation piping tips in Chapter 10, and/or have a plumber check your work.

For gravity sources, the plumbing that routes water from the fixtures to the outside will be conventional except for these few respects:

❖ **Rigorous conservation of fall**—This impacts the design of every joint and pipe run. You must have a specific benchmark and an ironclad agreement with your plumber as to the height where pipes will exit the house, in order for it to be possible to irrigate plantings right around the house.
❖ **Toilet water will be separate**—For new construction, I recommend *running greywater in separate pipes until outside the building*. This gives you flexibility to add a greywater system in the future.
❖ **Diverter valves**—Installed to enable greywater to be diverted to septic or sewer in case the soil is waterlogged, the system is down, or you want to use some nasty cleaners that you don't want on your plants. (Some states allow a higher-capacity greywater system instead of a backup system.)

Continue p. 41

***You may wish to skip the next two pages unless you are a builder or unfazed by technical stuff.** Still reading? These pages give a few examples of how collection plumbing can be done. Every installation is different. There is more on collection plumbing for new construction and slabs in our* Builder's Greywater Guide.[6]

The exact rules vary by state/county. In general, a homeowner can work on their own plumbing, but can't hire themselves out for plumbing, and in many places can't hire a non-plumber (neighbor's kid, migrant laborer) to do their plumbing.

FIGURE 4.3: HOW TO TIE INTO PLUMBING

Vent through roof

Vents tied together 12" (30 cm) above **spill point** of highest fixture (where water would overflow; lip of sink in this case)

Tub vent

Sink vent

Toilet vent

P-trap

Sanitary tee to merge flow into a vertical pipe

Combo tee-wye to merge flow into a horizontal pipe

P-trap

Always divert greywater downstream from vents and traps

Cleanout

To septic/ sewer

Cuts

Cleanout to snake clogs out of line

Pipe to garden

3-way diverter valve switches flow between garden and septic/sewer

←— **Inlet**

Swing check or backwater valve only allows water to flow one way, so toilet water can't back into GWS* likely clog point, only install if code requires

Pipe

No-hub connector

Street 45° bend (street= hub on one end, pipe-sized on the other)

To septic/ sewer

EXPLODED VIEW

To garden

To septic/ sewer

Wye replaced with street wye, glued to backwater and 3-way valve with silicone

DIVERSION INSTALLED

*GWS=greywater system

FIGURE 4.4: GREYWATER DIVERSIONS

Two drains merge right before diverter valve, septic line has to double back.

No-hub connectors on long pipe allow for valve reuse. 2" no-hubs fit directly on smaller ports of the valve we sell.

Well-labelled diversion.

Greywater line exits crawl space at proper slope...after chipping out concrete. Below-grade surge tanks like this need to be anchored against floating when it rains.

FROM CAST IRON DRAIN LINES

Cutting the old iron pipe with a sawsall.

Before: cast iron drainpipe for bathroom in an old New Mexico adobe.

Greywater plumbing subassembled (no glue).

New Mexico—required overflow to septic (a diverter valve is not required; this is full-time GW unless frozen/clogged)

After: Greywater collection plumbing installed.

Surge Capacity

For Laundry to Landscape and Branched Drain systems, all surge capacity is in the receiving landscape; the other sections don't apply.

Surge capacity, or the ability to handle peak flows, should be provided in every system. Systems without any flow bottlenecks (e.g., Branched Drain) have all their surge capacity in the receiving landscape (e.g., in mulch basins). Most other systems require tanks upstream of bottlenecks. We'll now look at all the sizes of surges (Table 4.2), and places surges can be accommodated: collection pipes, surge tanks, irrigation pipes, and landscape.

A bathtub can drain at 15 gpm, far in excess of what a pump or filter can accommodate. If the washing machine cycles on at the same time the bathtub is draining, 30 gal of water could flow out in 1 minute, followed by another 15 the next.[m] For most homes, 45 gal of surge capacity is sufficient. If you habitually launder while you are in the shower and your kids are in the tub, you need more. The overflow consequences of exceeding surge capacity have a major bearing on this decision. Systems that require a surge tank require more fall.

TABLE 4.2: GREYWATER SURGE VOLUMES

Water source	Typical surge	gallons	cubic feet	liters
Washing machine	1 min each cycle	15	2.0	57
Tub draining	3 min	45	6.0	170
Low-flow shower	10 min	20	2.7	76
High-flow shower	10 min	50	6.7	190
Bathroom sink (low-flow)	1 min	1.5	0.2	5.7
Kitchen sink (draining)	1 min	4	0.5	15

Surge Capacity in Collection Plumbing

This only matters if you have a filter before the surge tank.

Surge capacity before a surge tank filter is given little thought. In most designs it amounts to whatever space there is in the collection lines (see Table 4.3). Collection plumbing is usually sized to accommodate the flow if everything were draining at once. It is a rare greywater system that requires bigger than 2" pipe to achieve this.[*] The volume of prefilter surge capacity determines how soon you notice slow draining and need to clean your filter. A common amount is 10 gal *(40 L)*; if you have short collection lines and fall to spare, you can install a *pre*filter surge tank. Design it so solids are flushed through, otherwise it will need periodic cleaning. Bigger pipe could accommodate surges but may not purge solids afterward.

Surge Tanks

Typically surge tanks are located downstream of pressurized greywater sources and upstream of pumps, filters, and small irrigation orifices that slow the flow: in other words, anywhere surge capacity is needed to prevent a problematic backup from a flow bottleneck.

The simplest surge tank is a 30–55 gal plastic drum *(100–200 L)*. The most common application was the Laundry Drum, but that has been superseded by the Laundry to Landscape system, which uses mulch basins for surge capacity. Greywater corrodes metal drums after a few years. Empty plastic drums are UPS-able, increasing your scrounging range. Various industries generate surplus drums that they give away or sell cheaply. Reject any that held something toxic. Nurseries and hardware stores sometimes sell plastic drums. Inexpensive plastic trash cans *appear* to work as surge tanks. But, they soon become trash themselves when sunlight weakens them and the water weight splits them open. Drums with tight-fitting, large lids are ideal, but are much rarer than drums with two small bungholes. The latter work if you don't need to put a pump inside, or you can saw the whole top off, then rig it as a lid. Laundry sinks next to washers can be used as surge tanks.

Surge tanks that are buried during drought can suddenly pop to the surface when rains finally saturate the soil. If you bury a tank, anchor it well against floating. The upward force on an empty drum surrounded by water is considerable: almost 500 lbs *(200 kg)* for a 55 gal *(200 L)* drum. Certain soils also progressively cave in buried drums as the soil expands and contracts. Tanks designed to be buried don't have this problem.[s5]

Surge tanks often stink. Smell can be reduced by minimizing the holding time. Sealing the tank and venting it through the house's roof can minimize its noticeability. Storing greywater isn't a good idea; we cover the gory details in Error: Storage of Greywater, Chapter 11.

---

[m]**Metric:** *Bathtub can drain at 55 Lpm. If washing machine cycles on while tub is draining, 115 L can flow out in 1 min, and 55 L the next min. A 170 L surge capacity is enough for most homes.*

[*]*New codes that call for 3" greywater lines in large single family residences are more about flow of money than water.*

Surge Capacity in Irrigation Piping

Surge capacity in irrigation piping is rarely a limiting factor. It does, however, affect evenness of irrigation. Suppose you have 62 gal of surge capacity in 100' of 4" leachline and your pump cycles on with 8" of water in the tank and off at 3".[m] The few gallons it pumps out with each cycle will only wet the first few feet of the line. If it were 100' of ½" dripline, the first gallon would fill and pressurize it, and the rest would be pumped out evenly over emitters along the whole line. (The cost of this better distribution is more work for the pump.)

To water with large, infrequent doses, improve distribution, and give the soil resting time, set the <u>float switch</u> so the pump cycles on when the surge tank is nearly full, and shuts off when it is as empty as possible (p. 141). *Note: Greywater can go septic if it sits in a dosing surge tank while you're on vacation. Also, long float-switch tethers can tangle or hang up.*

Surge Capacity in the Receiving Landscape

The simplest place to accommodate greywater surges is in the landscape, as Branched Drain, Laundry to Landscape, and Landscape Direct systems do. For all systems, the surge capacity in the landscape—basins, swales, and soil—should be adequate to receive the largest expected peak flow (though some automated systems can be set to send excess greywater to septic/sewer). A few gallons of greywater landing on hard soil could run off into the street. But even 100 gal of greywater may not fill a deep mulch basin around a large tree to the point of surfacing or overflowing, even if the soil is full of rainwater.

As previously mentioned, the possible consequences of exceeding surge capacity affect system design. For example, if the whole area is mulched, any water that overflows a basin is still covered by mulch, so it's no big deal. For most systems, making the basins twice the volume of the expected surge is sufficient. For big systems, or stringently regulated systems, more sophisticated estimation of landscape surge capacity is described in Greywater Calculations in our *Builder's Greywater Guide.*[6]

Dosing Siphon

Note: these are rarely employed, and it is tricky to get homemade dosing siphons to work reliably.

A dosing siphon (Figure 4.5) turns many small doses of greywater into one large one, without a pump. If you try one, make sure the outlet line is small enough for an average surge to activate the siphon and not just dribble over the spill point; 1½" pipe should work. Accumulated sludge and scum could eventually block the outlet.

FIGURE 4.5: DO-IT-YOURSELF DOSING SIPHON

Inlet (must be vented)

Siphon spill point level should be between top of the drum and start of the curve on inlet pipe (thanks to Eric Hughes of Berkeley for this suggestion)

ABS slip by 2" male pipe thread

Watertight connections

Water flows in a little at a time...

...Water level rises in pipe as well...when water level reaches spill point and large enough surge comes through to fill full diameter of pipe, siphon starts and whole drum empties at once

ABS slip by female pipe thread

Outlet (must be unobstructed)

Manufactured dosing siphons are reputed to work well—a 2" one costs about $225[s3,s4]

ABS slip by male pipe thread

Ball valve open to drain or clean surge tank

[m]***Metric:** 0.2 m³ surge capacity in 30 m of 100 mm leachline, pump cycles on at 20 cm and off at 8 cm; 100 gal = .4 m³*

TABLE 4.3: GREYWATER PLUMBING PARTS

Env. impact	Parts	Gravity collection	Pressure collection	Filtered irrigation	Unfiltered irrigation	Sold by	$/ft or $/each	Flow rate gpm	Surge capacity gal/ft or gal/each	L/m or L/each	Normally used for; available from
	Rigid pipe										
•	¾" schedule 40 PVC			x		10, 20', 3, 6m	$0.25	12	0.025	0.31	
•	1" schedule 40 PVC		x	x	x	10, 20', 3, 6m	$0.40	15	0.041	0.50	
•	1½" schedule 40 ABS	x			x	20', 6m	$0.60		0.100	1.24	Drain-Waste-Vent
•	2" schedule 40 ABS	x			x	20', 6m	$3.00		0.164	2.04	(DWV); hardware store
	Flexible tubing										
.	½" HDPE dripline			x		100, 500'	$0.35	4	0.013	0.16	Drip irrigation;
.	¾" HDPE dripline			x	x	100, 500'	$0.20	8	0.022	0.27	hardware store
•	1" HDPE dripline			x	x	foot, 600'	$0.50	12	0.040	0.50	Potable water, land-scape; hardware store
●	1" Spa-flex[s6]		x		x	foot, 50'	$1.00	15	0.041	0.51	Hot tubs; pool supply store[s6,s12]
•	¾" garden hose			x	x	50, 75'	$0.60	7	0.025	0.31	Landscape; hardware store
	Emitters										
•	Underground dripline			x		187.5'	$0.12	1.15	0.013	0.16	Septic leachfield; plumbing supply
●	Standard recycled HDPE infiltrator w/2 end plates			x		each (6' long)	$130.00		76	287	
	Valves										oasisdesign.net[s9]
●	1" brass 3-way diverter valve		x	x	x	each	$50.00				
●	1½" – 2" 3-way diverter valve[s2, s9]	x				each	$50.00				Pools; pool supply, oasisdesign.net[s9]
●	Electric switch for 2" diverter valve	x				each	$120.00				
.	½" drip ball valve			x		each	$3.00				Drip irrigation; plumbing supply
•	Pair of RV dump valves					each	$15.00				RV supplier; if 3-way valve not obtainable
•	1" PVC schedule 40 swing check valve		x	x	x	each	$11.00				Hardware store
●	3" ABS schedule 40 backwater valve	x				each	$27.00				Sewer; plumbing supply
	Filters										
.	Pantyhose	x	x			pair	$2.50	.	4	50	Cover legs; drugstore
.	Airless paint sprayer bag	x	x			each	$2.00		1	12	Painting; hardware store
	Pumps										
●	Zabel p-se-12t (integral switch)			x	(x)	each	$289.00	17			Dewater basements, pump septic effluent, etc.; hardware store, Little Giant Pump Company,[s8] ReWater Systems,[s5] specialty stores
●	Little Giant 5.5asp (integral switch)			x		each	$273.00	35			
●	Little Giant 5msp (needs float switch)			x		each	$203.00	15			
●	Float switch					each	$45.00				

3-way diverter valve

Choosing and Finding Parts

Greywater collection plumbing parts are mostly the same as those for standard collection plumbing. Table 4.3 shows most greywater parts (except Branched Drain parts, which are in Table 9.2). Within the family of drain-waste-vent (DWV) plumbing parts, ABS or PVC plastic drainpipe works well. This system has a huge diversity of fittings and bends. (If you are working in the nonindustrialized world, see *PVC Sanitario*, p. 90.)

A few fittings from other plumbing systems are used in greywater systems; these are noted in Table 4.3. With those few exceptions, you don't want to use pipe and fittings designed for other purposes (such as potable water, for example; see Error: Freshwater Designs and Hardware Used for Greywater, Chapter 11).

Minimize Plastic Impact

Design to use the *least amount* of the least damaging materials. HDPE is the least environmentally damaging plastic, followed by ABS, your most likely choice. PVC is the most evil, but hard to avoid. Cement works. Unfired clay or earth channels work well in the nonindustrialized world. Other options aren't so practical: iron is rough inside and awkward to work with, copper is very expensive and damaging in its extraction, and bamboo would need frequent replacement.

Proper Fittings and Optimal-Sized Pipe

For gravity flows, use sanitary drainpipe and drain fittings. These have no shoulder on the joints and have nice sweeping curves (Figure 4.6). Pressurized and/or filtered greywater can go through freshwater supply fittings.

All greywater plumbing should be corrosion resistant and of the proper diameter.

What size pipe and fittings should you use? With gravity flow in too big a pipe, solids can form stationary islands in a thin film of water on the bottom of the pipe (not to mention the waste of plastic and money). Too small, and the pipe may fill to the top with water, overload, clog, and completely change the physics of flow splitting (Figure 4.7). A 2" pipe is plenty for the greywater main of any but the most palatial of residences and may take longer to clog. A 1½" pipe offers good scouring flows and economy.

With pressurized flows, solids can settle out of a slow flow in a big pipe. The same flow in a small pipe would be fast enough to scour solids through ("scouring flow" is the engineering term for a flow fast enough to mobilize solids and move them through the pipe; Oasis Greywater Extras[43] and Water Storage Extras[44] both have calculators for flow speed in different sizes of pipe).

FIGURE 4.6: SANITARY FITTINGS VS SUPPLY FITTINGS

Smooth

Sweeping turn

Sanitary drain

Raised shoulder clogs can form on it

Tight turn

Supply

FIGURE 4.7: EFFECTS OF PIPE SIZE ON SOLIDS IN GRAVITY-FLOW DRAIN WATER

½" *pipe would overload even if not blocked*

¾" *pipe: return airflow restricted*

1" *pipe*

1¼" *pipe*

1½" *pipe: solid still floats free*

2" *pipe: solid skims along bottom*

3" *pipe: solid rolls some-what*

4" *pipe: solid is an immobile island in thin flow*

Valves

Valves are expensive. However, they are critical, so don't cut corners. (If you need an inexpensive system, consider one of the simplest, valveless greywater systems, such as Landscape Direct or Radical Plumbing; or, skip diversion and just plumb for full-time greywater in a higher-capacity system.)

Diverter Valves

You can't shut off the flow of greywater in the usual sense—if you generate it, it has to go somewhere. So the valves in simple greywater systems are generally *diverter valves*. They direct a flow to one destination or another. In collection plumbing, the diversion is from the landscape to the septic/sewer system; in irrigation piping, it's from one irrigation zone to another, or to a dispersal field. In most cases, you want to use a 3-way diverter valve. Other options include operating two or more shutoff valves together or moving a pipe or hose between different drain lines (see photos).

Ideally, unique portions of the flow have their own separate diverter valves. For example, I like to divert the kitchen sink separately so it can be sent to the septic/sewer while the other greywater continues to go to the yard. You might want to do this at the first sign of system overload or if the yard doesn't need greywater at the moment, but you don't want all the greywater going into your septic tank. (Another option for a kitchen sink is to route the wash side permanently to the septic/sewer and the rinse side to the yard.)

Note: 3-way valves are rare even in well-stocked plumbing suppliers—look for them in pool supply houses or order from oasisdesign.net/greywater/divertervalves.[s2,s9]

Simplest possible diverter valve: *A coconut shell (rock, chunk of wood, dirt clod… whatever) is shifted by foot from blocking one greywater furrow to another.*

"Valve" (coconut husk)

Diverter for cheap labor conditions.
Slide the shroud shut, and water goes to trees. Slide it open, and water goes to treatment/dispersal.
The shroud can also be set partly open, so low flows go to dispersal and only high flows make it through to trees. This helps maintain aerobic conditions by providing more dry-out time. This valve was made in rural Mexico of PVC sanitario and cement. It could be done in ABS with an unglued wye, which rotates up to send the water straight or down to let it out.

Shroud closed, water goes through pipe to trees

Shroud open, water goes through lower pipe

which drains this register to alternative location

Inlet
Zone 1
Zone 2

Brass 1" 3-way valve *for washing machines.*

Diverter valve to switch between irrigation zones.
The interior of a plastic 3-way diverter valve would ideally be smooth, but it is not at all. It is one of the mysteries of greywater system design that these things never clog, while so many other things do.

Moving washer hose between multiple standpipes *achieves diverter valve effect.*

From washer

SEWER SANTA CRUZ RIVER
OLIVE + POMEGRANATE
ORANGE
FIG
WHITE SAPOTE

To various trees

A 3-way diverter valve is spliced in under a sink. Note that the trap had to be raised to make space.

Before   *After*

Diverter Valve Installation

The installation of 3-way valves to toggle between greywater destinations is likely to be unfamiliar but readily understandable to most plumbers.

The diverter valve must be accessible if you want it to get used. This is tricky with retrofits, as the valve must be positioned between the fixture vent and the septic/sewer connection...usually in an awkward corner under the house. Sometimes you can reach the valve from a hatch in the floor, or through a cabinet under the sink. Some diverter valves can be fitted with an extension handle so that a valve installed under the house can be turned from inside. Motor drives are available for diverter valves. These can be controlled remotely with the push of a button (if you've got $200 for the actuator, and provided there is power).

Verify access to turn the valve, access to remove the face, and that a bunch of fall is not squandered in its installation. If you can, route the greywater out of the house and put the valve there. If necessary, do a U-turn for the line connecting to the septic/sewer.

Note: the inlet on a 3-way valve can be shifted to any of the three ports by unscrewing and rotating the valve face. This handy feature opens more options for the design of this complicated junction. Also, if the inlet is the leg of the tee, and you position the valve so both outlets are open, the flow will split into both outlets, though not nearly as cleanly as with a double ell. Diverters are best installed with no-hub connectors or silicone sealer (see Build for Future Flexibility, p. 23). It's a nice touch to give pipes a tweak in the hub so they come out of the valve sloped (as in the photo "A 2% downward tweak on pipes," Chapter 10, p. 103).

Two Shutoff Valves in Lieu of a Diverter Valve

A common idea to cut corners is to use two shutoff valves (below) in lieu of a 3-way valve. However, if both shutoff valves are shut by mistake, an upstream pump can burn out, or water with nowhere to go may overflow. Also, the dead-end space before a closed valve goes anaerobic and accumulates crud (diverter valves don't pose these problems). If the space is deep enough and the valve shut long enough, the crud forms a solid plug so no water can pass when the valve is reopened. Using two RV dump valves is better; they take less space than ball valves, so the crud plug would be smaller. And, they disassemble to get the plug out.

Shutoff Valves

More complex greywater systems have shutoff valves that enable various functions such as draining a filter or surge tank, etc. Gate valves are less expensive than ball valves, but are far more likely to clog with hair or lint and fail to shut off completely. They are not recommended. RV dump valves work well. They are reasonably priced, and disassemble to provide complete access for service or replacement.

Check and Backwater Valves

Check valves prevent water in lines that slope uphill from running back into the surge tank and causing a pump to cycle endlessly. They can also be used to prevent blackwater from backing into a greywater line. Use *swing* check valves, not *spring* check valves, as the latter clog too easily. A fancy check valve called a backwater valve is designed for sewage.

Nicely labelled diverter valve for a bathtub *in a secret compartment between toilet and wall.*

An RV dump valve *is inexpensive, takes less space than a ball valve, and can be replaced without cutting pipe.*

Electric Valves

Most inexpensive electric solenoid irrigation valves don't work with greywater systems. There isn't enough pressure to operate their diaphragms, they corrode quickly, and soap sticks the diaphragms shut in greywater. However, a few do work. The Toro 2500t, for example, has a sensitive diaphragm that works at 15 psi and doesn't stick.

Very expensive motorized electric valves designed for wastewater are available, and motorized actuators for 3-way diverter valves also work.

3-way valve actuator *and indoor switch parts.*

Tools for Collection Plumbing

The following tools are almost always necessary for collection plumbing:

- ❖ tape measure
- ❖ levels—*for gauging correct slope*
- ❖ hacksaw, plastic pipe saw, sawsall, or plastic pipe cutter
- ❖ ABS glue
- ❖ drill and large bit or hole saw—*to make holes for pipe to go through*
- ❖ ¼" nutdriver, wrench, or cordless drill—*for tightening no-hub connectors*
- ❖ adjustable wrench
- ❖ knife—*to deburr pipe ends*

And these tools are sometimes needed:

- ❖ transit or water level—*for checking levels across long distances; see Appendix B*
- ❖ sawsall with metal cutting blade—*to cut cast iron drainpipes used in most pre-1970 homes*
- ❖ cordless drill—*for pipe hangers*
- ❖ narrow trench shovel—*for running pipes underground to yard*
- ❖ pipe wrenches—*for threaded fittings, if any*

Plastic pipe cutter *Makes fast, clean cuts–without plastic sawdust.*

Radical Plumbing: A Fraction of the Resource Use

No need to read this unless you are in the back woods. This is the way to get way ahead of the curve on living better with less resource consumption. You don't need or want a plumber if you go this route.

"Radical" means root. A radical solution addresses a problem—in this case, the drawbacks of septic and sewers—at its root.[15,16] The greatest benefits at the lowest cost are achieved when there is no redundant wastewater system—when a composting toilet/greywater system is not an add-on but replaces the septic/sewer entirely. That is the genesis of Radical Plumbing.

Elimination of a redundant backup system has implications for greywater system design:

The irrigation system needs to be designed to be able to handle all the greywater load, all the time. In practice, this won't change the design much. Most greywater-only systems are built in contexts with nonexistent regulations, where the perfection standard is simply shifted to accept occasional greywater system overload. By any rational analysis, greywater system overload is of little consequence, either absolutely or compared to septic or sewer system failure, so this isn't generally problematic.

Where a greywater-only system is permitted, the requirements generally include so much overcapacity that the absence of an alternative dispersal system shouldn't increase the design requirements.

The collection plumbing can be *greatly* simplified. An interesting snowballing of benefits occurs in collection plumbing design when you commit fully to your greywater system and forget about a septic/sewer connection.

Drainpipes have water-seal traps to keep sewer gas out of the home. To keep the water from being siphoned out of the traps, the traps need to be vented. Wastewater rushing down a pipe into a septic tank displaces air. Because that air has no place to go other than out the vent, it has to rush back up the drainpipe even as the water rushes down. One of the reasons drainpipes are so darned big is to accommodate this air countercurrent above the water flow.

Well, if there's nothing but green garden and blue sky downstream from your greywater lines, gas traps are not essential for habitability, which means you don't need vents. Moreover, any displaced air can head out into the garden *ahead* of the water, so the pipes can be considerably smaller. Then (by gosh), once you're freed from the fancy-schmancy turns and extra connections for traps and vents, you can switch from ABS (environmentally questionable) to HDPE (environmentally benign but tough to make smooth joints and tight turns with).

Bottom line: Instead of plumbing your house with a truckload of ABS that costs thousands of dollars to install, you can get your water out with about $100 worth of HDPE that you can install yourself. Instead of 1½"–2" pipe, you can use 1¼" HDPE, or even 1". (If you never thought of this before, you've got plenty of company. Thanks to Ianto Evans for expanding my thinking on small, unvented pipes.) *Note: You want to build a system that has no standing water (makes anaerobic smells) if you have no traps. Wind or solar heating of drainpipes can push drainpipe air into the room. A drain screen and/or S-trap is recommended to keep crawlers from crawling into your house through the pipe!*

FIGURE 4.8: RADICAL VS CONVENTIONAL PLUMBING

I am excited to move forward with the PE tubing alternative. However, none of the fittings are suitable for drain water. Both the compression fittings and the barbed fittings common in the US leave ragged, crud-trapping edges. Branched Drain systems with PE are attractive, uncharted territory. In Spain, where external couplings are the norm and PE tubing shares the same outer diameter as PVC, I recently did a number of Branched Drain systems with long HDPE runs slip fit into PVC flow splitters. This has worked so far. As mentioned, the easiest way to split the flow among many plants is to not combine fixture flows in the first place. For a high-volume kitchen in Spain we started the flow splitting with separate lines for each side of the kitchen sink; one went to a Branched Drain, one went to Twisted Tees. The ultimate expression of this principle, combined with Radical Plumbing, would be to give various different areas Landscape Direct irrigation: for example, one outdoor spot for dishwashing, another for laundry, another for bathing, and so on, with no pipes at all.

I've recently explored fabricating HDPE flow splitters (below). These featured bell ends to facilitate movement of solids, and some reduce pipe size as well—great for arterial branching. We went down to 1"; in a no-pressure system, ¾" is probably the smallest size worth attempting. On a big slope, ½" might work. Hand making these artisanal fittings one by one isn't practical; perhaps someday we'll be able to buy them factory-made.

PE is flexible and curvy, thus challenging to lay at a perfectly consistent slope of 2%. More slope is desirable than if you were laying out the same system in ABS. Uncoiling the tubing onto a hot flat surface helps it adjust to being straight. For the Spain systems we clamped some runs at perfect slope to the side of a stone wall, others we tied to perfectly sloped cables (p. 103).

HDPE tubing slip fit in PVC branch supported by brackets. Handwash water from a sink by a composting toilet splits and waters an orange tree that shades and provides privacy for the structure weights. I've only seen these 1" drain fittings in Europe. (See also picture of reduction, p. 109).

The ideal Branched Drain fitting
Wye rather than tee: splits and reduces one pipe size. Welding HDPE might be a way to open up the Radical Plumbing possibilities. It is unusual to weld pipe this small. These wyes were welded with considerable effort and expense (jig at left, welded at right, this may be a preview of the future of eco-plumbing—you saw it here first).

European HDPE fitting
No leaks, no tools. Perhaps not certified in US because it would lower income for the pipe trades.

TABLE 4.4: RADICAL VS CONVENTIONAL PLUMBING

	Radical Plumbing	Conventional plumbing
Toilet	Composting, Green Septic, or Watson Wick[24]	Flush toilet
Redundant wastewater system	None	Septic or sewer
Length of septic/sewer drain and vent pipe	Zero	30' 2", 20' 1½", 30' 3", 80 fittings, total weight ABS plastic = 150 lbs, total materials cost = $1,000, total labor for professional installation = $3,000
Greywater collection plumbing	100' 1" line, 20' 1¼" line, no fittings, total weight HDPE = 30 lbs, $100, owner installation labor = 10 hrs	30' 2", 20' 1½", 30 fittings, two 3-way valves, total weight ABS plastic = 100 lbs, total materials cost = $600, total labor for professional installation = $2,500±
(2015 costs) Greywater irrigation piping	Materials included in above lines, owner installation labor = 10 hrs	10' 2", 40' 1½", 30 fittings, total weight ABS plastic = 80 lbs, total materials cost = $300, professional installation labor = 10 hrs
Total plastic	30 lbs HDPE	330 lbs ABS
Total materials cost	$50	$1,450
Total paid labor	$0	$4,500
Total owner labor	10 hrs	10 hrs

Chapter 5: Greywater in the Landscape

Now that you've figured out how to get the greywater out of your house, it's time to consider how to handle it in the landscape. Key landscape design points were mentioned at the beginning of Chapter 3. Now we're going to get into more details. A primary consideration is whether you are designing a system only to treat and dispose of greywater (in which case you can read the paragraph below and then skip ahead to Plants for Greywater Treatment/Dispersal); or, whether you hope to reduce your freshwater consumption by using greywater for irrigation. In the latter case, we suggest you read this whole chapter carefully.

How Much Area Do You Need for Treatment/Dispersal?

Treatment/dispersal area is easy. Check the perk rate of your soil, and look up the needed area in Table 2.3, Dispersal Loading Rates. Unless your greywater flow is huge, your perk low, or your area really tiny, space shouldn't be a problem. It only remains to figure out how to disperse greywater over this area, using the greywater irrigation system of your choice.

Coordinate with Freshwater Irrigation, Actualize Water Savings

Note outdoor faucets and existing freshwater irrigation hardware on your site map. Consider how greywater use will dovetail with freshwater irrigation to actualize your water savings. In theory, a main benefit of greywater reuse is saving freshwater. To achieve this in real life, **you have to adjust your freshwater irrigation to account for the variable contribution of greywater**. The easiest way is to have zones where freshwater irrigation can be independently reduced or eliminated. In an automated system, this is done with valved zones and adjusting the controller. In a manual system, it's done by paying attention.

In sophisticated automated greywater systems, makeup irrigation water is added automatically, and greywater in excess of plant needs (if any) is automatically shunted to septic/sewer. Some systems control all irrigation with both kinds of water.

Applying the permaculture credo "the problem is the solution," greywater and freshwater can be set up to form complementary functions. Eighty percent of the root mass of most plants is in the top foot or so of soil. A drip system can keep this area at optimal moisture for optimal growth. Then, occasional large doses of manually applied greywater will flush salts and encourage plants to send roots farther than little spots right under the emitters. Deeper roots provide drought insurance and make use of stored rainwater. If you have an automated greywater system with a predictable supply, the roles can switch, with manual freshwater application providing the occasional deep watering or a different wetting pattern.

Also, greywater can be directed to new plantings, so the entire drip system does not have to be turned on more frequently to meet the temporary extra needs of a few plants.

Irrigation Efficiency

The percentage of applied water actually used by plants is the irrigation efficiency. The rest evaporates from the soil or is lost below the roots. Well-designed drip irrigation with a weather-based controller delivers a precise amount of water to the roots at the correct time. 80% of the water from a well-designed drip system is transpired by plants. With few exceptions, the irrigation efficiency of greywater systems is low: 50% or less.

The most intractable issue is that greywater generation is fairly constant, while irrigation needs may range from zero to many times the available greywater. Aside from that, the central challenge in greywater irrigation design (as with conventional irrigation) boils down to how to divide and distribute the flow.

The uniform, precise water distribution of drip irrigation is the result of relatively high pressure (15–20 psi, *100–140 kPa*) in a line with small emitter orifices.[s10] Greywater, in contrast, discharges from the house at zero pressure, full of orifice-clogging glop.

It is possible to finely filter the glop out of greywater, pressurize the water, and distribute it via drip irrigation. Filters need frequent cleaning, a disgusting job soon abandoned by all except the truly fanatical. You can, however, purchase an automated, engineered solution to this problem—for a few thousand dollars or more. Salesmen's claims to the contrary, an economical, durable greywater-to-drip solution remains elusive.

Get Your Freshwater Irrigation Under Control

You may be able to save more water by reducing freshwater irrigation waste than by reusing greywater:

❖ **Remove useless water-hog plants**—If people only walk on your lawn to mow it, replace it.

❖ **Irrigate to replace transpiration**—Check moisture and roots with a soil probe. Install a weather-based irrigation controller, etc.

❖ **Submeter your irrigation**—My new favorite conservation practice. Add a remote readout indoors where you can't miss seeing it every day (for irrigation and indoor use separately) and watch your water bill drop.

In general, only for high flows or new construction can the cost and complexity of filtering and pressurizing be justified. (For more on pumping and filtration, see the pumped systems in the System Selection Chart, and Appendix E.)

Low-tech systems sacrifice irrigation efficiency for simplicity, economy—and working long term. In the low-tech system example in Figure 5.1 (p. 40), 40% greywatering efficiency means only ⅓–½ of the total irrigation need is met by greywater, far short of what is possible in theory. But for most residential retrofit systems, this sacrifice is the best approach. In practice this means that you have far fewer outlets, with more water in each outlet. This in turn affects the choice of plants. With only a few outlets, it's a lot easier to irrigate trees than grass.

Choose the Proportion of Irrigation to Meet with Greywater

For most systems, applying greywater at a rate equal to the average year-round or average dry season irrigation demand is best.

Greywater generation is fairly constant. Irrigation need varies widely. The portion of plants' irrigation need you fill with greywater affects how many plants to plumb to, how much effort to put into supplemental freshwater irrigation, and the efficiency of greywater reuse.

If you apply enough greywater to cover peak need, most of it will be wasted most of the time. If you spread greywater widely so the application rate equals the lowest irrigation need, you will have to cover a huge area with greywater plumbing, and—unless you don't mind the plants being parched most of the time—freshwater irrigation plumbing, too.

In choosing among the options below, it can help to first draw out different scenarios for different irrigation proportions on the site map; that is, scenarios in which the greywater is distributed among more or fewer plants. Here are the advantages and disadvantages of different irrigation proportions:

TABLE 5.1: POSSIBLE MATCHES BETWEEN GREYWATER DELIVERY AND IRRIGATION NEED

Greywater application equals	Average wet season irrigation demand	Average irrigation demand (usually best)	Peak dry season irrigation demand or more
Effectiveness of water reuse	Maximized	Medium	Very low
System overload	Very unlikely	Possible in wet season with adverse soil and rainfall conditions	Likely without carefully considered design
Greywater irrigation shortfall	Large; supplemental irrigation system required	Moderate; some supplemental irrigation required	Little, none, or year-round surplus; no supplemental irrigation system necessary
Infiltration area required per 100 gpd *(376 L)* **greywater (approximately a conservative 4-person household)**	500–2,000 ft² *(30–200 m²)* outdoors in dry climate	200 ft² *(20 m²)* outdoors	Inside solar greenhouse: 40–200 ft² *(4–20 m²)* Outdoor mulch basins: 200–800 ft² *(20–80 m²)* Outdoor wetland system: 100–400 ft² *(10–40 m²)*
Greywater supply — Irrigation need .... Greywater in excess of irrigation need ▢ Freshwater irrigation ▆	Wet Dry Wet ◄······Months of year······►	Wet Dry Wet ◄···· Months of year ····►	Wet Dry Wet ◄···· Months of year ····►

❖ **All else being equal, greywater delivery should equal the average dry season irrigation demand**—This ratio represents a good overall balance between irrigation efficiency and plumbing effort. This is what I aim to achieve with a typical residential system. Supplemental irrigation will be required in the driest times.

❖ **To avoid the necessity of an alternative irrigation source, greywater delivery should equal the peak dry season irrigation demand**—Much greywater is "wasted" in this scenario, as it is delivered in excess of plant needs. On the other hand, you save the effort of making any other irrigation system; it's all covered by greywater.

Example: An institutional system with a large greywater flow irrigating a modest landscape through subsurface drip. Saving the cost of a freshwater irrigation system helps pay for the greywater system. The high efficiency of drip irrigation effectively increases the greywater supply, helping ensure that the landscape is adequately watered. Also, with numerous, closely spaced outlets, each applying water at a very low rate, greywater is so evenly distributed that excess watering is less likely to create sodden conditions.

❖ **For dispersal only (that is, for systems with little or no reuse), greywater delivery often equals or exceeds the peak dry season irrigation demand**—This ratio is most often found in wet and/or cold climates, or in areas with large wastewater flow in a small area. The primary goal is to get rid of the water in an ecologically sound way, with reuse after treatment or not at all. Plants can effectively treat an amount of greywater that is many times their irrigation need. However, applying excess water to ordinary plants in low-perk soil would likely suffocate the roots. Wetland plants don't have this problem (see Constructed Wetlands, Chapter 8). Suffocation can also be reduced by making "high-island" mulch basins. Putting the outlet a considerable distance from the trunk, possibly outside the canopy of the mature tree, would help too (see Mulch Basin Design, p. 47).

Examples: Constructed Wetlands, sometimes soil beds in a greenhouse (purified excess water seeps out of drain tiles to reuse, or through the bottom of the beds to groundwater).

❖ **For maximum reuse, greywater delivery should equal the average wet season irrigation demand**—This is most attainable in dry climates, and with a fair amount of land (see Table 5.1 for area requirements). There isn't any point in designing a system to deliver *less* than the average wet season irrigation demand; just spread the water over fewer plants and save your plumbing effort.

Example: Branched Drain to Mulch Basins, with evergreen fruit trees, in a desert (evergreens transpire at least some water in the wet season). Extensive supplemental irrigation will be required.

How Much Area Should You Irrigate?

Irrigation ability is limited when irrigation need is high but greywater generation is low. I used to calculate irrigation need with the formula in our *Builder's Greywater Guide*.[6] Then I realized that this level of precision is highly desirable for people irrigating vast fields with freshwater, but useless for small-scale landscape irrigation with greywater. First, irrigation need can vary by a factor of 10 depending on whether the day is foggy, or hot with a dry wind. Moreover, what are you going to do about it? Greywater generation does not vary according to irrigation need. There's only so much laundry you can save for a hot day, only so many dishes you can wash (I suppose you could take more showers). The best you can do is match your greywater to some sort of seasonal average need for the landscape (as discussed in the preceding section), then make up any shortfall with freshwater.

Even if you use the coarsest of guesses for irrigation need, don't forget to account for tree growth. For a Branched Drain system, I suggest planning for how big the trees are going to be in ten years. That's a reasonable balance between current and future needs, considering the difficulty of changing the system and the likelihood that further in the future, everything else may have changed (kids grown and gone, etc.). For other systems, which have a shorter life or are easier to change, you could plan for fewer years of growth. How big will the trees be? Check out other trees in your area, ask a nursery, or research this at your library or on the Internet.

Take the irrigation need you calculated in Assess Your Irrigation Need, Chapter 2, and multiply it by the proportion you just chose in the previous section.

For example, if your irrigation need is 1,000 gpw for 2,000 ft² of tree canopy (per the rule of thumb in Assess Your Irrigation Need), and you have 500 gpw of greywater, you could:

*A **soil probe** (or excavation with a post-hole digger) casts light on the mystery of what is happening underground. See where the root hairs actually are, where the soil moisture actually is. This empirical data is the foundation of effective irrigation.*

- water all 2,000 ft² through two zones, alternating between freshwater and greywater irrigation in each zone during the high-irrigation season, and watering all 2,000 ft² with greywater alone when irrigation needs aren't high
- water 1,000 ft² with greywater alone, with no backup irrigation system.

FIGURE 5.1: MATCHING GREYWATER SOURCES TO IRRIGATION NEEDS

GREYWATER SYSTEMS USED:

- **Washer:** Laundry to Landscape system to downhill and slightly uphill plants
- **Tub plus bathroom sink:** Branched Drain to Mulch Basins around large trees
- **Shower:** Movable Drain to Mulch Basins, plumbed to opposite side of house, where irrigation need is greatest
- **Kitchen sink:** Drain to subsoil infiltration chamber by one big tree
- **Reverse osmosis water purifier drain water** (clearwater): Through ½" drip irrigation tubing to water garden (*Note: this small line would clog with greywater*)

% Irrigation Efficiency

Drip irrigation can reach 80% efficiency, about the highest attainable. The average irrigation efficiency in the example in Table 2.4 is 40%, so 864 gpw of reused water reduces freshwater irrigation by 350 gpw (25%).
Metric: *3.8 m³/week irrigation need; 190 m² tree canopy; 1.9 m³/week greywater.*

FIGURE 5.2: EFFECT OF SOIL TYPE ON SOIL-WETTING PATTERN

Try different scenarios for connecting your greywater sources with irrigation need on your site map. Then do a mock-up using uncut, unglued pipe laid out on the ground. (See Figures 5.1, 9.4, and 12.1, and Table 2.4 for sample diagrams.)

Effect of Soil Type on Irrigation Design

The smaller the soil particles, the more water will spread in the soil, so the farther the emitters can be from each other (Figure 5.2).

Effect of Rainwater Harvesting and Runoff Management

Beside beneficially flushing salts, infiltrating stormwater can reduce irrigation need. Account for this in your irrigation calculations.

WETTED AREA APPEARING ON SOIL SURFACE

Sandy   Loam   Clay

CROSS-SECTION OF THE WETTED AREA IN SOIL PROFILE

Sandy   Loam   Clay

2'–3'   3'–5'   5'–7'
0.5–1 m   1–1.5 m   1.5–2 m

What to Do with Greywater When Plants Don't Need It

Is there any reason to route greywater to the yard when it's pouring rain? It depends. If your septic is failing, absolutely yes. If greywater dispersal is impossible due to, say, ultra-low percolation or high population density, first maximize conservation, then consider a wetland or indoor greywater reuse[34] or cascading: using laundry rinse water for the next wash or using shower water to flush toilets, for example. (See The Household Water Cascade, Appendix F.) In dry climates, all the reasons to use greywater still apply until the soil has absorbed all of the moisture it can store, whether it's raining or not...and application beyond that can help flush salts out.

Even when plants' water needs are met by rain, onsite greywater treatment is ecologically preferable to centralized treatment. Sewage treatment plants consume energy and chemicals. Their leftover nutrient-laden water pollutes surface waters instead of returning nutrients to the soil and recharging groundwater. During very heavy rainfall, runoff leaks into sewage treatment systems and totally overwhelms their capacity. They release raw sewage into natural waters in these circumstances. People who don't know what to do with greywater during heavy rain are in good company—the local treatment plant doesn't know either.

If your greywater would otherwise go to a treatment plant, getting it into the ground instead is beneficial almost no matter how wet the soil is. *(Exceptions: On bare, saturated soil, greywater can flow over the surface, posing a potential mild health hazard.[1,3,6] On an unstable slope, greywater could help oversaturate the soil, causing the land to slide. And if soil remains saturated for more than a day, plant roots can suffocate.)*

Greywater reuse can often continue under a blanket of snow (extreme cold is covered in Appendix C).

If you have the option of diverting greywater into a septic tank at times when soil is saturated, that's a good option; the treatment level is good, nearly all of the water returns to groundwater, and sewage plant loading is not increased.

Preserving Soil Quality

This is a consideration for all systems. The drier your climate, the higher the percentage of greywater irrigation, the higher the clay content of your soil, and the more fruit you eat from the greywatered area, the more critical preservation of soil quality is.

When you irrigate with greywater, you think more about what you put down the drain. <u>Biodegradable</u> means "breaks down," whereas <u>biocompatible</u> means the breakdown products are good for, or at least not harmful to, the environment.

A substance's biocompatibility depends on the environment to which it is being added. Phosphate is good for plants on land, but causes harmful algae blooms in the ocean. No-phosphate biodegradable detergents are designed not to hurt aquatic ecosystems, but contain salt; salt doesn't hurt the ocean or its plants, but is toxic to land plants and soil (Table 5.2).

Insensitive plants may be watered for years with greywater containing non-biocompatible cleaning products. However, once damage is finally evident, it can be a really big job to repair the soil—definitely a case where an ounce of prevention is worth a pound of cure.

Most of the substances in household greywater (for example, lint from natural fabrics, dead skin, sweat, hair, food particles, dirt, grime, etc.) biodegrade into plant nutrients. Household cleaners are the main exception. Also, salt from urine can be problematic with low rainfall and/or clay soil. Finally, for a society used to pouring any unwanted liquid down the drain, the absence of a convenient means of dumping toxic waste without feeling like that's what you are doing can be puzzling. We'll look at each of these issues in this section.

Garden-Friendly Cleaners

The chemical and biological composition of greywater varies greatly, based on numerous factors including the original quality of the water coming to the home, the habits of family members, the plumbing fixtures connected to the system, and the soaps used. After excluding obvious toxins and unplugging the water softener, choosing plant and soil biocompatible cleaners is the major factor you can control to improve greywater quality.

Cleaner breakdown products vary in toxicity, and different soil types and plants vary in their susceptibility.

Permanently Reduce Your Energy Bill and Carbon Footprint in 5 Minutes

Just shut off the hot water supply to your washer. The hot water wash habit is from when soap was made from pig fat and wood ash. Modern detergents work just fine in cold water. Your clothes will last longer, too (more on p. 61).

Tip:

You can have cleaner clothes and happier plants if your washwater <u>always</u> goes to terrestrial ecosystems. Add a tablespoon of potassium tripolyphosphate to each load. It is sold as fertilizer...and it increases the effectiveness of detergents in hard water. (Can't send it to aquatic ecosystems; the nutrients will throw the balance off; see Table 5.2)

Continue p. 43

TABLE 5.2: BIOCOMPATIBILITY OF MATERIALS IN WASTEWATER WITH DIFFERENT DISPERSAL ENVIRONMENTS

Material	Dispersal environment			
	Terrestrial		Aquatic	
	Arid land soil	Tropical and temperate soil	Ocean	Freshwater
Water	Highly beneficial	May be beneficial	No consequence	Little consequence
Organic compounds	Beneficial food for soil microorganisms Fast biodegradation times desirable		Must be removed by oxidation in pre-treatment to prevent depletion of oxygen dissolved in water Fast biodegradation times essential	
N—Nitrogen	Extremely beneficial; N is beneficial plant growth's limiting nutrient	Beneficial; may leach into ground-water if added in excess	Probably OK; N is harmful algae growth's limiting nutrient, but dilution makes measurable effect unlikely	Highly undesirable; N is second-most limiting nutrient for harmful algae growth
P—Phosphorus	Beneficial; leaching into ground or surface waters unlikely due to low mobility in soil and plant uptake	Extremely beneficial; P is beneficial plant growth's limiting nutrient	Probably OK; P is harmful algae growth's second-most limiting nutrient, but dilution makes measurable effect unlikely	Extremely undesirable; P is most limiting nutrient for harmful algae growth
K—Potassium	Beneficial at washwater concentrations		Effect unlikely	
S—Sulfur	Beneficial		No consequence	
Na—Sodium	Highly undesirable; toxic buildup likely Directly toxic to plants, destructive to soil structure	Undesirable but partly flushed from all but clay soils by rain	No consequence; this is where sodium from land should be dispersed	Little consequence in moderate concentration; surface water can be used as conduit to ocean
pH—Acidity/alka-linity	pH lowering desir-able—acid OK	pH raising desir-able—alkali OK	No consequence	Little consequence
Cl—Chlorine	Undesirable		No consequence	Little consequence
B—Boron	Highly toxic to plants at washwater concentrations		No consequence	Undesirable
Pathogenic micro-organisms	Harmlessly biodegrade under proper conditions		Diluted but could spread disease	Likely to spread disease
Industrial toxins	Disastrous unless biodegradable (like, for example, trace of motor oil in run-on to mulch basins)		Highly undesirable; diluted but may bio-concentrate	Disastrous

Some cleaning products are toxic to plants, people, and the environment and should not be used. Products designed to open clogged drains or clean porcelain without scrubbing **must** be sent to the sewer or replaced with alternative products or boiling water and elbow grease. (Acid, though, isn't bad in dry climates, nor alkali in wet climates; they will neutralize in the soil.)

Most hand and dish soaps and shampoos don't damage plants at low residential con-centrations. Laundry detergents, on the other hand, need to be selected carefully. Powdered detergents and soaps include "filler" ingredients (not essential to clothes cleaning), which are usually some compound of sodium. Liquid soaps contain water as the filler, thus less sodium.

"Eco" claims on cleaners, even if true, apply to biocompatibility for *aquatic* dispersal, and guarantee nothing about biocompatibility with land plants and soil. Oasis and Bio-Pac soaps are formulated for use with greywater systems. (They are free of sodium, chlorine, and boron, and do not significantly affect soil pH.)

Few cleaners are so bad that they immediately kill plants. Water is a big plus for thirsty plants, toxins from ordinary biodegradable cleaners are a small (but cumulative) minus. Nutrients from biocompatible cleaners are a small plus. To minimize impact on plants and soil from cleaners, take these measures (in descending order of priority):

❖ Avoid washing more often or using more cleaner than needed.
❖ Avoid cleaners that contain boron (borax), a potent plant toxin.
❖ Avoid using chlorine bleach or non-chlorine bleach containing sodium perborate, a potent plant toxin. Send bleaches to septic/sewer when used. Liquid hydrogen peroxide (e.g., Liquid Chlorox II or Ecover) is a less powerful, more expensive, but nontoxic alternative bleach. Do **not** use detergents "with bleach"; it's actually sodium perborate.
❖ Avoid detergents that advertise whitening, softening, and enzymatic powers.
❖ Use cleaners that contain little or no sodium. Liquid cleaners and laundry detergents contain less sodium than powders. A buildup of sodium is toxic to plants and destroys the structure of clay soils.
❖ Use plant and soil biocompatible cleaners, which contain no sodium, chlorine, or boron and do not adversely affect soil pH or structure.[17,s11]

Urine and Salt Balance

Everyone should read this.

A certain amount of salt can be flushed from the soil each year. As long as you don't add more salt than this, your irrigation is sustainable. Two ways to help the salt balance: add less salt, flush more salt. We'll look at each.

The sources of salt in a greywater system are the water itself, sweaty bathers, cleaning products, water softeners, and urine. Water softeners add high levels of sodium chloride that will adversely affect most soils. (Use of potassium chloride water softener salt[s1] makes softened water far less damaging, as plants will take up the potassium, slowing buildup. But—pulling the plug on softener is still the best idea.)

Urine is where the vast majority of the body's salt ends up. Urine may find its way into your greywater reuse system via toilets, a composting toilet leachate line, pee jars dumped into the system, or people peeing in the shower.

The tricky thing about urine is that it is half super-concentrated fast-acting fertilizer...and half super-concentrated slow-acting poison.* It is full of plant nutrients, primarily nitrogen, but also potassium and phosphate. The bad news is that it is equally full of sodium; it's half as salty as seawater. Each person whose urine goes into the soil adds 7 lbs (3 kg) of salt a year. That is a lot of salt, especially if it is distributed over less than a quarter acre. (That's about how much area you need to get the full value of the urine as fertilizer—the same area it takes to grow the food for one person.) Salt accumulates in soil, potentially to the level where it will kill plants. Worse, while the nutrients can easily be lost to the air or groundwater, the sodium is immutable and difficult to flush below the root zone—the only way to get rid of it.

Urine enthusiasts gloss over this dark side. Diluting urine with water before application or binding it to high-carbon material won't solve the sodium accumulation problem. (These measures can, however, reduce the loss of the fertilizer value.) The rate of sodium accumulation is slower the higher the rainfall and the lower the soil's clay content. If you have high rainfall and low clay content, urine is likely more of a long-term benefit than a liability to your plants. On the other hand, with clay soil and/or low rainfall, you're best off excluding urine as much as possible from your garden and routing it instead to the septic/sewer or to a sacrificial disposal field.[18] The disposal field can be as simple as a post hole with a lid.

How do you know whether you've got enough rainfall to not worry about salt? If precipitation exceeds evapotranspiration—that is, if a barrel left in the open forever would overflow at some point in the year, rather than evaporate entirely—you've got a lot of rain. It's a continuum, but I relax a great deal about salt in climates that receive more than 30" *(75 cm)* of rainfall annually.

Effect of sodium-containing cleaners (center) vs biocompatible cleaners (left) on tomato plants at high concentration. Control (no cleaners) is at right. (From a study I did at UC Berkeley, which led to the development of the first plant- and soil-biocompatible cleaners. I sold this business in 1996 and Oasis cleaners are now distributed by Bio-Pac.[s11])

Salt-sensitive avocado suffers from being too convenient to the path. Humans don't urinate evenly over the landscape, but rather concentrate urine on instinctually attractive hot spots. With modern population densities, plants suffer.

Read about urine to your heart's content in the Oasis Greywater Extras packet.[43]

The Key Role of Rainwater

In arid lands, freshwater irrigation raises the salinity and pH of the already too salty and alkaline soil. This simple, irresistible trend has been implicated in the collapse of all irrigation-based civilizations, including the impending collapse in the American West.[19] Unfortunately, greywater tends to do the same to an even greater degree.

This is a case where an ounce of prevention is worth hundreds of pounds of cure. To minimize the damage, don't soften water using sodium chloride, choose cleaners carefully, and direct urine appropriately for the soil and climate, as mentioned previously. In addition, **use concentrated rainfall and/or runoff to flush salts from irrigated areas.**

Rain is effective for flushing excess salts from the root zone. In rainy climates with free-draining soil, flushing is automatic. Otherwise, run rainwater from the roof downspouts or from hardscapes into the mulch-filled basins that receive greywater. Give each basin several inches in a short period of time, then divert the rainwater to the next basin. Mulch helps too, by reducing direct evaporation from the soil. Lawns or planting areas can be graded perfectly flat, with a surrounding berm, and filled with concentrated rain runoff like a rice paddy—just make sure it drains in a day or so.

Monitoring and Repairing Soil

If your soil is damaged, all is not lost. If you see salt burn on leaf tips, add gypsum and flush deeply with water according to instructions from your local nursery. The application rates are high: hundreds of pounds of gypsum for a suburban lot. For highly sodium-laden soil, hard water containing calcium is more effective for flushing than rain.

If your plants seem to be suffering, test the soil pH. If pH is over 7.5, it will benefit from adding mulch, gypsum, and/or elemental sulfur to lower pH.

After repairing damage, kick your soil problem prevention program into high gear. (Gypsum can also be added at lower rates as a preventative measure.)

Toxic Waste Disposal

Obviously, you don't want to use a greywater system as a toxic waste disposal, even if you're accustomed to using the septic/sewer this way. So what do you do with the nasty stuff? Here are some options:

❖ **Don't let dangerous toxins into your home**—Reducing or eliminating toxins is far and away the preferred option. The Washington Toxics Coalition,[20] among others, has good suggestions for nontoxic alternatives to just about everything. In many cases the nontoxic alternative is cheaper and performs as well or better. Most of the "need" for toxic junk has been conjured into existence out of thin air, along with brainwashing that the more toxic and expensive the product, the better. If you simply banish toxic products from your home, you're not going to diminish your quality of life.

❖ **Route toxins into their own industrial re-cycles**—Used motor oil, for example, can be re-refined into perfectly good motor oil.

❖ **Send toxins to a toxic waste dump**—Check with local government/industry for options.

❖ **Route toxins elsewhere**—For example, by diverting them to the sewer, or burning them. The problem with this approach is that there isn't really such a place as "elsewhere." Even if *you* don't swim in or drink the water your waste contaminates, someone will.

❖ **Make a dedicated low-level toxin disposal field**—This can be very small, as the volume is typically miniscule: the occasional latex paintbrush washout, excess urine (see above), and whatnot. On the upside, you're taking responsibility for your own waste; on the downside, you're creating your own little low-level toxic waste dump.

❖ **Evaporate the liquid and landfill the solids**—Particularly if you live in a hot, dry climate, it may be feasible to dump nasty/undesirable liquids in a bucket, then landfill the minute amount of solids left after the liquid evaporates. This still has the "no elsewhere" problem, but less acutely.

❖ **Sell them**—I once cleaned all the household toxins out of my parents' house and had them cued up in front to take to the toxic waste disposal. We were also having a garage sale, and I'll be darned if people didn't swarm over and *buy* all those pesticides, old paint, drain cleaner...a powerful illustration of the "toxic = good" brainwashing mentioned previously.

Plants

If dispersal is your only interest, you can skip to the Plants for Greywater Treatment/Dispersal section. Conversely, if you are only interested in reuse, you can read the Reuse section and skip the Dispersal one. If your climate has both a dispersal and a reuse season, read both.

Using greywater on ornamentals that don't require acid conditions is safest, followed by fruit trees. As mentioned elsewhere, greywater should not be used on vegetables (p. 115) or on the surface of lawns (p. 15, 115). Plants can be used to perform multiple system functions. For example, a solid ring or spiral of plants can provide privacy screen and shade for an outdoor shower or washing area, as well as absorbing excess water and nutrients.

If your soil is high perk and there is irrigation need in the wet season, you can probably greywater the same area year-round. Otherwise, you may need to make a separate zone for dispersal during the wet season.

TABLE 5.3: SOME PRODUCTIVE PLANTS FOR GREYWATER REUSE

1 = best
5 = worst

Plant	Wet tolerance	Dry tolerance	Self-mulch/barrier	Keeps leaves (transpires all year)	Salt tolerance	Benefits	Comments
Banana	2	3	3	Y	1	Delicious fruit, ornamental	Premier plant for greywater in warm climates. Clumps will expand until they are using all available water. If they need more water, chop a few down and the rest will do better. For maximum fruit production, each clump should have a mature, medium, and small stalk.
Mango	2	3	3	Y	3	Delicious fruit, ornamental	Grows into an enormous tree.
Avocado	4	4	3	Y	4	Delicious fruit, ornamental	Grows into an enormous tree. Make sure you have an idea of how to water it when it is four stories tall! Susceptible to root rot—use high-island mulch basins (Figure 5.7), best to use 50%+ freshwater.
Citrus	3	4	4	Y	2	Delicious fruit, ornamental	Great plant for greywater in subtropics. Highly fire-resistant, so good by the house.
Pineapple guava	3	2	4	Y	3	Delicious fruit and flowers, hedge, ornamental	Can be maintained as a chest-high hedgerow, or shaped into a two-story specimen tree.
Fig	1	2	5	N	1	Delicious fruit, ornamental	No paradise is complete without figs. While deciduous, there is a shorter interval between dropping old leaves and growing new ones than for most deciduous fruit trees.
Clumping bamboo	2	3	4	Y	3	Structural wood, ornamental, slope stabilization	Wide variety of climates with different properties. Use clumping rather than running bamboos—much easier to contain or eradicate.[21] Can eat shoots, great for building, fuel.
Blackberry, elderberry, currants	2		2	N		Delicious fruit	Nothing like a stand of blackberries to attract people to the edge of your basin, but keep them out of the middle! Too bad most berries lose their leaves. Hard to eradicate.
Peach, plum, apple, pear, quince	4	4	2	N	4	Delicious fruit, ornamental	Good in cold climates; may require diversion of greywater at times to avoid waterlogging.

Warm climate ↑ / ↓ *Cold climate*

Plants for Greywater Reuse

Trees and shrubs are the best things to irrigate via low-tech greywater systems with few outlets. Water delivered anywhere in their root zones benefits the whole plant. It is a heck of a lot easier to hit a few big root zones than numerous small ones. Anything less than a large shrub is just too small for a system capable of supplying only a dozen or so outlets (as compared to hundreds with drip irrigation).

My philosophy is that if I water something, I want to be able to eat it. In my opinion, fruit trees are the logical thing to irrigate with greywater, especially in warm climates. For outdoor greywater systems in cold, severe climates, it's a different story. As you can see in Table 5.3, productive reuse options are mostly limited to plants that drop their leaves in winter. You may need a winter dispersal zone, or forget about productive reuse and settle for ecological treatment.

If you've got fruit trees already planted, water them if you can. If you have evergreen fruit trees, they are the priority. They transpire and benefit from greywater year-round. If your trees are not yet planted, then you have the opportunity to optimize coordination between the greywater system and the layout of the edible landscaping.[22,s9]

TABLE 5.4: ACID-LOVING PLANTS
(DIFFICULT TO KEEP HAPPY WITH GREYWATER)

Azalea	Begonia	Bleeding Heart (*Dicentra*)
Camellia	Fern	Foxglove
Gardenia	Hydrangea	Impatiens
Wood Sorrel (*Oxalis*)	Philodendron	Primrose
Rhododendron	Violet	Zylosma
Blueberry		

Plants for Greywater Treatment/Dispersal

For dispersal, theoretically you don't even need plants. The bacteria on the soil particles can take care of pathogens by themselves (as in a sand filter). However, it's better with plants. They will remove the nitrate, phosphate, etc. from the water, and help maintain aerobic conditions.

In high-perk soil with a high water table, groundwater contamination could occur if wastewater moves through too fast. In very low-perk soil, ponding and anaerobic conditions can occur. Plants improve physical soil conditions including perk rate, and add their own substantial contribution to water dispersal by transpiration. A given area's treatment capacity is storage plus evapotranspiration plus percolation. Deepening mulch basins and choosing plants with higher water uptake can increase treatment capacity. The ideal plants for greywater dispersal:

❖ are tolerant of wet conditions
❖ generate their own mulch or physical barrier so you don't have to (preventing greywater from being seen or played in)
❖ keep their leaves all year (so they transpire water all year)
❖ look beautiful and/or make fruit or some other useful thing (the plants in Table 5.3 work for treatment as well as reuse)

More Plants

There is a list of 150 subtropical and low-chill deciduous fruit trees for mild climates, and 100 greywater plants for harsh, freeze-dried New Mexico conditions, at *oasisdesign.net/ landscape/fruittrees*.

TABLE 5.5: SOME PLANTS FOR GREYWATER TREATMENT/DISPERSAL

Note: all Table 5.3 plants work for treatment as well, particularly banana and bamboo.

Plant	Wet tolerance	Self-mulch/ barrier	Keeps leaves	Benefits	Comment
				1 = best Y = yes	
				5 = worst M = maybe	
				N = no	
Ivy, vinca, et al.	2	2	Y	Ornamental	Can be noxious scourges in the wrong spot, but do a good job of covering greywater basins so that added mulch is not needed.
Wetland plants	1	?	M	Pump oxygen into saturated soil	Most likely to be appropriate in cold and/or very wet climates.
Redwood	3	Y	Y	Timber	Conifers vary in wet tolerance, redwood can take a lot.
Willow, ash, cottonwood	2		N		All wet and cold tolerant.

If the perk is low and the loading rate high enough, you'll end up with a <u>bog</u> or wetland. Wetland plants literally pump oxygen down through their roots, maintaining aerobic conditions in mucky soil. For this reason, they are ideally suited for a heavily loaded treatment area. Also, many form such a dense stand that the need to add mulch is obviated; the plants themselves preclude access to the water (this matters because if there is even the tiniest area of open, standing water for more than a week or two, mosquitoes will hatch from it). For more on wetlands, see Constructed Wetlands, Chapter 8. For bogs, see the end of Chapter 10. To plant a small wetland, go to your nearest natural wetland and (with great care and conscientiousness) transplant *one or two* of each kind of plant that is abundant. Any of them appropriate to your greywater context will reproduce in great abundance.

Mulch Basin Design

If I had to improve the world's handling of greywater in just two words, they would be **mulch basin.** Even wastewater flowing over the surface of the soil is purified to a surprisingly high level.[3,6] However, the simple measure of covering and containing the greywater in mulch basins assures a spectacularly high level of treatment. Contouring the ground helps contain runoff and concentrate irrigation water where needed, especially on slopes. Mulch basins and <u>swales</u> (long thin basins on contours across a slope, like terraces) are also perfect for capturing stormwater and storing it in the soil: swales on slopes and basins by downspouts. Imagine you are a terrestrial beaver, shaping the earth so that it could hold water like rice paddies.

Mulch

Mulch (ideally wood chips) *covers the greywater* so kids and dogs can't play in it. Greywater coming from a free-flow outlet or hose quickly vanishes under mulch and is contained by the basin. Mulching softens soil's surface and slows the flow of greywater over it, allowing greywater to infiltrate much more quickly.

Mulch basins are a good way to reuse organic waste such as leaves, straw, prunings, weeds, and tree chips that might otherwise be landfilled. In many areas, truckloads of wood chips can be delivered for free (or close to it) by tree trimmers or road crews. Build your soil by tossing these reclaimed materials in mulch basins. Place the unchipped prunings at the bottom and the most attractive material on top. It will all biodegrade over time.

Mulch soaks up greywater, then time-releases it, which smoothes irrigation peaks and reduces erosion. Mulch slows the movement of runoff, retards evaporation (reducing salt buildup), helps lower pH, and provides habitat for beneficial organisms. Mulch reduces loss of water through gopher holes. Mulch adds beneficial organic matter and, eventually, nutrients to the soil. If you spread fertilizer on top, mulch binds it and then time-releases it. Mulch is basically *gold*. Spread mulch over all exposed soil in your yard and fill basins to the level of the surrounding soil.

Cautions: Dug-in mulch, which typically has a very high carbon: nitrogen ratio, can tie up nitrogen, starving plants. In areas to be seeded, avoid mulch from trees with germination-inhibiting (allelopathic) properties, such as eucalyptus and black walnut. (This same property helps inhibit weed growth where desirable plants have already germinated.)

Basins

A **basin** is formed by scooping a doughnut-shaped hole in the earth and piling the <u>tailings</u> from the hole in a ring around the basin. Tailings can be piled downhill to make a basin on a slope. The walls of basins tend to get worn down, so they should be dug deep initially—10" *(25 cm)* at least—then filled with mulch. Size them to accommodate the surge volume they will receive: a bathtub and washer cycle's worth, for example (Table 4.2 gives surge volumes). The basin should be at least as wide as the dripline of the tree (the diameter of the canopy) and can be much wider. Most tree roots extend farther than their branches. Making the basins bigger than the tree makes it easier to expand them without hurting the roots as the tree grows (Figures 5.3, 5.4).

The basin *contains the greywater* where it is needed, within the dripline, and prevents it from escaping where it would be wasted or a nuisance. Equally important in wet climates,

Infiltration Capacity of Greywater Mulch Basins

Septic leachfield infiltration capacity or Long-Term Acceptance Rate (LTAR) typically drops by 99% compared to adjoining soil, due to clogging by anaerobic bacteria.

Meanwhile, mulch basins typically have dramatically better LTAR than the original soil. This really needs more study, but in at least a few cases LTAR has increased by a factor of 50 or more.

Coarse wood chips over rough mulch (unchipped sticks) are best in greywater and rainwater basins. Fine mulch (in hands) is good on the surface between basins and, for uniform appearance, on the top layer of the basin.

FIGURE 5.3: STANDARD MULCH BASIN FOR NEW PLANTING

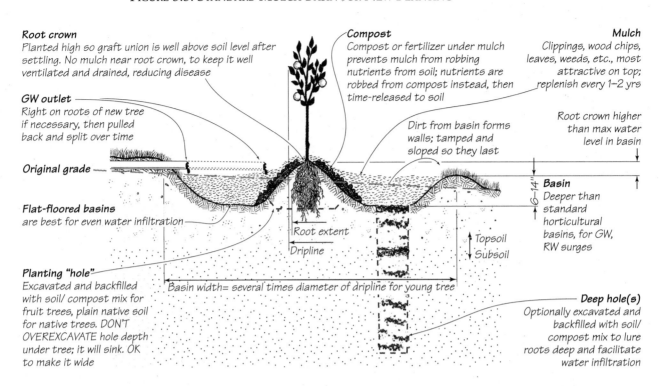

Root crown
Planted high so graft union is well above soil level after settling. No mulch near root crown, to keep it well ventilated and drained, reducing disease

GW outlet
Right on roots of new tree if necessary, then pulled back and split over time

Original grade

Flat-floored basins
are best for even water infiltration

Planting "hole"
Excavated and backfilled with soil/ compost mix for fruit trees, plain native soil for native trees. DON'T OVEREXCAVATE hole depth under tree; it will sink. OK to make it wide

Compost
Compost or fertilizer under mulch prevents mulch from robbing nutrients from soil; nutrients are robbed from compost instead, then time-released to soil

Mulch
Clippings, wood chips, leaves, weeds, etc., most attractive on top; replenish every 1–2 yrs

Dirt from basin forms walls; tamped and sloped so they last

Root crown higher than max water level in basin

Basin
Deeper than standard horticultural basins, for GW, RW surges

6–14"

Root extent
Dripline

Topsoil
Subsoil

Basin width= several times diameter of dripline for young tree

Deep hole(s)
Optionally excavated and backfilled with soil/ compost mix to lure roots deep and facilitate water infiltration

FIGURE 5.4: MULCH BASIN MAINTENANCE/ SAME TREE 30 YEARS LATER

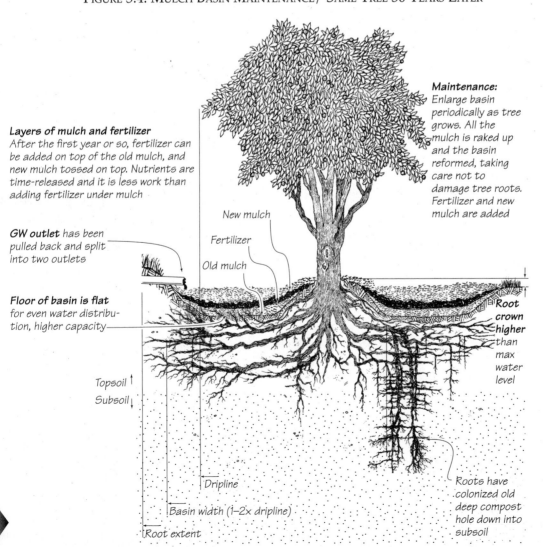

Layers of mulch and fertilizer
After the first year or so, fertilizer can be added on top of the old mulch, and new mulch tossed on top. Nutrients are time-released and it is less work than adding fertilizer under mulch

GW outlet has been pulled back and split into two outlets

Floor of basin is flat
for even water distribution, higher capacity

New mulch
Fertilizer
Old mulch

Maintenance:
Enlarge basin periodically as tree grows. All the mulch is raked up and the basin reformed, taking care not to damage tree roots. Fertilizer and new mulch are added

Root crown higher than max water level

Topsoil
Subsoil

Dripline
Basin width (1–2x dripline)
Root extent

Roots have colonized old deep compost hole down into subsoil

Tips
For greywater mulch basins compared to regular mulch basins for fruit trees:

- Basins should be deeper.
- Basins should be wider.
- Walls should be compacted water-tight by stomping or tamping.
- Mulch should be a thicker layer of woodier (i.e., more durable) material.
- Trees should be planted in taller islands.

More info: p. 104.

FIGURE 5.5: MULCH BASIN TERRACE OR SWALE ON A SLOPE

FIGURE 5.6: NO-ISLAND MULCH BASIN
FOR WATER-LOVING, ROT-PROOF PLANTS (E.G., BANANA)

Greywater applied to **cut** side, rather than **fill** side

Cut on uphill side, **fill** on downhill side

Dry-laid rock wall in crescent or full terrace form retains soil, water, mulch, and fertilizer on steep slopes. Footing must extend into undisturbed soil, deeper for a taller wall. Mortaring rocks with clay/compost mix will bind them in living mortar over time

If there is room for a bucket under the pipe, water can be manually spread evenly around the root zone

Former grade

Greywater outlet

Flat-bottom basin for even water distribution

No island in the middle

FIGURE 5.7: HIGH-ISLAND MULCH BASIN
FOR WATER-AND-ROT-SENSITIVE PLANTS (E.G., AVOCADO), AND/OR PLANTINGS IN HEAVY CLAY SOIL

Clay pot by newly planted tree.
Filled by hand until roots reach greywater outlet.

Greywater outlets well away from trunk, ideally at drip edge

↓ **Extra-tall island**
18–30"

the rim around the basin *excludes runoff* from entering the basin, helping to keep the roots from drowning or the greywater from escaping in a flood of runoff. The island in the middle of the mulch basin protects the sensitive root crown from becoming waterlogged and diseased. In low-perk/high-rainfall conditions, the mulch basin may need an overflow armored against erosion, or even a drain on the downhill side (see Real World Example #4).

Mulch basin construction is especially critical for greywatered trees, as the trees will often get too much or too little water. Most trees like to be on the edge of the basin or on an island in the middle. Plants resistant to waterlogging can inhabit the bottom. See the mulch basin figures and photos for specific geometry of mulch basins and islands for different trees, soil, and climate conditions. The basin geometry also may be affected by what kind of greywater outlet you use.

Swales

Swales are long, thin basins (or blind-ended ditches) that run on contour, that is, on the same level across a slope. Their downhill tailings are an ideal place to plant fruit trees. (Figure 5.5 could be a section through a swale with a tree on the tailings.) Roots can seek water in the bottom of the swale during drought and air in the top of the tailings during flood. As with basins, swales should be filled with mulch.

Post Holes and Auger Holes

Post holes are like tall, narrow "basins." They are particularly suited to tight locations such as under a downspout between a house and walkway. Auger holes can be punched down through the soil with a 2" *(5 cm)* auger bit, available in 2'–5' *(0.5–1.5 m)* lengths. Auger holes amount to very little in terms of volume, but provide a proportionately large surface area for water to soak into lower layers of soil. These holes can completely change the infiltration characteristics of a soil underlain by a thin hardpan. They also allow roots to reach reserves of water and nutrients they could not otherwise. Fill them with mulch or compost. With plants nearby, the composting organic matter will turn into roots that help keep the soil open and infiltrating long term. In Australian hardpan, dynamite has been used to create fracture patterns that fruit tree roots then follow.

Newly formed basin with tree.

Deep area of mulch basin adds surge capacity

Peach tree

Greywater outlet; ⅛ of flow

"Shrubbler" adjustable drip irrigation emitter can be shut off when greywater is available

Basin with mulch, two years later *(note tree growth).*

Greywater outlet

Mulch basin with fertilizer added over mulch. *Nutrients bind to the mulch, then time-release.*

You can adapt greywater to any aesthetic. *Here, rocks serve as mulch for greywater basin in Japanese garden. (Less capacity due to lower biological activity.)*

Chapter 6: System Selection Chart

Take some time with this chart; it is your best tool for choosing a system.

Greywater systems consist of <u>collection plumbing</u> (C) in the house, <u>irrigation piping</u> (I), and the <u>receiving landscape</u> (R): mulch basins, soil, and plants. In the next three chapters we'll help you decide which systems are right for your context.

Keeping in mind your context and the design considerations mentioned earlier, peruse the System Selection Chart that follows, with an eye for a system that meets your needs and your site.

A complete system provides for greywater collecting, distributing, and receiving. Some of the systems in the chart are complete, others are subsystems that can be combined with each other or with generic collection plumbing to make a complete system.

It is likely that at least one of the systems here will be adaptable to your situation. If not, each system's elements can be rearranged to make a wide variety of other possible systems, or to serve as an inspirational starting point for an as-yet-unconceived variation.

Note that some designs are cautioned as being unproven. Clearly, with experimental designs, the risk of wasting time and money is higher, so proceed with care. An incremental approach can reduce this risk. For example, one fixture set could be connected to a single hose for a Movable Drain to Mulch Basins system. If everything worked well, the remaining fixtures could be connected, and then a Branched Drain system added later.

For best results, choose the simplest possible design and build it as well as you possibly can.

The next chapter describes the most simple greywater system options. Simple systems have the advantage that they work. The overwhelming majority of systems that are more than five years old and still working are very simple. Simple systems are ecologically benign, as they take little material to construct, no energy to operate, and generally last longer.

On the other hand, the more complicated and expensive systems in Chapter 8 offer more efficiency or convenience. All have applications, so they're all worth checking out.

Consider each set of fixtures individually; it may be best to employ a few different greywater systems, even in a small house. Quite often the laundry gets its own system, as does any fixture set that, because of collection plumbing issues, is not practical to unite with the other greywater flows.

Around 1995 I developed the Branched Drain in an effort to achieve some of the performance of a complicated system with the low cost and high reliability of a simple system. Branched Drain systems can automatically deliver greywater to plants without using a surge tank, filtration, pumping, or any moving parts. People can make this system themselves with off-the-shelf components.

Within a few years I found that I recommended the Branched Drain system for about 75% of installations. I ended up writing a whole book about it in 2000. After selling several thousand copies, I began to feel that everyone who bought *Create an Oasis* should have the *Branched Drain Greywater Systems* book too—and now you do, because that book has been completely incorporated into this edition of *Create an Oasis*.

Chapters 9 and 10 cover Branched Drains in great detail. Even if you choose a different kind of system, you may find it useful to look at all design issues through the lens of the Branched Drain system.

The Laundry to Landscape system (L2L), a promising new washer-pressurized greywater system I developed in 2008, has proven *very* popular. I see it recommended in the majority of installations now. In California alone, more than 20 cities offer rebates specific to this system, and it was included in the Federal Stimulus Job Training Program. As we go to press there are 17,200 hits in Google for "Laundry to Landscape," including a whole new cadre of professional installers specializing in this system (L2L is the first simple greywater system that can be professionally retrofitted economically). We're promoting this business model as a free open source franchise. See oasisdesign.net/greywater/laundry for design updates and our two hour Laundry to Landscape instructional DVD, which includes very complete design, installation, and maintenance instructions. It has largely replaced the classic Laundry Drum system.

TABLE 6.1: SYSTEM SELECTION CHART

Legend:
m = maybe   1 = most satisfactory
y = yes   5 = least satisfactory
Y = yes, very much so
blank = no (or not applicable)

Pages, refs to read (bg = Builder's GW Guide)	System Name	System provides for: C = greywater collection / I = greywater irrigation / R = greywater receiving	Overall score in optimum application	Renter's construction?	Can distribute upslope of greywater source?	Collection possible with fixture plumbing under slab? (I only / C only)	Suitable for nonindustrialized world?	Possibly legal under CPC/UPC? All are legal in AZ, NM, etc.	Ease of construction (1=easiest, 5=hardest)	Ease of use
	Simple Greywater Systems									
54	Landscape Direct	CIR	1	m		y	**Y**	m	1–5	1
55, 84, 87	Drain to Mulch Basin/ Drain Out Back	CIR	1	m			y	y[B]	2	1
55-56	Movable Drain[A]	IR	2	m			m		2	3
84-109, bg	Branched Drain[A]	IR	1				y	y[B]	4	1
57	Laundry Drum	CIR	2	y		y	y		2	3
57-71[41], bg	Laundry to Landscape (L2L)[A]	CIR	1	y	3 ft/ 1 m	y	m	y	2	1
72	Garden Hose through the Bathroom	CIR	3	y	m	y	y		1	5
72, 117, 119, 124-125, 137	Dishpan Dump/ Bucketing	CIR	1	y	y	y	**Y**		1	5
47–50, 55, 85-86, 95-96, 98, 104, 106--107, 127	Mulch Basins	R	1	y			y	y[B]	1	1
72, 137-140	Greywater Furrow Irrigation	CIR	1	y			**Y**		2	3
	More Complex Systems									
24, 73-75	Drum with Effluent Pump	I	4	m	y			y[B]	3	4
70, 74-76, 87, 95-98	Subsoil Infiltration Chambers[A]	R	1				m	y	4	2
75-76[25,26], bg	Solar Greywater Greenhouse	R	1		m			y[B]	5	2
77[24], bg	Green Septic: Tank, Flow Splitters, and Subsoil Infiltration Chambers [A]	CIR	2		y		m	y	4	1
78-79[27],124, bg	Constructed Wetlands	I(R)	2		y		m	y[B]	5	2
79-81, 128-129, bg	Automated Sand Filtration to Subsurface Emitters	IR	1		y			y[B]	5	2
81–83, bg	Advanced Treatment System to Subsurface Drip	CIR	2		y	y		y[B]	5	2

[A]Oasis original design
[B]With outlets shielded or buried

Comment	Greywater Sources				Cost range (for the functions that the system performs; add $200–$1,000+ for collection plumbing if system is I or R only) (2015 costs)	Requires electricity?	Adapted for freezing?	Suitable for large flows?	% Irrigation efficiency (Drip = 80%) I only	Degree of filtration provided or required	Proven?	Year current version developed (as far as we know)
	Laundry, dishwasher	Tub, shower, bathroom sink	Kitchen sink	Toilet (blackwater) capable								
Good for earthy lifestyle		y			$0–$1,000+				20–60a	None	y	BC
Very simple, easy, reliable, cheap	y	y	y		$10–$20		y		0–60a	None	y	≤1990s
Simple, good temporary system; flexible PVC very bad environmentally	y	y	y		$75–$150		m		10–70	None	y	1996
Simple, reliable; most recommended system for all but laundry	y	y	y		$100–$3,000+c		y		30–60a	None	y	1998
Superseded by L2L except where manual irrigation is desired	y				$20–$100	b			10–50	None to coarse	y	≤1970s
Simple way to water slightly uphill or on level; most recommended	y				$50–$1,500c	b	m		30–70	None	y	2008
Good place to start		y			$0-$150	m			10–50	None to coarse	y	≤1970s
Good place to start	m	m	y		$0				10–80	None	y	BC
Receiving landscape for most simple systems	y	y	y		$0		y	m	20–60	None	y	BC
For village conditions; very simple, easy, reliable, cheap	y	y	y		$0				20–50	None	y	≤1995
Simplest system for uphill irrigation	y	y	m		$500–$1,500	y			20–50	None	y, but mixed	≤1980s
Safe; requires batch dosing or Branched Drain	y	y	y	y	$200–$2,000		y	m	10–50a	None	y	1987
Best system for cold; an asset to a cold-climate home in many ways	y	y	y	m	$300–$1,000 +greenhouse		Y	m	10–80a	None to fine	y evolving	≤1990s
Very promising, unproven system	y	y	y	y	Septic tank +$300–$3,000		y	y	20–40a	Fine provided (by settling)	y evolving	2000
Most common in wet climates, familiar to regulators, expensive	y	y	y	y	$500–$15,000		m	Y	10–40	Medium to fine provided	y evolving	1900±
Elaborate mechanics soothe health officials; safe for watering turf	y	y			$2,000–$15,000	Y	y	y	30–80	Very fine	y, high-end only	1992
Elaborate mechanics soothe health officials; safe for watering turf	y	y	y	y	$10,000–$50,000	Y	y	Y	30–80	Super fine	y	1988

[a]Water path cannot easily be changed
[b]Electricity needed for washer pump
[c]For professionally installed, turnkey system

Chapter 7: Simple Greywater Systems

These simple systems are the easiest. Each has its pros and cons—see whether one fits your needs.

Each system is coded with its function(s): C = Collection, I = Irrigation, R = Receiving. Most of the simple systems are complete (CIR); some are subsystems (IR, for instance) that need to be combined with whatever piece is missing (C, in this case) to make a complete system.

Landscape Direct (CIR)

Nice in mild climates and in the nonindustrialized world. I personally love *these systems.*

Perhaps you don't need to plumb the water through the house in the first place. Landscape Direct greywatering can be as simple as using the garden hose to take a shower under a fruit tree, or as beautiful as an elaborately landscaped bathing grotto amidst an edible jungle. (These systems may slip through a legal loophole in some areas: because the water never enters a drain, it may not fit the definition of wastewater.)

Refined Landscape Direct systems use variations in topography and permeability of materials (such as sand or clay) to guide runoff to carefully sited plants.[22] The treatment level is high because there are no pipes or dark anaerobic corners in which pathogens could survive and multiply. These installations are especially nice inside a solar greenhouse in cold climates.

For a fraction of the cost of a structure, you can make a really nice bathing garden. An Eden-like Landscape Direct system could be designed and built by a landscaper (Figure 7.1). Construction of a bathing garden is part artistry, part intimate knowledge of local conditions and materials. To work out optimally, science should go into it as well. Consider when and how much greywater will be generated, and how to bring it to the plants or the plants to it. Ideally it should all be made out of natural materials, as much as possible from on site. It is crucial that the system be adapted to local conditions, so design variation from place to place will be extreme. One bathing garden may be a place to cool off, another to warm up. One design may take great pains to prevent waterlogging, another to concentrate water as much as possible.

The paths should be raised, and paved with something that you can walk over without getting your feet dirty. Likewise, the immediate shower area should be well drained, directing water above or below ground with materials of varying permeability. To get maximum irrigation utility from a shower on free-draining native soil, for example, a low-permeability clay lens can be poured beneath the shower so the water doesn't just fall straight to the center of the Earth, but is directed outward to a ring of plantings. Privacy and shelter from wind should be provided. (If you make a bathing garden, please send us a photo.)

Simplest of all greywater systems: *bath under hose in garden.*

FIGURE 7.1: BATHING GARDEN

Plantings and screen *sized to amount of greywater expected; provide privacy/shelter with a view out but not in*

Dressing area *w/ shelves and towel pegs, paved with flagstones*

Clay lens *diverts water to surrounding plants, avoids clogging in center*

Hot water pipe *insulated along entire length*

Attractive river rock *w/ gap around shower paving. Water disappears below rocks, hair etc. disappears in this gap*

Former grade level *Shower and path are on raised mound. Ring-shaped cut and fill around shower prevent greywater runoff even in heavy rain*

Path *high and dry atop extra fill from basin*

Flagstone   Sand

Mulch basin   Tailings

Drain to Mulch Basin/Drain Out Back (CIR)

The Drain to Mulch Basin is an improved version of the Drain Out Back, the simplest system for just getting rid of greywater.

Probably 90% of the world's greywater systems are just drains pointing out the back of a house. Some are gross, and most have low irrigation efficiency. The simple refinements of adding slope (to move the water from the outlet) and a mulch-filled basin eliminate most grossness. The ability to alternate channels is a nice refinement (photo bottom of p. 138). Plants with irrigation needs that match the water source can efficiently reuse it. Cover the outlet with rocks and mulch, and install a screen over the drain (or a vent and trap) unless you want the true backwoods feel, complete with vermin entering the house via the drainpipe. The line can run any distance with continuous downhill slope and is installed the same way as a Branched Drain irrigation line (see Laying Pipe, Chapter 10).

Drain Out Back in Costa Rican rainforest. *The water rains into the mini-jungle below, which absorbs and treats it. There isn't even a drainpipe. This system has worked for decades without intervention or problems.*

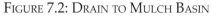

FIGURE 7.2: DRAIN TO MULCH BASIN

- Vent
- Plants enough to use water
- P-trap
- Diverter valve
- Greywater retrofit (shaded pipe)
- Cleanout
- Earth slope away from house
- Rocks as mulch shield
- Mulch
- Basin
- Septic/sewer
- Separation adequate from foundation

Movable Drain (IR)

An excellent provisional system to use while building a new home. As the permanent landscape is installed it can be changed to a Branched Drain or other system. Unfortunately, flexible PVC is an environmental disaster in its production and disposal. Any PVC is bad, but the flexible version has plasticizers, which make it worse. HDPE or 1" garden hose work, but not nearly as well. A good scenario is for an installer or community to have one set of flexible PVC hoses that are passed through many temporary systems. (An Art Ludwig original design.)

From the collection plumbing, route 1½" drain line at ¼" per foot (2%) slope to the edge of a mulch basin. Run the greywater into this basin, or route it to other downhill basins through press-fit lengths of 1" flexible PVC (Spa-flex).[s6]

Flexible PVC is inexpensive, makes nice sweeping curves, and is impossible to kink. The dark brown version looks better snaking around the yard than the brilliant white variety. At 1" diameter the line will quickly drain a tub, eliminating the need for a surge tank.

Flexible PVC is a working Tinkertoy set for moving water or wastewater without glue (or leaks) at pressure or vacuum up to two stories.

SVANTE VAN BART

Collection plumbing for this system is tedious and expensive (as gravity collection plumbing always is), but the irrigation is simplicity itself. All of the crud that would choke a filtered system flows harmlessly out into the landscape and becomes compost.

There is a bit of a learning curve for laying hose for nonpressurized greywater. Hose lengths should be no longer than needed, and the slope as constant as possible, so air and water can drain freely. The main obstacle is an "airlock," where air trapped in an inverted U-section blocks the flow of water. Right-side-up U's appear to work fine, at least with low-solids, high-volume greywater, and occasional moving of the hose.

This flexible line wasn't moved for just six months, and an arm-length root plug was the result.

FIGURE 7.3: MOVABLE DRAIN

- Sink and tub vent
- Toilet vent
- 45° bend (straight down)
- Double ell (optional to split flow)
- 3-way diverter valve
- ABS drain line ¼" per foot slope (2%)
- Adapter bushing
- These fittings are press fit, not glued
- 1" flexible PVC
- Mulch-filled basins *Slope style (trees planted on tailings)*
- Mulch-filled swale

Branched Drain (IR)

The system I recommend most frequently if the area to be irrigated is downslope from the greywater source and the volume is residential-scale. It is not simple to build—with lots of greywater and little slope, it is quite challeng- ing—but it is easy to use and maintain. (An Art Ludwig original design.)

Branched Drain systems improve on the Drain Out Back by splitting, containing, and covering the flow. The flow is split by <u>double ells</u> or other flow-splitting fittings in a branching network (right). The output is contained in basins covered by mulch, or in <u>subsoil infiltration chambers</u> (Figure 9.8).

For sites with continuous downhill slope from greywater source to irrigated areas, **Branched Drain systems provide inexpensive, reliable, automated distribution with almost no maintenance.** Branched Drains have no filter, pump, surge tank, or openings smaller than 1" *(2.5 cm)*.

All variations of this system meet legal requirements in Arizona and other states that regulate greywater rationally.[4] A friendly inspector can issue a permit for this system under the CPC/UPC. Chapters 9 and 10 explore every aspect of Branched Drain systems in detail.

FIGURE 7.4: BRANCHED DRAIN NETWORKS (PLAN VIEW)

Laundry Drum (CIR)

A classic, but 99% superseded by the Laundry to Landscape system. The application remaining is keen, hands-on gardeners who fill the drum, then open the valve and manually, meticulously dole out the water plant by plant. (Construction details in Oasis Greywater Extras.[43])

With a Laundry Drum (photo at right), even distribution is achieved by moving the hose from mulch basin to mulch basin. This deceptively simple approach elegantly solves a host of problems, in exchange for one ongoing task: someone has to move the dang hose. If you're a person who spends time in the garden and will move the hose with every load, year in and year out, seek no further—this is a reliable way of delivering laundry water to your plants and requires virtually no maintenance, decade after decade.

¼" (6 mm) screen · Rain↓

Laundry water

Full port ball valve for manual distribution

Raised for more pressure

¾" garden hose to fruit trees

A Laundry Drum supplied by a washer drain hose run through a hole in the wall. This drum also catches rainwater, which runs through a screen mesh and helps flush salts from the mulch basins (reminder: greywater is not to be stored more than 24 hours).

Laundry to Landscape (CIR)

The Laundry to Landscape (L2L) system is the simplest, least expensive, lowest-effort way to get the most greywater onto the home landscape. It is the greywater system most suited for professional installation by landscapers, yet it is also DIY and renter-friendly. Odds are it makes sense for you…and even if not, like the Branched Drain chapters, this section intersects some important greywater design principles from a new angle and is worth reading. (The L2L is an Art Ludwig original design, developed to address the need for a more prime-time-ready laundry greywater system when California agreed to our request to make laundry-only systems permit-exempt.)

The L2L system uses a washing machine's own pump to send water through lightweight, inexpensive, easily worked polyethylene tubing (the most "eco" plastic) to 1–20 outlets, without moving a hose. It can irrigate areas level with, downhill from, or in some cases even slightly uphill from the washer. It is much easier to reconfigure than a Branched Drain System, which is often installed for non-laundry greywater on the same site.

From what I can see, this system, which we developed in 2008, is now the most commonly installed greywater system in California—perhaps in the Western US. More than 20 agencies in California offer rebates for them, the federal government has sponsored job trainings for L2L installers, etc. The California Plumbing Code specifically exempts it from needing a permit or inspection if it meets a short list of requirements. This has had the predicted effect of improving quality and safety of systems: the proportion of systems installed by a growing cadre of professional installers and landscapers is skyrocketing.

Providing that no toxic chemicals are used in the laundry, washing machines offer the most convenient source of useful greywater in most households. To take advantage of this source for irrigation, many people used to simply attach garden hoses to the drains of their washers. There are several issues with this practice (listed on p. 116), which the L2L system addresses. This system also replaces the venerable Laundry Drum for most applications.

On the other hand…the L2L system is not without its downsides. Getting the water out to the yard is easy; but really getting even, useful irrigation takes some fiddly attention to detail that is different in every context. Splitting the very low flow of some high-efficiency (HE) washers is especially challenging with only inches of pressure to work with…and there's less water gained when you are done (see suggestions for HE washers near the end of this section). These are not cookie cutter, one-size-fits-all systems…but they are well within the range of just about any do-it-yourselfer, and the quest for more efficient irrigation offers lots of systems-thinking practice.

In this section we'll take a quick overview of the system elements; look at how L2L fits in the greywater design and implementation sequence; consider the broader context of how to clean clothes in the most ecological way; then go through the system elements in detail one by one. We also offer a two-hour instructional DVD—see inside back cover—which explains in more detail how to design and install this system, with lots of visuals.

The current state-of-the-art design follows. Check <u>oasisdesign.net/greywater/laundry</u> for updates.

Elements of the Laundry to Landscape System

These are the elements of an L2L system (numbers key to these elements in the L2L centerfold on the following pages)—

GREYWATER BASICS ❖ GREYWATER BASICS ❖ GREYWATER BASICS ❖

FIGURE 7.5: LAUNDRY TO LANDSCAPE SYSTEM

3 DIVERTER VALVE
BLU-LOCK OPTION

1" male pipe x Blu-Lock

Bends... as needed

1" 3-port diverter valve

1" male pipe x barb adapter

Hose clamp

Washer hose

1" HDPE tubing

8 Automatic bypass
water can escape here if lines are frozen

Note: Numbers key to the list on p. 60 and the headings on the following pages. Numbers for optional elements are grey. Letters after numbers are for options.

Irrigation zone diverter valve: indoor option

Upper Orchard

Lower Orchard

2 Biocompatible cleaners

4 Signage

Ocean via sewer

Orchard

5a

7b Air admittance: vent tube option

7a Air admittance: auto-vent option

Watch out for plumbing, electrical, and gas lines when drilling through wall; look for studs to attach diverter to

3 Diverter valve

6 Transition to outdoors

1 Washing machine (pump for system)

To septic/sewer

11 Rainwater inlet
direct to mulch basins (or added to L2L distribution piping through filtered connection)

Outlet: drilled
easiest and cheapest to make/unmake; may clog, but easy to clean

9 Hose service connection

5b Irrigation zone diverter valve: outdoor option

13b

13 OUTLET OPTIONS
1–20 per zone

Backflow valve **10**
only needed if pumping uphill

Outlet: valved **13a**
easy to tune and clean

15 OUTLET CHAMBER OPTIONS
Outlet shields may be required for a permit, and/or be necessary to keep mulch away from the outlet

Outlet chamber:
none—easiest to inspect, service (not allowed in all areas) **15a**

16 Mulch basins

5b DIVERTER VALVE POLYETHYLENE OPTION

1" barb x male pipe adapters

1" hose clamp

1" PE tubing

1" 3-port diverter valve

7a AIR ADMITTANCE

1.5" auto-vent

1.5" female thread x 1.5" female slip

1.5" male slip x 1" female slip

1" tee

1" PVC pipe

1" slip x 1" female thread

1" male pipe x barb adapter

1" PE tubing

9 HOSE SERVICE CONNECTION

1" barb x ¾" female hose adapter

¾" male hose x 1" barb adapter

Male end of garden hose

1" PE tubing

Anti-siphon device

10 BACKFLOW VALVE

1" PE tubing

1" threaded check valve, transparent

1" hose clamp

1" barb x male pipe adapter

17 Productive trees/plants

14 Failsafe overflow
open outlet, main line size, above normal working pressure level, ideally at end of line

utlet: reducing
ee w/ extension
ood; movable
xtension to feed
arious root areas
onger extension=
wer flow); ⅜"
ner diameter
ubing can slip
nugly inside ½"
ubing

13c

13d Outlet: reducing tee w/out extension

13a Outlet: valved this one has extension

15e Subsoil Infiltration Chamber—major pain to service, only recommended in special cases, e.g., to bear traffic load under path, or where it is necessary to have system hidden

12 Irrigation piping outside basin on solid ground

15d Mulch shield: valve box
ideal...except for containing massive amount of newly made plastic

15c Mulch shield: section of plastic culvert super strong

15b Mulch shield: recycled plastic bucket—durable, good size; hole cut in bottom for inspection/service

Outlet shield: plastic flowerpot—not durable, but suitable for meeting legal requirement when outlet shield isn't otherwise needed

Metric: 2" = 5 cm; 12" = 30 cm; 8"= 20 cm; 1½" = 4 cm

1. **washing machine pump**—directly pressurizes the irrigation lines; the key to the simplicity of this system
2. **plant and soil biocompatible cleaners**
3. *diverter valve (optional)—between landscape and septic/sewer; not needed if your system is full-time greywater*
4. **signage**—to inform users what cleaners to use and when to switch valves
5. *irrigation zone diverter valve(s) (optional)—right by the washing machine (preferred) or outdoors*
6. **transition to outdoors**—from inside to outside, and past whatever hardscape or other obstacles await between washer and plants
7. **air admittance**—to break a siphon that could empty the washer as it tries to refill
8. *automatic bypass (optional)—in case the line freezes, or someone closes the valves to every zone*
9. *hose service connection (optional)—to facilitate adjustment and unclogging*
10. *backflow valve (optional)—only needed if the line runs higher than the washer*
11. *rainwater inlet (optional)—for supplemental water, flushing of salts*
12. **irrigation piping**—to convey water to where it's needed
13. **outlets**—one to twenty per zone
14. **failsafe overflow**—above normal operating water level
15. *outlet chambers (optional)—for legal compliance and/or keeping mulch/ soil/ kids/ dogs away from outlets*
16. **mulch basins**—or other receiving landscape for containing and covering the flow, accommodating and infiltrating surges of greywater
17. **productive trees/ plants**—for using and purifying the water

> ## Professional Installation of Laundry to Landscape Systems
>
> *Why bother with any of this when there is an emerging cadre of professional L2L installers to help you? Want to become an installer? There are trainings and resources to support you.*
>
> *Greywater Action (the new incarnation of the Greywater Guerillas, now that greywater is legal) is the pioneer in training homeowners as well as professional installers of L2L systems.[42] They list graduates of their course on their website. Ecology Action pioneered greywater training in their Green Gardener Greywater curriculum as well.*
>
> *Between this book and our L2L instructional DVD[45] there's enough info for landscapers to add L2L systems to their business offerings. We're compiling evolving best practices and resources for L2L systems, as well as free open source franchise information for running a business installing them, at oasisdesign.net/greywater/laundry. If you have design tips or photos, please share.*

Laundry to Landscape in Sequence

Many of the integrated water reuse/irrigation systems I hear of these days feature a combination of diverse irrigation water sources. These systems would ideally be designed together, as per Chapter 3. The most efficient sequence is to design irrigation in order from the least flexible to the most flexible source:

❖ **Green Septic**—Water must flow continuously downhill; large subsoil infiltration chambers should be within root reach of central landscape trees, not too close to tree trunks, out of the way of accidental digging, easy to locate, and not too disruptive to dig up and service, for example, under pathways or near lot edges (regulations vary).

❖ **Branched Drain**—Must be downhill, not too close to tree trunks, out of the way of accidental digging, easy to locate, and not too disruptive to dig up and service. Under paths is often a good location for pipes.

❖ **Rooftop rainwater and hardscape runoff/run-on**—See where stormwater can best infiltrate into the ground. There should be provision to direct stormwater to greywater basins or to its own basins separate from greywater (if the climate is very arid, rainwater can be plumbed full time to appropriately sized combined greywater+rainwater basins).

❖ **Laundry to Landscape**— Once you've figured out where the Green Septic, Branched Drain, and stormwater have to go, send the L2L water where the other sources can't reach; it can go farther, even slightly uphill, and be changed more easily. If it makes sense to switch to an HE washer, do that first so you don't have to redo your system. An L2L system designed for a standard washer won't work well for an HE washer and vice versa.

❖ **Drip irrigation**—There's nothing like working with greywater to make you appreciate the ease of sending freshwater through drip irrigation wherever you want it.

❖ **Hand watering**—In our sandy soil we'd literally need drippers one foot apart in every direction to wet all the soil. Instead, we go around once in a while with a hose and fill up the soil sponge where the drip and greywater don't reach.

Once you have designed the L2L system last…it often makes sense to install the L2L system first. Why? It is the quickest and easiest, and if you need to dig other trenches later you can just lift the tubing out of the way and put it back.

Ecological Laundry

Much like the "reduce, reuse, recycle" hierarchy, there is an array of measures you can take to reduce the impact of washing clothes…usually bigger than the impact of washing anything else in the house. Don't feel bad about the things on this list that you are not doing; just look for any actions you might want to take now or in the future:

❖ *Give your dryer a rest or get rid of it*—Use a solar clothes dryer (clothesline). Drying uses the majority of the energy for laundry and is the major climate impact. In Northern Europe—hardly the world's preeminent drying climate—you see clothes drying quickly indoors on little racks more commonly than you see a dryer.

❖ *Turn off the hot water to your washer*—Heating accounts for 70% of the carbon footprint of domestic water. Yes, you read that right: the multiple and complicated processes of pumping your water from far away, treating and pressurizing it to deliver it to your home, then—after it falls from tap to drain—pumping it again to sewage treatment, stirring it, mixing in chemicals, then pumping it one more time out to a river or ocean, all adds up to 30% (on average) of the carbon impact of your household's water usage. Heating a small portion of that water in your house costs the other 70%! You can dramatically and permanently reduce your energy bill and carbon footprint simply by shutting off the hot water to your washer. The idea that hot water is necessary to get clothes clean is a holdover from the days when soap was made from pig fat and lye. Modern detergents work just fine in cold water. Your clothes will last longer, too.

❖ *Don't use more laundry detergent than necessary*—More soap does not equal cleaner…it equals harder to rinse, and more yucky leftover detergent irritating your skin. It's a titration reaction; once the detergent has reacted with the dirt and grime, more detergent just sits there with nothing to react with. Measuring with a hand pump or measuring cup will help get the manufacturer-recommended amount.

❖ *Dye your whites pretty colors*—White clothes require much more energy and chemicals to clean. Colored clothes look good longer with less impact.

❖ *Don't wash more often than necessary*—One family of three plus a live-in maid did seven loads of laundry a day. Not sure how this is even possible, but we're guessing that every bed and towel was stripped and replaced daily. They did reuse the water, but a responsible system designer would at least point out that dialing back the inexplicably excessive washing by half would be a step to consider.

❖ *Go naked*—At the opposite end of the lifestyle spectrum from the family in the previous example, you can minimize laundry by not wearing clothes. This dramatically lowers the laundry work load with little kids.

❖ *Launder in bathing water*—This works well with a small volume of clothes. We like to travel super-light, with about 1½ changes of clothes. We wash the clothes with us in the shower and air-dry them overnight.

❖ *"Suds Saver"*—A rare but clever system in which rinse water is drawn back into the machine for use as wash water in the next load.

❖ *Don't buy any cleaning products you wouldn't want to eat*—Whether you send it to the groundwater, river, ocean, or fruit trees, it all will come back to you eventually.

❖ *Dispense with fabric softener* and other made-up laundry needs.

❖ *Reuse your washer water for irrigation*—Got that covered here…

❖ *Convert to a horizontal axis washer*—This is a case where simply throwing money at an environmental issue actually works. HE horizontal axis washers are a bona-fide technological improvement. By dropping and lifting clothes in and out of a puddle of water instead of sloshing them in a giant tub of water, they use 30–50% less water. They require less detergent, are higher capacity for a given sized drum, clean better, and are more gentle on clothing. You can stack a front-loading washer easier, and good ones are so quiet they can be in occupied rooms. Because they spin the water out of clothes first (at 1,000+ rpm) you will use 50–65% less energy for drying…if you need a dryer at all.

TABLE 7.1: STANDARD VS HIGH-EFFICIENCY WASHER COMPARISON

Washer comparison	Water-hog washer	HE washer
Water use per load	30–50 gal	8–25 gal
Peak flow	10± gpm	7± gpm
Water per discharge (gal)	15–25 gal	2–5 gal
Emitters per zone	6–20	1–10
Max flat length	50–100'	75'
Max lift above top of washer	1–3'	0.5–1'
Optimum main line size	1"	1" (or ¾"?)
Check water use per load	optional	yes
Check flow, gal/ spurt?	optional	yes
Detergent use per load (oz)	2–4 oz	1–2 oz
Washer operating costs	$525/yr	$300/yr
Washer cost	$0–$50*	$7–$1,500

*No reason to spend $700 on a new one; get one of the millions that are being replaced by an HE machine. GW-using households are a good place to use these up.

High-Efficiency Washer or Reuse—Which to Do First?

If you have limited irrigation need or season, and/or do a lot of laundry, you should probably switch washers first. If you plan to make your L2L system yourself, line-dry your clothes, and have a lot of irrigation need, it probably makes sense to do the L2L system first and then modify it once you've sprung the big bucks for a horizontal axis washer down the road.

Measure Washer Flow Rate and Gallons per Load

Step 1 to designing a L2L system is to get an idea of how much water comes out of the machine and how fast. If this sounds too science-y and you have an old vertical axis machine, you can skip this step. The gallons per load are likely to be between 30 and 45, and the vast majority of the water will come out at a high flow rate, between 6 and 10 gpm. The difference in how you design the system depending on which end of this range you are on is not huge.

For modern HE washers, both the total water per load and the rate that it comes out vary quite a lot. Could be 25, but it seems like every day I hear about machines with lower gallons per load: as little as 15 for an advanced vertical axis washing machine with wash plates, and 8 for a horizontal axis machine. The low water use is lovely, and may improve your water budget more than reusing greywater from a water-hog machine…but it sure complicates the work of getting useful irrigation out of the system.

You can sometimes find the gallons per load online, or you can check the difference in your water meter reading before and after a standard load with no other fixtures going. Or, you can fill up a trash can or drum of known volume and multiply this by the number of uses per week, and you know how much water you have to distribute.

To measure the flow, catch the water in a gallon container, timing how long it takes to fill. The flow rate is useful for two reasons. First, if you know the washer flow, you can adjust a hose to the same rate and use that to tune all the outlets. When the outlets are tuned to the machine this way they are much more likely to work as intended.

Second, with some machines the flow and/or amount of water per discharge is so low it can be really hard to split. If the flow rate is less than 5 gpm, or it discharges less than 3 gal in one go, consider the design adaptations discussed later in Experimental Adaptations for High-Efficiency Washers. Now we'll look at each system element in turn:

1. Washing Machine Pump

L2L systems use the washing machine pump to distribute the water. It is practical to irrigate any distance downhill, or pump up to the elevation of the top of the washer some distance away. See Table 7.1 for approximate design guidelines for standard and HE washers. *Note: there is a lot of variation both in washers and opinions about what works best.*

The resistance the pump has to overcome should ideally be about the same as in a standard installation, where the hose discharges at the height of the top of the machine. For example, if a washing machine empties through 100' of 1" pipe that ends 18" lower than its lid, the effective resistance is the same as if it discharged 2" above its lid (100' of horizontal 1" tubing

FIGURE 7.6: STANDARD VS HIGH-EFFICIENCY WASHER FLOW AND CUMULATIVE DISCHARGE

HE washers are the way to go overall. However, they send out less intense, smaller discharges of water over a longer period of time. Each of these factors makes it harder to accurately split the flow.

FIGURE 7.7A: GEOMETRY FOR LEAST FORCE ON PUMP AND LEAST STAGNANT WATER

No inertia—best
Tubing drains completely

Low inertia—OK
Only a few feet of water in tubing to get moving

High inertia—not good
Several times as much stagnant water to get moving

offers the same resistance as 20" of vertical rise at 6 gpm). At considerable risk to the pump, I've seen people irrigate up to 6' above the top of a standard washer.[m] HE washers appear to be less practical for pumping uphill. *Note: washer pumps are cheaper to replace than effluent pumps are to buy, so a design that likely will result in needing to replace a washer pump isn't out of the question.*

The variables that affect the load on the pump are:

Height differential—The less rise, the easier on the pump. I wouldn't go more than the rise or run indicated in Table 7.3 (but you can go any distance with downhill slope).
Pipe flow resistance—The main line should not be less than 1" diameter for a vertical axis machine or ¾" for a horizontal axis machine, and should not kink.
Low inertia—If possible, route the line up as soon as possible, then continuously down from there.
Pump model—Higher-quality pumps perform better. However, the rate of L2L-induced pump failure seems to be quite low: only a handful out of thousands of systems.

Washer hose diversity
Slip over nipple, with heat or clear tube adapter if necessary.

2. Biocompatible Cleaners

Biodegradable cleaners break down…biocompatible cleaners break down into stuff that is good for the ecosystem. For laundry, use liquids rather than powders; avoid products with sodium, chlorine, or boron. For more, see Preserving Soil Quality, Chapter 5.

3. Diverter Valve *(optional)*

The diversion occurs upstream of the standpipe (the drain the washer outlet hooks into). The fact that you don't have to mess with the house drain plumbing was a key point in our successful campaign to have California allow the installation of L2L systems without a permit or an inspection.

The laundry diverter valve is usually mounted on the wall behind the washer, or where it is easily visible and convenient to turn. It should be solidly screwed to the wall using metal pipe brackets or steel plumber's tape, so that it does not wiggle with the force of turning the handle (they can get sticky over time). One side of the valve diverts water into the standpipe (regular house drain), and the other side through the wall or window (or floor, if you must) to the outdoors (photos at right).

The universally used diverter valve is a 1" brass 3-port ball valve (the other materials vary—see Types of Pipes, p. 66). These aren't always easy to find (we sell them in our online store). Unlike the pool valves used for larger plastic pipe, you can't change the inlet port: it is always the leg of the tee. Any orientation will work but the best is with the inlet at the bottom, and the outlets to the left and right. This sets the stage for the least water in the lines to rush back into the machine.

Sometimes the washer hose fits right over the nipple on the male adapter, sometimes it needs some persuasion (photo, top right). Heating can be effective, also using a short piece of tubing that adapts between the two.

Note: Full port valves have a larger hole for the water to flow through. They offer lower resistance, but the few full-port and standard port valves we tested had only inches of difference in resistance. In these valves the difference between water going left and right was also a few inches; it was less with the water going to the right, as in the photos above.

Diverter valves installed.

4. Signage

Signage at the machine is useful both to help the system get used correctly, and for the consciousness-raising opportunity it offers. The most important usage points to convey are:

PVC

LDPE

[m]*Metric: can irrigate 50 cm below washer top 30 m away. 30 m of 2.5 cm hose = 45 cm vertical. 30 m of 2.5 cm pipe 45 cm lower than lid = resistance of 50 cm above lid. 2 m vertical possible with pump risk.*

Where the water goes with the diverter valve positions—I am a fan of specific labels. For example, rather than "sewer" and "landscape" it could say "East Beach" and "citrus trees."

What the indicators are for what the valve position should be—For example, "Send to beach if using bleach," or "Send to septic when ground is frozen."

How to manage the irrigation zone valves—For example, "Switch valve position with each laundry load."

5. Irrigation Zone Diverter Valve(s) *(optional)*

An **irrigation zone diverter valve** (5a and 5b in Figure 7.5) enables you to give one area a rest while you irrigate another. It is recommended for high-use washing machines, low-perk soil, or better irrigation efficiency with low-flow HE washers. The ideal place to put zone valves is indoors, where every user of the machine will see them. Just switch zones after starting each load. You can put one air admittance upstream of the valves or have a separate air admittance for each line. Either way you'll need to get at least two pipes through the wall (one for each zone, or one for the greywater and one for the air admittance).

If there is an attentive gardener who will switch it, the zone valve(s) can go outdoors. The plumbing for this is so much simpler that most systems with multiple zones are built this way…though there are almost always problems with remembering to switch.

6. Transition to Outdoors

The transition to the outside of the house is the part of the system that is most demanding of construction skill (unless your washer is outside to begin with).

The first step is to determine the best location for this transition. The best location is through an exterior wall right next to the washer, at a height between the top of the washer and 6" higher. If your washer is against an exterior wall that you don't mind drilling a hole through, then consider no further. Otherwise, you'll have to get creative. You can put the air admittance indoors and go out through the wall lower down, or go through the floor into a crawl space and then pop out of the house wherever you want. If your washer is stranded in the middle of a house on a slab, there may still be creative options:

Snake the line through a utility corridor such as the space under a bathtub or a closet.
Run the line through a dryer vent.
Run the line along the bottom corner by a wall, and score it into the concrete under the threshold to get it past a door.

Before making a hole through a wall, check for studs and carefully assess whether you'd be drilling through electrical, water, drain, or gas lines. How? Look for visible signs (switches, outlets, hot and cold water taps, drains, gas connection), and use a stud finder or tap to find studs. Wires will usually either be affixed to studs, or loose enough that they will move out of the way of a drill bit. Measure two or three times to establish where you'll be coming through on the other side of the wall, then drill a pilot hole through the wall with a long, small-diameter bit to establish where you're coming out on the other side (photos at right). For a 1" pipe the hole should be 1⅜" in diameter.

A hole saw from each direction makes nice work on the exterior finishes, and allows you to peer into the hole after removing each layer to confirm that you are not about to go through a gas line. A diamond hole saw can cut the most cleanly through stucco or concrete.

7. Air Admittance

Breaking the siphon by admitting air into the drain line is essential to keep the line from continuously siphoning water out of the machine as it tries to refill. This is not a problem with every machine or load, but it only takes one load continuously refilling overnight to blow a lot of water savings—best to just add it. (The loose fit of the washing machine drain hose into the standpipe provides air admittance in conventional plumbing.) You can see

Tools for Transition to Outdoors

- ❖ tape measure
- ❖ marker
- ❖ drill
- ❖ stud finder
- ❖ safety glasses
- ❖ ear protection
- ❖ long thin drill bit—*for pilot hole*
- ❖ hole saws—*for wood*
- ❖ masonry bits—*for stucco or concrete*
- ❖ tape—*to reduce splintering and chipping around hole*
- ❖ caulk gun—*to seal around hole*

Choose hole saw slightly bigger than the pipe...

measure, cut hole in drywall, peer inside for utilities, studs...

coast clear? Drill pilot hole to other side...

drill w/ big bit back to interior...

slip pipe through, caulk the hole...done.

air admittance options in Figures 7.5, 7.7a, 7.7b and the photos at right. The first shows an auto-vent, the second a vent tube that extends above the highest level the water could attain when the pump kicks on (about 8' *(2.5 m)* above the washer in this case). If your washer spurts water out the top of the tube, reduce the resistance of the irrigation piping, extend the tube higher, or put a check valve or auto-vent on the top. To work right:

The air admittance must connect above the upper rim of the washer tub—Or it could siphon water despite the air admittance downstream. It is usually situated evenly with the top of the washer to a foot higher.*

As little water as possible should be poised to flow back into the machine—Up to several feet of 1" line between the washer and the air admittance are working in practice. More than that, and the dirty water could rush back into the machine when it shuts off. Thus, the air admittance should be close to the washer, usually just outside the house. If the line must dip down before leaving the house, it could siphon even with a vacuum breaker outside; in this case, mount the vacuum breaker inside.

To avoid the possibility of spillage indoors through the air admittance—You can put it over a utility sink or route a tube from the top of the vacuum breaker outlet back into the septic/sewer drain standpipe. The auto-vents commonly have not been failing. But, the oldest systems are from 2008 and auto-vents do have a finite service life.

Air admittances installed. Auto-vent option at left, vent tube at right. After painting the color of the house these blend right in.

FIGURE 7.7B: CHARACTERISTICS OF LAUNDRY TO LANDSCAPE GEOMETRIES

Perfect—
Siphon: **nope**
Volume that will run back into machine: **none**
Extra standing water: **none**
Way to leak inside: **none**
Air ad. moving parts: **none**
Irrigation bypass if frozen: **yes**

Air admittance (AA)

Good—
Siphon: **nope**
Volume that will run back into machine: **none**
Extra standing water: **none**
Way to leak inside: **auto-vent**
Air ad. moving parts: **auto-vent**

Good—
Siphon: **nope**
Volume that will run back into machine: **none**
Extra standing water: **none**
Way to leak inside: **auto-vent failure**
Air ad. moving parts: **auto-vent**

Okay...in theory****—**
Siphon: **nope**
Volume that will run back into machine: **none**
Extra standing water: **6'**
Way to leak inside: **none**
Air ad. moving parts: **none**

BAD—
Siphon: **yes**

Ultra-low-plastic air admittance version pioneered by Fred Hunter. Note that the air admittance tees off to the side, so the inertia of the water moving past doesn't push the water higher into the vent tube.

8. *Automatic Bypass* (freezing climate only)

If the distribution lines slope downhill continuously they probably won't freeze (photo, p. 70). If your lines can freeze, you must have an automatic bypass. This is a pipe through which the water harmlessly overflows when the main line clogs with ice, instead of burning out the pump or flooding the house. The ideal bypass makes an audible splash so you know what's up. The vent tube air admittance option mentioned above (and in Figure 7.5, item 7b) could double as an automatic bypass if it is 1" or more in diameter. You'd certainly notice if greywater fountained off the side of your house. Perhaps a reader from a freezing climate will come up with a better design with less drastic notification of frozen lines.

9. *Hose Service Connection* (optional, for easier tuning and service)

A hose service connection makes tuning the outlets easier (you won't have to do load after load of laundry to check and tune outlet flows: a process guaranteed to drive you crazy if you try to do it with the intermittent flow from washer water). It is also good for

---

I suspect the lower height limit for air admittance is the spill point of the washer tub. I haven't seen this proven or disproven in the field.
**Another unproven theory: The main can dip down to get outside, then back up to an effective air admittance at the height of the washer drum. Should work to prevent siphoning, at the cost of stagnant water in the line.*

blowing out lint, if needed...or blowing the system apart if you pressurize it more than the 20 psi *(140 kpa)* that this type of plumbing is designed for. The hose service connection should be upstream of as many potential clog points as possible to ensure it can do its clearing job. (But it's not recommended to attach the hose indoors, as this scenario could go bad too easily.) The hose service connection must be properly installed so there is no chance of greywater backflowing into the freshwater lines. The layers of protection against this are: 1) the washer has to be disconnected to connect the hose; 2) the swing check valve (below); and 3) a backflow prevention device (below) at the hose bib.

To tune the outlets perfectly, check the flow from the washer by timing how long it takes to fill a bucket. Then adjust the hose to the same flow. Each fitting adds resistance—often as much as a long run of smooth tubing. For example you can see at right that a 90° fitting adds as much resistance as 6' of tubing for an outside coupling and about half that again for a barb (inside) coupling. Flow turning through a tees—see table. Try to minimize the number of fittings, so the total resistance adds up to pumping to the height of the top of the washer. Two things will help you: outlets reduce flow, and for an HE washer the line only gets a few gallons of water at a time.

10. Backflow Valve (optional)

If the drain line runs (or can be lifted) above the top of the washer, a swing check valve should be included as close as possible to the washer, to keep water in the line from rushing back into the machine when it shuts off. Get a clear valve with 1" pipe thread so you can watch what is happening inside. If you have a hose service connection, a swing check valve adds backflow protection. If you are pumping uphill it is doubly important to minimize inertia from standing water in the lines. Figures 7.7a and 7.7b show how to do this.

0.75'

11. Rainwater Inlet (optional)

It's desirable in dry climates to run rainwater into the same mulch basins as greywater to help flush salt and provide supplemental water...when there's not so much water that plants suffocate or a landslide is caused. This can be done by routing the water over the surface. *(Or, rooftop rainwater could be routed directly into all the L2L zones at once through some kind of plumbing connection. This could be a desirable addition to the state of the art; let us know if you come up with something, and check our website for possible further developments.)*

Design considerations: The downspout flow should be filtered of leaves and debris that could block the small-orifice emitters in the L2L system. The pressure and portion of the flow should match what the L2L system can handle.

12. Irrigation Piping

For optimal flow and distribution, as well as minimal ecological impact, pay attention to the size, geometry, and material of the piping.

The preferred material (sidebar) is 1" polyethylene tubing, ideally the kind with a purple stripe to indicate non-potable water. Bigger tubing traps more septic water and crud and is a waste of plastic. PVC pipe destroys the environment, and is ugly outdoors. (It is common to use PVC indoors for a sleeker look.)

For low-flow HE washers, ¾" tubing may work, though there is limited experience with this as yet. Definitely test the washer's

Preliminary results.

TABLE 7.2: RESISTANCE OF FITTINGS
(IN FEET OF WATER COLUMN; 2.3 FT= 1 PSI)

Fitting	10 gpm	7 gpm (HE washer)*
50' of 1" PE tubing	4'	2'
50' of ¾" PE tubing	16' (!)	8'
3-way valve flow left	1'	0.5'
3-way valve flow right	0.75'	0.4'
1" barb male x ¾" male pipe	0.75	0.4'
1" barb coupling x ¾" female hose adapter	2'	1'

(IN EQUIVALENT LINEAR FEET OF PIPE)

Fitting	Outside fitting	Barb fitting (approx)
90° bend	5.3'	10'
Flow through branch of tee	6'	12'
Flow through run of tee	1.7'	2.5'
Male or female adapter	2	4

Types of Pipes

It's always desirable to minimize the plastic in a system. First, choose the minimum diameter and length of tubing for each part of the system. Then, choose the least-bad plastic. PVC is one of the worst plastics and its use should be minimized. Polyethylene (PE) is one of the best; a nice thing about the L2L system is that it can be made mostly or entirely from PE.

Opinions vary on the desirability of low- vs high-density polyethylene (LDPE vs HDPE; both—confusingly—referred to as polyethylene or poly tubing). The difference is how hard/stiff it is. 1" LDPE tubing can be squished between thumb and forefinger...and easily sliced through with a shovel. HDPE is astonishingly hard by comparison—so hard that getting barbed fittings into it is difficult without heating. LDPE is less expensive and easier to find and work with. If you are a homeowner, I recommend LDPE. If you are installing systems professionally, I suggest trying each and deciding which you prefer for various applications. Personally, I lean toward HDPE for buried lines and lines attached to the house. For aboveground lines I go with LDPE. A type of HDPE called "Blu-Lock" is a viable alternative to PVC for the indoor part of the system.[24]

GREYWATERACTION.ORG

Getting Even Distribution

Goal: the right amount of water for each plant, from rain, greywater, and supplemental freshwater irrigation.

For effective L2L irrigation, first choose the best plants to irrigate: not too many, not too few, in good locations (Chapter 5). Then balance the irrigation piping sizes and lengths with the number, size, and elevation of outlets so the water is distributed widely, yet evenly.

❖ **Too many outlets**= some won't have as much or any water.

❖ **Total flow from all outlets too low**—the pump will work harder and may need to be replaced sooner.

❖ **Too few outlets or outlets too big**= a few waterlogged plants and a lost opportunity to use the water on more plants.

❖ **If outlets are too small**—they will clog.

❖ **Low outlets followed by high outlets**—Low outlets will drain the water before it gets to the higher ones, especially with HE machines, where sometimes the first discharge fills the line, then the second discharge comes out the outlets...if a low outlet hasn't drained it all.

Unlike a Branched Drain system, a change to any L2L outlet changes the pressure, flow, and total water that comes out of every outlet. Unlike drip irrigation, adding more outlets won't increase the amount of water; one way or the other, you're going to get one laundry load's worth of water per load.

FIGURE 7.8: LAUNDRY TO LANDSCAPE IRRIGATION PIPING ELEVATIONS AND OUTLET FLOWS

Each outlet takes pressure out of the line. Too many outlets, and the water won't reach the end...

too few, and the pump works harder than necessary...

just right...and you get the most even irrigation with reasonable load on the pump

Here an HE washer that only puts out 3 gal, then another 3 gal 15 min later, fills the first part of the line...which drains out the first two outlets before the next discharge, leaving the part of the line beyond the little bump high and dry

You can't irrigate along an uphill run...

first go uphill with a solid line, then run the line with outlets downhill

Gentle slope adds pressure at the same rate that friction and emitters reduce it. Result: even flow, amount of water per outlet

On a steep slope, you either need to slalom the pipe side to side down the slope, or reduce the tubing size (in this case from 1" to ¾" to ½")

With a 1" line the whole way, the water just rushed down the big slope and geysered out the outlets at bottom, leaving the plants at the top high and dry

Changing the downslope section to ½" tubing, then going back to 1" evened out the flow perfectly flow rate before doing this; ¾" tubing has half the flow capacity of 1" tubing; 7 gpm seems to be working in the few trials I know of. Attractive features of ¾" tubing: it uses about half the plastic of 1", is easier to find, and can be joined with a wide variety of compression fittings that go on the *outside* of the tubing. Thus, the smallest opening in a ¾" system with compression fittings would be the ¾" tubing itself, which is *bigger* than the opening in the barbed fittings that go inside of 1" tubing. This gains back a bit of the resistance differential between ¾" and 1".

You can run a single or multi-trunk line, with or without valves or branches. An arterial progression of branching and reduction, where the tubing gets smaller as the flow divides, is a promising way to go. You can attain the aforementioned advantages of ¾" tubing without sacrificing flow capacity by dividing the flow from a 1" line into two ¾" lines. Branches can be 1", ¾", or ½". ¼" is definitely too small: ⅜" may be ideal for the smallest legs, but experience is limited.*

If you have lots of greywater and/or low-perk soil, use two or more irrigation zones with the flow directed by valve(s) (photo at right, Figure 7.5). The outlets must be under 2" *(5 cm)* of mulch or shielded for a California-legal system (Figure 7.5). Otherwise, outlets can go on top of the mulch where you can see them and know whether they need service.

To avoid freezing, bad smells, and pump strain, it's best that the line slopes downhill continuously.

However, because the line is pressurized, if need be it can dip up and down, trapping water in the line between uses. (I have heard from some installers that a geometry that leaves lines filled with water between outlets improves the irrigation evenness from HE machines; it effectively reduces the amount of water it takes to refill the lines if they are already filled.) Unless the line might freeze, this is acceptable. The water can go mildly septic if it sits for more than a day. But, the volume of water in even a long run of 1" pipe is so small that any objectionable smell is only detectable for the first moment of discharge. In an installation that includes both some rise and a long horizontal run, the quantity of trapped water will be minimized by sending the pipe up to the maximum height as quickly as possible, then running the pipe continuously down from there (Figure 7.7); this drains most of the run after each use. The same geometry works to get water from a basement washer up to the yard in a freezing climate, as this places the part of the line that holds standing water inside the thermal envelope of the house. Finally, the less water in the line, the less inertia needs to be overcome by the pump.

13. Outlets

The capacity of all the outlets should be enough that the pump will not be strained trying to push too much water through too small or too few holes. On the other hand, too many or too large holes will result in pressure loss that may leave some outlets high and dry. The total cross-sectional area of all the outlets in a zone should be 1–2 in² *(650–1,300 mm²)* (the L2L Calculator in Oasis Greywater Extras[43] can be used to find the total cross-sectional area from a variety of outlets).

Note that outlet flow in this pressurized system, unlike a gravity-flow system, depends on the height, size, and number of outlets, as well as the length and diameter of the tubing. You can tune the flow by making the outlets different sizes, or adjusting the outlet ball valves (photo at right). If your line runs uphill between outlets, the lower outlets will get way more water than the upper. To avoid this, run a solid line to the high point, then do a U-turn and put all the outlets in the downhill run. This takes twice as much plastic, but is essential if you want even irrigation.

❖ **13a) Outlet: valved**—These are easy to tune, easy to clean...but clog easily. Plastic drip irrigation ball valves are very economical: a few bucks each. "Green back" brand valves work well. You can tune the flow by adjusting the valves so the total amount of water from each valve is what you want. Once you've done this, you can score the valve handle with a hacksaw to mark the right setting. Then, if you open it all the way to purge lint, or close it all the way when the tree loses its leaves, you can reset it correctly without retuning everything all over again.
How to clear clogs: Usually, opening and closing the valve while water is running through it is enough. If not, poke something through the open valve. Still clogged? Blast water

Crimping clamp: *the quickest, cheapest way to get a moderately secure connection.*

Zone valves in valve box *made from recycled plastic drum.*

Valved outlet *inside irrigation valve box mulch shield.*

Hole drilled in tubing as emitter. *Seems like cheating, it's so easy. They do clog more quickly, but they are easy to clear.*

*½" Eco-Lock tubing inserts snugly into ½" poly drip line; its inner diameter is ⅜."

through the system with the hose service connection. If that doesn't work, take the tee out of the main line and clean it.

❖ **13b) Outlet: drilled**—These are really easy and cheap to make, and easy to change. They clog more easily than fancier outlets, but are easy to clean. A $\frac{7}{32}$" *(5.5 mm)* hole is the perfect size to fit a drip irrigation goof plug, enabling you to plug and relocate holes at will. It's best to have the holes on the side of the pipe; pointed up they make geysers, pointed down they are vulnerable to root intrusion and difficult to check.

How to clear clogs: Poke at the lint with a stick or wire and it will usually blurp out immediately. A paper clip with a hooked end could make sure it is dragged out rather than pushed in. If you don't have washer flow to flush the lint, use the hose service connection.

¾" main to ½" drip to ½" light-colored Eco-Lock tubing (⅜" ID). *Long branch from upper left, short one at bottom.*

❖ **13c) Outlet: reducing tee with extension**—These are a really nice option. They can be valved, or the flow can be reduced by using a longer length of smaller-diameter line to increase resistance. It's nice that the end can be moved around to feed roots in different areas. Promising but unproven variation: slide thick-walled ½" outer diameter (OD), ⅜" inner diameter (ID) tubing inside the ½" ID drip tubing to lower the flow.

How to clear clogs: Just slide the smaller tubing out of the bigger tubing. If that doesn't do the trick, try the escalation in 13a).

❖ **13d) Outlet: reducing tee without extension**—Another super-simple option: just cut in a 1" x ½" reducing tee and off you go. You can adjust the flow a tiny bit by rotating the tee so the outlet points upward—yes, these systems can have such low pressure that a couple of inches makes a difference in the flow.

How to clear clogs: Pull the lint out with a paper clip with a hooked end. If you don't have washer flow to flush the lint, use the hose service connection.

1" x ½" barbed tee outlet.

14. Failsafe Overflow

You never know when some nasty blanket covered with fur balls might clog every outlet in the system. By leaving a raised end of the main line wide open, you protect your pump by ensuring that the water will always have a place to exit. To keep it from gushing with every load, it should be higher than the usual water level. The end of the line is a perfect place for this; there is rarely more than a few feet of pressure by the end. This also offers an exit for pennies and paper clips and whatever else finds its way into the laundry but is too large to escape through the emitters. An open end of the main line also facilitates scouring the system with water from the hose service connection.

How to clear clogs: This shouldn't ever clog.

15. Outlet Chambers *(for legal compliance or keeping mulch at bay)*

Outlet shields are necessary to comply with the code in California and/or keep mulch and roots away from the outlets. Let's look at the options:

❖ **15a) No outlet chamber**—This is the way to go if you are in a state and context that allow it. It has the lowest failure rate because the emitters are easy to find, inspect, and service. Eventually all jurisdictions will likely allow these for residential installations.

How to inspect/service: Whenever you are in the garden you'll see and hear whether the outlets are working.

❖ **15b) Mulch shield: recycled plastic bucket or flowerpot outlet shield**—Plastic buckets are strong and durable. Plastic flowerpots are legally accepted but are not as durable; they will likely buckle within a year. Both buckets and flowerpots are available in 1–5 gal sizes. To speed drainage, you can make thumb-sized holes around the lower portion.

Mulch shield *in mulch basin (5 gal pot).*

How to inspect/service: They are installed upside down; cut a hole in the bottom (now the top) for inspection/service. These can be covered with stepping stones for aesthetics and to facilitate finding them (you'd be amazed at how easy it is to lose outlets...especially years later). If you can hear the water falling that will greatly simplify inspection: nothing to take apart.

❖ **15c) Mulch shield: section of plastic culvert**—These are super strong. You might be able to find a mountain of short cutoffs perfect for outlet chambers in the service yard of a contrac-

HDPE culvert outlet shield *with ⅜" tube from ¾" main.*

tor who installs storm drains. Cut in half and set lengthwise, the bigger diameters work like infiltration chambers, below.

How to inspect/service: Same as previous, except there's no bottom to cut through.

❖ **15d) Mulch shield: valve box**—Beloved by professional installers for their strength and the nice lid, these are ideal...apart from the cost and the massive amount of newly fabricated plastic. These are generally deeper than needed. You will need to drill one or two holes in them to allow the tubing to get inside/through at the right height.

How to inspect/service: Same as previous.

❖ **15e) Subsoil infiltration chamber**—In the right context these are a dream; they provide invisible, odorless, 100% sanitary subsurface irrigation. They are great in public installations, under paths (they can take traffic loads), or in tight side yard setbacks (as they can go under a path). The cost of this dream: much more digging for installation (all the surge volume is in the chamber instead of a simpler, cheaper basin) and major pain to service. Put ½" welded wire mesh under them to keep gophers at bay. Only use subsoil infiltration when you have to.

How to inspect/service: Map and mark locations well. Take photos as they are going in. Mark inspection ports with stepping stones. Lift the stone and open the port to inspect. For major service—for instance if gophers have filled the whole volume with dirt, and roots have made this into a solid mat—you'll need to completely exhume the infiltration chambers, and cut loose and remove the roots and soil. If you managed to not break them, set them back in; otherwise replace them.

16. Mulch Basins

Mulch basins are the way to go (Chapter 5). The greywater tubing can go on the solid ground near the basins and the outlets can be directed into the mulch. No room for basins? See 15e, above.

17. Productive Trees/ Plants

If your goal is to irrigate, plants are the point. If you want to disperse greywater, they provide good treatment. It's always a good exercise to visualize what roots are doing, and to refine your mental root map with observation when you dig and service the system.

Tuning the System

When you have your L2L system built you can tune the outlets with water from the hose service connection, as described above under 9. Hose Service Connection and 13a. Outlet: valved. Then you're ready for that glorious first load of wash, with all the water coming out of a bunch of outlets at once, automatically.

Servicing the System

These systems generally fail in a soft way; the splitting just becomes less and less perfect. If you see or hear that an individual outlet isn't flowing properly, you can often clear it with nothing more than a paperclip and the pressure from the washer, as described under 13. Outlets, above. If the whole system seems clogged, you can blast lint out with the hose service connection. Service on these systems is roughly annual.

L2L ancestor I made for a school in Tijuana in 2000. A 1" main line feeds six ½" lines, which feed separate mulch basins. Pressure from the washer pump yields fairly even splitting, especially with the outlet heights and line lengths approximately equal.

Leveling an L2L line buried 4" (10 cm) deep in a hard-freeze climate. This line ran fine all winter, even though the plumbing inside the house froze!

Valve box mulch shield with drilled hole for outlet extension to come in high, holes to facilitate exit of water.

Clogged infiltration chambers.
These infiltrators did not have anti-gopher mesh. Gophers filled them with dirt, which roots then colonized. They clogged within about three and eight years, respectively. The more excess capacity you have, the longer the service interval. The biggest hassle with bought infiltrators is roots growing through the side louvers and pinning the infiltrator to the earth. The repurposed half culvert infiltrator at top does not have this issue.

Per-fect im-print of infil-trator shape

Experimental Adaptations for High-Efficiency Washers

Getting an L2L system to irrigate efficiently with the low, sputtery flow from an HE washer requires special adaptations. My colleague Fred Hunter of <u>dreamscapesb.com</u> describes the issue well:

"The lower total volume from horizontal axis machines is tough but even more challenging is the irregularity of the flow. The low-volume front loaders tend to expel the water in fits and spurts that don't allow for easy balancing of the flow. I have achieved as many as ten emitters on a system on a relatively level site where the client always uses the lowest quick-wash setting which only uses approximately 8 gal. The machine pushes out the first 1½ gal in a nice strong flow that only lasts for seconds. Then the machine tumbles and waits for more water to drip out of the clothes, spitting a little bolus of water here and there. Getting these dribbles to spread evenly through the irrigation lines requires careful balancing and leveling of tees much like Branched Drain work. Maddening and definitely not for the novice. Favorable slope conditions would help."

HE washing machine sales skyrocketed from 5% of washer sales to 50% between 1995 and 2012. We're going to face these issues more and more. Here's some thoughts on how to address them. These ideas are new and unproven as we go to press; they are here more to stimulate experimentation than to provide a recipe (check our website for updates):

❖ **Several zones with manual switching by the washer**—With a manifold by the washer (photo below), water could be sent to, say, four zones supplied with ¾" tubing. There is so much less plastic in ¾" tubing that this would not use much more than a 1" system with a single zone.

❖ **Lots of zones with manual switching by the washer**—With a manifold by the washer, water could be sent to say, a dozen zones supplied with ½" tubing. In this instance, at least three valves would need to be open at once to take all the flow. In the case of operator error with not enough valves open, overflow through the 1" air admittance tube could take the extra flow back into the lines downstream of the valve. This would require a lot of plumbing, but would provide excellent control and certainty of irrigation without a lot of demand on the user, and would be easier for the installer to tune.

❖ **Lots of zones with automatic splitting**—A manifold could be set to have all the spill points at the same elevation, such that a flow could be split into 4–12 zones *at once*. Each zone would get a trickle, but the trickle would be sure to reach the plants as it would have nowhere else to go. This could work normally by gravity, but be sealed so that if pressure built up, the clog could be pushed through the lines. This would be functionally similar to the dipper distribution box used in Branched Drain systems. To work properly, the splitting manifold should be at atmospheric pressure, at the high point of the water path. Thus, this system would probably work best with a washer high above the garden.

Check our <u>oasisdesign.net/greywater/laundry</u> for updates...

Small HE washer discharge reaches far because it doesn't have to fill the tube, which is already full

A **copper hydronic heating manifold** could be used, or a manifold could be assembled from PVC or copper. For the "all valves open at once" scenario it's important that all the spill points of the tubing to each zone are the same height.

Garden Hose through the Bathroom (CIR)

Commonly used as a temporary drought-emergency measure.

In the bath or shower, block the drain with a flat rubber drain stopper, then siphon the water through a hose from the bottom of the tub or shower stall into the garden after you bathe or as you shower. Use the "warmup" water (the cold water that comes out of the tap at first) to start a siphon. The "pro" way to start a siphon is to fill the hose completely with water (using a shutoff valve on the end, if necessary), then open the outlet while the inlet is underwater. A sump pump can be used as well (do not siphon greywater by mouth—duh!).

Dishpan Dump/Bucketing (CIR)

A good choice when water is extremely tight and time is abundant, in a drought emergency, or if the water supply system goes down and you need to make the most of greywater to keep plants alive.

The most time-honored of all greywater systems: when the dishpan water gets dirty, dump it in a mulch basin next to plants. No system can equal the efficiency attainable by Bucketing, even at a thousand times the cost. It can be the perfect greywater solution for those rare applications where water is truly precious, gardens need irrigation, and people have energy to haul buckets around daily...all the way to where it's needed. The Achilles heel of this system is laziness; the tendency is for plants near the door to get way more water. Improvement to help irrigation efficiency with less work: Branched Drain or Twisted Tees pipes that take water almost the whole way to where it needs to go, and then Bucketing it the last bit of the way. (A refined variation I call the Multimode Greywater Tank is described in Real World Example #3.)

Mulch Basins (R)

The simplest, best receiving system for greywater.

This is what receives the greywater from all the systems mentioned up to this point. Mulch basins are discussed at length in Mulch Basin Design, Chapter 5.

Greywater Furrow Irrigation (CIR)

Continue p. 84

An excellent system for nonindustrialized countries.

This is a greywater system reduced to its simplest elements: soil and plants. It consists of narrow channels formed in the soil which direct greywater to plants. Greywater Furrows can be owner built with a shovel, hoe, or rake. This system is best adapted to nonindustrialized world conditions where exposed greywater flows are the norm and mulch is unpopular (details in Appendix D).

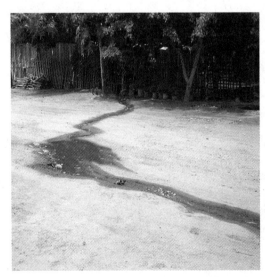

Before: *Greywater puddles in public street in Mexican village; habitat for dengue mosquitoes.*

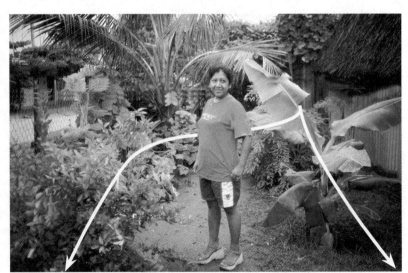

After: *Village women have made Greywater Furrows (arrows) that channel laundry water and bathwater to several thriving fruit trees.*

Chapter 8: More Complex Greywater Systems

The simple systems in Chapter 7 may not be an option if your plants are uphill from your greywater source, your greywater flow is high, it makes sense to reuse your blackwater as well as greywater, automated high-efficiency irrigation is desired, codes are strict, or some other reason. If this is the case, check out the systems that follow...

Drum with Effluent Pump (1)

The cheapest uphill distribution system. The pump quality and design details greatly impact its reliability. Virtually every one of these that includes a filter and a cheap pump is eventually abandoned due to maintenance hassles. If you choose this system and want it to last, go for an expensive, high-quality effluent pump capable of passing ¾" solids, and forget the filter.

This system consists of (surprise!) a plastic drum for a surge tank, a filter (optional, and emphatically *not* recommended), and a pump (Figure 8.1). You'll also need some means of distributing and receiving the water in the landscape, such as Mulch Basins.

If your garden is downhill from the drum, which may be up to 5' *(1.5 m)* higher than the washing machine, a Laundry Drum (that is, drum *without* pump or filter) that costs $20–$100 is best (see previous chapter). Otherwise, I recommend you bite the bullet and purchase an effluent pump. These are not cheap (see Appendix E).

If the irrigated area is uphill, you'll want a backflow prevention valve (p. 91).

You can distribute the water in the landscape via a movable hose (most people will quickly tire of moving it) or a branched network of permanent HDPE black drip irrigation tubing similar to a Laundry to Landscape system. This could consist of main lines of ¾–1" diameter, with branches of ½". For "emitters," use open-ended ½" drip tubing. Or, follow Larry Farwell's idea of using inexpensive ½" plastic inline drip ball valves to reduce the aperture size at the outlets, and/or to direct the water among different zones; these may clog, but you can just open the valves wide once in a while to free them. *Caution: Don't use drip irrigation emitters, as they will clog on the first use. Go with ½" minimum openings, as other greywater clogs more than laundry water.*

Note: The flow won't split predictably as it does when greywatering at atmospheric pressure through a Branched Drain network. Instead, the flow has to be fine-tuned so that outlets at different heights and at the end of different lengths of tubing emit an appropriate amount of water.

To receive the effluent in the landscape, you can use Mulch Basins or adequately sized subsoil infiltration chambers.

Drum with Pump and Mesh Filter is a discredited technology at this point due to longevity problems. It may make sense as a temporary system. Few of them have lasted more than a few years. But...they remain so popular that against my better judgement I'm including this brief description:

The surge tank is the same, but the pump is a cheap sump pump (see Appendix E). To prevent clogging and hair from wrapping around the pump rotor and killing it right off, tie pantyhose to the inlet as a filter. Some discard and replace the inexpensive pantyhose rather than clean them. The filter bags from airless paint sprayers work as reusable filters. This system costs

Effluent pump. *The expensive ones are well made. The $500 Zabel pump pictured supposedly has a service life of 27 years average, for pumping septic tank effluent. $100 pumps require filtering and rarely last five years.*

FIGURE 8.2: MESH FILTER BAG

FIGURE 8.1: DRUM WITH EFFLUENT PUMP

Inlet *from house*

Surge tank

Overflow line (2")

Power cord *(grounded)*

Swing check valve

To mulch basins *via HDPE tubing*

1" PVC flexible shown; rigid OK too

Float switch *where it won't wedge against tank wall*

Effluent pump *capable of passing ¾" (2 cm) solid*

Filter bag

$500–$1,500. Design it so that when the cheap pump fails or you tire of filter cleaning, you can easily upgrade to the effluent pump mentioned above. Mesh filtering allows reliable greywater irrigation via the irrigation tubing system described above. *Caution: Don't use drip irrigation emitters with mesh-filtered greywater. It will work for a while, but then they will clog—this has been firmly established. If you want to use drip irrigation, you'll need an auto-backwashing pool sand filter or media filtration, which are discussed toward the end of this chapter.*

Subsoil Infiltration Chambers (R)

Simplest method if subsoil irrigation is required. Sizing is important, as is access for service in the distant future. I often use these for kitchen sink effluent even if not legally required.

Subsoil Infiltration Chambers are open spaces under the soil into which you can pour effluent for treatment and reuse or dispersal. They provide surge capacity equal to their volume and wastewater infiltration area equal to their open floor area (and open wall area in the case of infiltrators, described below). They are so safe they work for raw blackwater.[24]

Greywater can be supplied to Infiltration Chambers via a gravity Branched Drain network, a Drum with Effluent Pump, or a Laundry to Landscape system. They do not require filtration, although an impermeable biomat may form in the absence of active earthworms. They must be supplied by multiple outlets, or be perfectly level and dosed in large batches for even distribution (see Dosing Siphon, Chapter 4). The optimum size dose (greywater surge) would fill the entire chamber 1½" *(4 cm)* deep. Dosing prevents an accumulation of solids at the inlet. Otherwise, progressive infiltration failure can occur as successive small areas are overwhelmed and clogged with solids. If greywater loading is not enough to make the inside disgusting all the time, gophers may fill them with dirt. To avoid this, cover the bottom with ½" *(13 mm)* welded wire mesh.

Consider Infiltration Chambers' ability to support the weight of soil and traffic, ease of inspection/service access, resistance to clogging by roots, and environmental impact/cost of materials. The various means of making these spaces include infiltrators, box troughs, and half pipes or drums.

Infiltrators are manufactured gravelless infiltration chambers now used for the majority of new septic leachfields in the US. Their form resists the weight of traffic, and they are designed to emit water not only through the open bottom but also halfway up the louvered sides, without soil leaking in. They are made from partially recycled HDPE plastic, a fairly benign material. You need to cut your own larger service access and make it a soil-tight lid (see images on this page). *Note: Infiltrator Water Technologies[s13] has redesigned these with narrower lower slots to reduce migration of soil into the chambers.*

FIGURE 8.3:
MANUFACTURED
INFILTRATION
CHAMBERS

Standard SideWinder
17 ft² area, 76 gal volume

High-Capacity Infiltrator
17 ft², 103 gal

Equalizer 24 Chamber
10 ft², 34 gal

Making a lid, access port: Cut out a section between structural ribs with a sawsall or keyhole saw. Put it back as a form.

Fill the cut-out section with concrete. This lid includes a smaller inspection port.

Finished access lids, one per infiltrator. They will have pavers over them on the surface to mark their location.

Photo taken by holding the camera down inside the access. Note the bamboo feeder roots coming up through the earth floor.

Box troughs are narrow, rectangular chambers made of flat material such as rot-resistant wood (Figure 8.4).[s14] They can water a planter in a greywater greenhouse, for example (photo at right). The advantage of box troughs is completely open access for inspection/service. A Branched Drain network for distributing the dose internally could possibly be concealed inside the box trough. (Contact us for the latest on this variation, which is promising but untried as yet.[s9])

FIGURE 8.4: BOX TROUGH

- Removable lid 2" x 12"
- Use redwood or cedar for longer life
- Sides 2" x 8" wood or 1" ferrocement
- Greywater from dosing tank
- Flooding dose = 1½"
- Water/ nutrient uptake
- Splash block
- Greywater/soil interface

Metric: 2" = 5 cm; 12" = 30 cm; 8" = 20 cm; 1½" = 4 cm

Box troughs water a greywater greenhouse in Maryland.

FIGURE 8.5: HALF PIPE LEACHING CHAMBER

- PVC half pipe 6–12" diameter, 5–20' long (1.5–6 m)
- Flooding dose- 1½" deep (4 cm)
- Mulch
- From dosing siphon
- Plastic mesh to keep pipe from settling

Half pipes or **half drums** can be made from 8–24" pipes or 15–55 gal plastic drums cut in half lengthwise (Figure 8.5).[m] Check with big contractors who build and repair roads; they may have a giant pile of 3-6' cutoffs of corrugated plastic drainpipe. Cut in half, it's perfect. Rest the half pipes on 1" plastic mesh or bricks to keep them from sinking into the soil, then cover with soil or mulch. If covered with mulch, service will obviously be easier. The ends should be capped or sealed so mulch doesn't leak into the chamber.

Solar Greywater Greenhouse (R)

The way to go in really cold climates. Successful with box troughs supplied by a Drum with Effluent Pump.

No finer synergy can be obtained between the different systems of a home than with an attached Solar Greywater Greenhouse. Not only does it provide an optimal microclimate for year-round greywater reuse/treatment in the harshest of climates, it also helps heat your house, grows food, and frequently ends up becoming the most popular hangout all winter (see sidebar next page).[25,26]

Compared to outdoor irrigation, a greenhouse's water need is relatively constant throughout the year, and generally, so is greywater supply. Greywater use/treatment may be feasible in a greenhouse even when the ground outside is frozen solid. A solar greenhouse can dramatically reduce space heating requirements.

According to Carl Lindstrom, several greywater-irrigated greenhouses in New England have been in operation since the 1970s. One greenhouse uses a clear fish pool with a waterfall and biofilter plates on the bottom as the final treatment. Deep soil beds store heat from the sun and from the greywater itself. This greenhouse was the highest cold-weather producer of greens in the US. These soil beds operate odorlessly and can provide salad greens throughout the long New England winters[s15] (photos next page, front cover).

[m]*Metric: 8–24" = 20–60 cm, 15–55 gal = 50–200 L, 3-6' = 1-2 m, 1" = 2.5 cm*

FIGURE 8.6: ATTACHED SOLAR GREYWATER GREENHOUSE

Sunny side
of house

House

Greenhouse

Hot-weather vent

Warm air to house
through one-way
vent

Sliding glass door
to house through
massive, uninsulated
wall (e.g., adobe)

House floor level
well above greenhouse
floor; 3' is good
(1 m)

**Cool air from
house**

Thermal mass
water in 55 gal
(208 L) drums

**Subsoil
Infiltration
Chambers**

Insulation

Greywater
Gravity flow or
pressure dosed

Excess water drains to
native soil or drain tiles

Metric: 2" = 5 cm; 12" = 30 cm; 8" = 20 cm; 1½" = 4 cm

Greenhouse with Clivus infiltration beds in
Massachusetts.

CLIVUS MULTRUM

Doug and Sara Balcomb's Solar Greenhouse in Santa Fe, New Mexico

The heating for the house is 93% solar: 73% direct passive and 20% active, from rock beds under the greenhouse. The owners estimate that this design would fulfill more than 50% of the heating needs for a home with good solar exposure anywhere in the US.

The two-story, well-insulated house has a 14" adobe wall between house and greenhouse. The home generally stays between 71° and 75°F in the summer and between 65° and 71°F in the winter (35 cm adobe wall, 22–24°C and 18–22°C, respectively). Because the floor and walls are warm, the owners found themselves more comfortable than in a forced-air-heated home. Here's a quote:

"It is important to emphasize the quality of life that a well-designed solar greenhouse affords the owner. Imagine a blustery, snowy winter day...cold and raw. Then imagine what it is like to step directly into a room where roses and petunias are in full bloom, where lemons are ripening on the tree, where the smell of fresh flowers and green plants pervades. Imagine what it is like to sit in a space like that and sunbathe when it is below freezing outside. Finally, and best of all, imagine picking all the fresh vegetables you and your family need for your winter dinners… This 'impossible dream' is a reality for us, one we hope every family in America will share."[25]

Green Septic: Tank, Flow Splitters, and Infiltrators (CIR)

Especially suited for new construction, replacement leachfields, and water reuse from homes with a large amount of space per person, as it eliminates the need for costly dual plumbing. This promising type of system can recycle blackwater as well as greywater, and may be the best way to go for a legal system in areas with lousy greywater codes. (An Art Ludwig original design.)

Much as the Branched Drain system is a more evolved, refined version of the venerable Drain Out Back, this system is inspired by the "grass is always greener over the septic system" phenomenon. A Green Septic consists of conventional combined greywater and blackwater collection plumbing, a conventional septic tank, a dipper distribution box (Chapter 9), and a 2" Branched Drain irrigation system that leads the effluent to subsoil infiltrators (see Subsoil Infiltration Chambers, this chapter and Chapter 9). With outlets 9" *(23 cm)* below the surface, the system is sanitary enough for the reuse of septic tank effluent. This is similar to the standard for secondary treated effluent.

A Branched Drain–Green Septic system promises economical, low-maintenance, sanitary, predictable, even distribution of clarified septic effluent for irrigating and feeding a bunch of trees. The system's capacity, longevity, and ease of service might well be better than those of a conventional septic system.

Caution: Trials have been limited and short term (since around 2000). It will take decades for this system to prove its reliability. The stakes of experimentation are high, as replacing a leachfield costs a bundle. Think twice before trying this with low-perk soil; better to let this system prove itself and have the kinks worked out in high-perk soil first. Current information on this new design can be found at oasisdesign.net/greenseptic. The only issues so far: 1) Inspection ports "lost," as in can't find them. This problem is common to all buried systems. Take photos that include stable landmarks as the system goes in, make a good map, and store a digital and hard copy for the ages. 2) Gophers filled the chambers with dirt in Southern California. Proposed fix = underlay with ½" (13 mm) welded wire mesh. 3) Undersized systems clog. These are not mulch basins; their capacity lowers with time. Interesting idea: put mulch inside them to encourage worms and bugs to open the soil (unproven).

Note: You don't have to have a full-blown septic system to use the "filtration by settling" principle for greywater only. Any tank with more than two days' capacity coupled with any subsurface irrigation system should work.

Blackwater Reuse Health Warning

Don't try blackwater reuse unless you really know what you're doing. Gross misuse of greywater is common. Typically there is almost no health threat because greywater is just not that dangerous in an industrialized world context. This is not the case with septic effluent. Greywater might have 50 coliform bacteria/100 ml, which is not an unusual level for drinking water in the nonindustrialized world; septic tank effluent might have a million. Put another way, your blackwater reuse system must be thousands of times more effective to achieve the same level of safety.

FIGURE 8.7: GREEN SEPTIC: TANK, FLOW SPLITTERS, AND INFILTRATORS
(NUTRIENT AND WATER REUSE FROM A NEARLY CONVENTIONAL SEPTIC SYSTEM)

Greywater and blackwater from house

Septic tank

"Dipper" distribution box

Disposal field

Flow splitter (double ell)

All pipe unperforated

Subsoil infiltrators

DANIEL WILSON WELDESIGN.NET

2 ft

Green Septic with passive distribution to 12 outlets, 1 per infiltrator (*close-up of dipper on p. 78*).

Constructed Wetlands (IR)

Good for responsible dispersal of greywater in wet climates, where perk is low and space tight, and for treatment of large flows prior to reuse. Constructed Wetlands work for blackwater as well as greywater. In dryland climates, reuse efficiency may be lowered considerably by water loss through wetland plants, possibly to zero when evapotranspiration is highest and irrigation most needed.

There are two types of Constructed Wetland: with open water and with water hidden under gravel, with plants coming up out of it (Figure 8.8).[27] Common sense dictates that the hidden-surface type be used for the first stage of wastewater treatment.

Wetland capacity is a function of temperature, evapotranspiration, rainfall, influent volume, Biological Oxygen Demand (BOD), and effluent legal standards. A typical size for a wetland in a mild climate is ½–1 ft²/gal/day *(24 m²/m³/day)*, and two or three times this in a cold climate. Wetland depth depends on plant species (see "Water level," Figure 8.8). Although all plant roots extract nutrients from wastewater, *only* wetland plants function as solar-powered

FIGURE 8.8: CONSTRUCTED WETLAND

Aquatic plants of locally appropriate species

Waterproof membrane protected from sun. Use EPDM or construct wetland from cement. Unlined wetlands OK in appropriate soil (low perk) and groundwater conditions (adequate separation)

Water level 2" below surface of gravel, 12–30" deep depending on plant root depth: 12" for cattails, 24" for reeds, 30" for bulrushes

Raw greywater or clarified septic effluent in

Rhizome network

Outlet manifold covered with 1" rock

Treated water out

Infiltrator 2–3' wide half pipe or half drum covered with 1½–3" rock, across width of wetland. Total wetland width should be about half of length

Gravel ½–1" Uniformly sized, double washed

Thermal baffles prevent short-circuiting of effluent

Level control Pulling plug once a month lowers water level, aerates, and establishes roots in lower part of system

DRAWING BASED ON US EPA WETLAND MANUAL

Metric: ½–1" = 13–25 mm; 1½–3" = 38 mm–8 cm; 2" = 5 cm; 12" = 30 cm; 24" = 61 cm; 30" = 76 cm; 2–3' = 60–90 cm

THANKS TO NATURAL SYSTEMS INTERNATIONAL, LLC, AND TAD MONTGOMERY FOR HELP WITH THE WETLAND SECTION.

Mini-Constructed Wetland in Mexico turns blackwater from two toilets into irrigation water. The plants are, from left to right: papyrus (taller than a person), canna lilies, and, on the tiny open-surface portion, water hyacinths.

6' (2 m)

Eco-Machine® at Omega Center for Sustainable Living, Rhinebeck, New York. Eco-Machines blend science and engineering with plants and beneficial bacteria to efficiently treat and reuse wastewater. Based on the principles of wetland ecology, Eco-Machines have been built since the 1980s and the longest-running machines have been operating continuously for more than 20 years. This installation treats wastewater in seven steps: 1) Solid Settlement Tanks, 2) Equalization Tanks, 3) Anoxic Tanks, 4) Constructed Wetlands, 5) Aerated Lagoons, 6) Recirculating Sand Filter, and 7) Dispersal Fields. It processes up to 52,000 gal of water per day when the campus is open in summer, and about 5,000 gal of water per day in winter.

TODDECOLOGICAL.COM

pumps that push oxygen out through the roots. This oxygen keeps Constructed Wetlands from "anaerobic meltdown." Amazingly, wetlands don't stink. Despite a constant inflow of raw sewage, the oxygen pumped during daylight hours prevents anaerobic conditions and odors, especially at the surface, where it matters most. Root hairs also provide growth medium for beneficial microorganisms.

Treatment is effective. In a toilet-only wetland I made in Mexico (photo facing page), the septic water going into it had 3,000,000 fecal coliform bacteria per 100 ml, the wetland effluent just 50—the same as the tap water in the house, and theoretically well within the standard for swimming. Nonetheless, disinfection may be required, depending on what you do with the effluent.

Eco-Machines (formerly Living Machines) are a design pioneered by John Todd.[s16] They are a wetland variation enhanced with the addition of a solar aquatic greenhouse, carefully crafted and balanced guilds of organisms, and attention to the disposition of each nutrient in the system. Eco-Machines range in flow from 500 to 5,000,000 gpd *(2–20,000 m³/day)*, require a land area sufficient for two-day retention time, and cost 30% less than a package treatment plant to build, 60% less to operate. These constructed ecosystems are especially appropriate in environmentally sensitive sites that don't offer much naturally occurring treatment capacity: for example, a ski resort surrounded by snow and rock. Some institutions choose this system for its teaching potential.

Notes: Wetlands are proven for cleaning large flows of partially treated municipal wastewater or septic tank effluent. They are less common for raw, unfiltered household greywater by itself; questions remain about clogging, high oxygen demand, and nutrient balance. Systems are reported to work with pantyhose prefiltration or a large-area infiltrator at the inlet, but a septic tank is better proven. Design guidance from an engineer with Constructed Wetland experience is highly recommended.[s17,s18] Wetland service is backbreaking and gross: remove all the roots and gravel, wash the gravel, and put it back.

Automated Sand Filtration to Subsurface Emitters (IR)

Expensive and complex, but beloved by regulators. These systems start to make sense for new construction with at least 100–200 gpd of greywater. Emitter cone installation does not get cheaper with larger irrigated area. Subsurface drip does, but more research is needed to establish whether subsurface drip works long term with filtered but otherwise untreated greywater. **This system and the next are the only acceptable ways to greywater turf.** *With more than 500 gpd, Advanced Treatment System to Subsurface Drip may be better (next section).*

Automated greywater-to-drip irrigation is the holy grail of greywater systems. Many have tried, few have succeeded, and none thus far have managed to open wide the gates between Americans' indoor water use and their lawns. Reliable greywater-to-drip is elusive. Unless you enjoy destroying expensive equipment as a hobby, breathe deeply and buy a system from an outfit that knows what they're doing—if you can find one.[53,85,]

Although the next big drought will no doubt spawn numerous new entries in this system category, ReWater Systems is the most solid representative in the US at the moment (Figure 8.9, Real World Example #5). They are the sole survivor of the numerous greywater system

FIGURE 8.9: AUTOMATED SAND FILTRATION TO SUBSURFACE EMITTERS

FIGURE 8.10:
IRRIGATION CONE
EMITTER

start-ups born from the big California drought of the 1990s. If you buy a system from an outfit that has been around for a long time, you'll hopefully get a more evolved design—and a better chance they will be there when the system needs an overhaul. Failure points for this type of system include inadvertent cutting of tubing when digging (easily done, easily fixed) and pump failure; about 4% fail early.

The ReWater computer-controlled, automatic backwashing sand filter system handles every conceivable aspect of greywater irrigation automatically—it even coordinates freshwater irrigation. The idea is that it is your sole irrigation system.

125 gpd of greywater can water a 1,000–2,000 ft2 lawn through emitter cones for roughly the same cost as sprinklers: about $1.25/ft2, installed.[m] Sprinklers are cheaper on big turf areas up front, but cost more long term due to higher water costs from overspray and evaporation losses.

Subsurface drip tubing has clogged with sand-filtered greywater. There may be a fundamental incompatibility between the small orifices of subsurface drip emitters and greywater that has both high mineral and soap content, even after fine mechanical filtration. Or, these failures may be due to absence of maintenance—more research is required. You can open up subsurface drip tubing by flushing it with acid, but not if it is completely clogged.

ReWater has developed proprietary one-piece recycled plastic irrigation cone emitters (Figure 8.10), approved by the Center for Irrigation Technology (as required by California greywater code). These cones have relatively large orifices that don't clog easily. They are about 2½" x 2½" version is coming out. [m] They can be supplied with ¾", ½", or ¼" drip tubing. Roots grow into the emitters, but don't block the inlets thanks to air pruning (the reluctance

---

[m]**Metric:** *0.4–0.75 m³/day; 2 m³/day. ReWater: 0.5 m³/day can irrigate 100-200 m² lawn. Costs $12.50/m².
9 cm x 9 cm, 6 cm x 6 cm.*

Installation of ReWater emitter cones for a new lawn. *A tedious process, but at least they seem to work long term.*

ReWater Systems controller, backwashing sand filter, and surge tank

of roots to grow more than a short distance straight up without soil, even though roots will go hundreds of yards horizontally along irrigation pipes). According to ReWater, hundreds of thousands of these emitters are in the ground. The oldest, in use since 1990, are still working. Many of these systems are in San Diego, California, where the mineral content in tap water is among the highest in the US.

Steve Bilson, the owner of ReWater, has been nothing if not tenacious, not only to simply survive so long in the industry, but in pursuing official recognition of greywater systems. With an effort of staggering proportions, he managed to get the US EPA State Revolving Fund (SRF) program to qualify ReWater systems for loans, which had previously only been available to cities for conventional centralized sewer systems, one of the century's greatest ecological disasters.[2] His multiyear effort generated a thick stack of paper and a rigorous life cycle analysis showing that if you take everything into account, even as complex and expensive a system as the ReWater will pay for itself through savings on water, wastewater, and non-point source pollution prevention, despite lost interest, operations and maintenance expense, and system replacement costs. According to Steve's analysis, sewer districts would save more water and money by installing gold-plated greywater systems in every new home than with the multimillion-dollar reclaimed water plants that the engineering lobbies are getting built instead. Interesting food for thought.

Caution: A halfhearted attempt at an automated greywater system is doomed. Components that work reliably with wastewater are expensive, but anything less will fail.

Advanced Treatment System to Subsurface Drip (CIR)

These are well proven for treatment and reuse. Secondary treatment is overkill for a residential site unless it is required for some reason, but this is the way to go for multifamily- or institutional-scale flows. Very expensive, uses a lot of electricity and materials, but is beloved by regulators. Also, this is a rare case of a truly turnkey system. If you can write eye-popping checks for installation and the (required) maintenance contract...that's all you have to do. You can reuse blackwater with this system, obviating the need for dual plumbing. These are regulated under septic system regulations, not the greywater code, which can be an advantage. Orenco developed this class of system.

Here's a general recipe for success in reusing combined greywater and blackwater for irrigation with Advanced Treatment Systems (also called Advanced Treatment Technology):

❖ **Settling and anaerobic digestion**—Combined greywater and blackwater are filtered of most solids by settling in a strong, watertight septic tank (fiberglass or concrete). Anaerobic treatment reduces sludge, scum, and some nutrients (settling can be compromised in Aerobic Treatment Units (ATUs); systems that bubble air through the septic tank itself).

❖ **Effluent filter**—A simple mesh filter protects the system from glop that might otherwise escape the septic tank (these are recommended for any septic system).

* **Secondary treatment**—Clarified septic effluent is stripped of biological and chemical oxygen demand (BOD and COD measure the amount of compost in the water) and nutrients in a well-designed, well-built, and well-maintained suspended growth aerobic treatment unit or packed bed media filter.
* **Effluent pump in pump tank**—Pushes effluent through the filter and into the dispersal field.
* **Drip filter**—Mechanical filtration in a 100 micron, self-cleaning drip irrigation filter.
* **Subsurface drip irrigation**—The effluent is distributed through well-designed subsurface drip irrigation.[s10] The whole drip system has to be a closed loop, the ends of which flush back to the pretreatment or the pump tank to prevent clogging. This flush can be achieved through ball valves that are cracked open to leak continually and are fully opened at intervals, manually or by electrically operated solenoid valves.
* **Proper operation and regular maintenance**—More important than the specific choice of hardware is choosing hardware that can, and will, be serviced.

*Orenco AdvanTex®—a deservedly popular **secondary treatment system**. By using engineered textile instead of sand as the packed bed media filter, it takes about a quarter as much area in the yard. I've tracked their work since 1990; Orenco has been very dedicated to the goal of getting these systems optimized.*

Drip dispersal of primary treated effluent is somewhat simpler and cheaper, but is allowed only in some states, may be problematic with clay soils, and requires more area.

Secondary treatment adds expense and complexity. The water is still an infection hazard, but it will not clog drip irrigation hardware as easily as primary treated (even finely filtered) greywater, especially in clay soils. It also allows higher loading rates and less separation to groundwater. Secondary treatment options are rapidly multiplying and evolving as large-scale solutions are adjusted to residential scale and vice versa.

In the ATU version of secondary treatment, air is bubbled through septic tank effluent to facilitate aerobic decomposition. This is the cheaper option.

In packed bed media filtration, effluent filters through textile, sand, or gravel (peat and foam have been used less successfully). Trillions of aerobic bacteria on the surface gobble the dissolved nutrients and anaerobic bacteria, yielding a sweet smelling, highly polished effluent.

Thus, for the high price of buying and maintaining these filters, pumps, and controllers, the dream of long-term, maintainable greywater-to-drip irrigation can be achieved. As toilet water needn't be excluded, you have more water available for reuse, don't need to pay for a backup wastewater system, and might be able to downsize or even eliminate the need for a freshwater irrigation system.

As much as I dislike pumps, a pressure-dosing/drip system can distribute water far more widely and evenly than a gravity system. Orenco Systems[s3] suggests using a high-head effluent pump, protected by an effluent filter, to pressure-dose subsurface drip irrigation lines. (For dispersal, shallow Infiltration Chambers consisting of 12" *(30 cm)* PVC half pipes in 10" *(25 cm)* deep trenches

Orenco sand filter system being pressure tested in Stinson Beach, California. The pipes will be covered with sand and plants.

are an option.) People are also experimenting with ozone disinfection, which may someday permit this effluent to be used for sprinklers or garden ponds.

A residential Orenco Advantex packed bed media system can cost $12,000–$30,000 installed, plus about $200 a year for the required maintenance contract. An ATU unit could be a few thousand dollars less. Primary treatment only is not much less than that, because the cost savings on treatment are offset by greater requirements in automation and dispersal field size.

Notes: Under some wastewater rules, it's better to call a wastewater reuse system a "dispersal" or "disposal" system and not an "irrigation" system. Despite movement toward acceptance of irrigation, a disposal mentality still hangs on. In most cases the system size and rate of application is based on soil acceptance formulas for the wettest month, not on irrigation need. This means that supplemental water will be required during the peak irrigation season.

This class of system is being pushed by industry profiteers and regulators as a universal substitute for septic systems, which would be a colossal waste of resources. Better to make simple, passive Green Septic systems (p. 77) for low flows in good soils.

Marin's Stinson Beach, a long, very narrow, low sand spit with the Pacific on one side and an ecologically sensitive estuary on the other. The spit is covered with large houses, all on septic tank/sand mound systems, all working. As part of one of the most stringent monitoring programs in the country, Stinson Beach inspects all onsite wastewater treatment systems annually.

Cont. from p.72

Chapter 9: Branched Drain Design

I recommend Branched Drains for most residential-sized flows where the greywater sources are located above the irrigated area. This chapter and the next slice through the whole of greywater system design along the axis of this one system—an interesting exercise even if this particular system isn't for you. (Branched Drains are an Art Ludwig original design.)

Most commercially sold greywater systems are elaborate affairs featuring filters, pumps, tanks, valves, and sometimes disinfection, electronics, etc. They cost $3,000–$30,000 (gasp!) for a single-family residence. Most are newly installed, abandoned, or failing to meet their original goals. However, commercial systems account for only a tiny percentage of the greywater systems in use: 1% or less.

What about the other 99%? Many have worked for decades without the users even thinking about them. The vast majority are nothing more than a drainpipe pointing down the nearest hill. The classic Drain Out Back has some serious shortcomings, but its durability and spectacular simplicity give one serious pause for thought.

Lessons Learned from the Drain Out Back

From a holistic perspective, an overly complicated, expensive system is doomed from the start. At best, all it can do is shift the impact from waste of water to waste of resources used to produce pumps, valves, tanks, piping, and electricity.[15]

How about scrapping all this delicate, expensive technology, which is nearly impossible to make ecological, affordable, or durable, and instead concentrate on learning from and improving the humble Drain Out Back?

Advantages of the Drain Out Back

❖ **no filtration is necessary**
❖ **no pumping is necessary**
❖ **no surge tank is necessary**
❖ **very little pipe is needed**
❖ **little or no maintenance is required**
❖ **economic and ecological costs are low**
❖ **anyone can build it**
❖ **the failure rate is low** (that is, they are no worse in year 100 than year one)
❖ **they last forever**

Shower water

Drain Out Back in Southern California. *Most likely installed with the cabin in the 1920s, a shower drain waters an old-growth orange tree. Despite the fact that the outlet is quite close to a road that wraps around the mulch basin only a few paces away, no runoff is ever encountered. Leaves from surrounding oak trees automatically replenish the mulch.*

Drawbacks of the Drain Out Back

❖ **Low reuse efficiency**—With all the water dumping in one spot, the result tends to be one overwatered patch and everything else underwatered. Usually nothing is planted to utilize the water, so the reuse efficiency is zero. Even when there are plants at the outlet, they might utilize only a fraction of the water available. In a few lucky instances there is a conveniently situated fruit tree, which grows until its water need equals the flow, in which case the reuse efficiency is high.

❖ **Poor sanitation**—Without a basin to contain it and mulch to cover and slow it, greywater applied to the surface could flow into a creek or onto the street, especially during rain. In older installations near natural waters, the pipe typically discharges directly into them (see Error: Discharge of Greywater Directly to Natural Waters or Hardscapes, Chapter 11). Without mulch or soil covering it, greywater could be lapped up by dogs, played with by children, or prowled for food bits by vermin. (This litany sounds worse than it really is in most industrialized world installations. A thin sheet of wastewater just flowing over the ground for even 20 paces receives spectacularly high treatment by the same beneficial bacteria that live in soil.[3] But in nonindustrialized world conditions, especially in shanty towns where people live in appalling intimacy with their greywater, it is just as bad as it sounds above.)

❖ **Soil overload/poor aesthetics**—With a typical Drain Out Back, a mucky, grey-white material on the ground indicates where the soil's purification capacity is overloaded. This patch can measure from a few inches to several feet in length. If the ground slopes so the greywater runs off and infiltrates the surrounding soil, there is usually no odor unless you stick your face in it. If the greywater pools at the outlet, odor is likely and mosquitoes are possible. Some plants may be harmed by root suffocation.

❖ **Illegal**—Though common throughout the world, the Drain Out Back is not allowed in many areas because the effluent is exposed on the surface (actually getting busted, however, is virtually unheard of). Drain to Mulch Basin, a more refined version, is allowed in a small but growing handful of jurisdictions including Arizona, New Mexico, and Texas.[4] Greywater Furrows are like Drains Out Back with greater irrigation efficiency and less anaerobic muck. (Drain to Mulch Basin and Greywater Furrows are superior variations that can be substituted virtually anywhere a Drain Out Back could go; see p. 55, 72.)

Branched Drain ancestor.
In Cuernavaca, Mexico, a cement channel on a steep, seasonally dry slope distributes greywater more evenly than if it were simply dumped on the ground. However, due to imprecisely formed splits, numerous cracks, and blocking from roots and leaves, it is not as predictable as a Branched Drain network. Shaping the splits precisely with a form would help.

Branched Drains to the Rescue

A Branched Drain system solves most of the drawbacks above while retaining most of the advantages. Like the Drain Out Back, it has no pump, filter, surge tank, electronic controls, or any opening smaller than 1" *(25 mm)*, and has maintenance intervals of a year or more. Unlike the Drain Out Back, it can automatically disperse greywater to several trees with satisfactory efficiency, it is much more sanitary, and you can get a permit for it. The difference is that it *splits* the greywater in a branching network of pipes, then *contains and covers* the greywater in the landscape by means of mulch-filled basins.

Split the Flow

The most intractable problems of the Drain Out Back stem from an unmanageably high flow to one place. The Branched Drain system addresses this by splitting the flow (Figure 9.1).

Contain and Cover the Flow

Mulch basins contain and cover the flow (Figures 9.2, 9.3). They are common in horticulture and could hardly be simpler to make and maintain. Don't let this fool you: Though nature takes care of their inner workings, they are fantastically complex biologically, far more than a municipal sewage treatment plant. What's more, the treatment level that mulch basins provide is much higher.[3] Finally, instead of consuming copious electricity and chemicals to pollute natural waters and create toxic sludge,[2] mulch basins run on sunlight and yield drinkable groundwater and fresh fruit. Convinced yet? (Mulch Basin Design is covered in depth in Chapter 5.)

FIGURE 9.1: FLOWS SPLIT VIA BRANCHED DRAIN
(PLAN VIEW)

Greywater outlets can be arranged so the water falls through the air for a few inches before disappearing under the mulch in the basins (simplest, lowest maintenance, most durable). Or, outlets can be shielded, or fully enclosed in chambers under mulch (more legal, more sanitary) or in chambers under soil (most legal, most expensive). These options are fully described later under Branched Drain Outlet Design.

Continue ▶ *p. 110*

Advantages and Disadvantages of Branched Drain Systems

Overall I'd characterize them as "surprisingly involved to design and install optimally, with surprisingly little to do afterward." The upfront investment (primarily labor) is substantial but then it's mostly over, possibly for the life of the house. In contrast, most other systems cost more, lack the opportunity to save much by doing the labor yourself, and require significant ongoing inputs of electricity, maintenance, and system replacement—or, they require much more effort in use.

All versions of the Branched Drain system are permitable in states with rational greywater regulations: Arizona, New Mexico, and Texas. If you use one of the subsurface versions, it is possible to get a permit under the CPC/UPC. If you're dealing with permits, I suggest you get our *Builder's Greywater Guide*.[6]

Limitations of the Branched Drain System

Carefully consider the limitations below and make sure what you are setting out to do is possible.

Cannot Deliver Water Uphill

If the irrigation or treatment area is located above your greywater sources, you're stuck. Look at the System Selection Chart for other system options.

Non-exception: Conceivably, a washing machine or an effluent pump could deliver greywater to an uphill, gravity-flow Branched Drain network. But you'd be better off with a smaller-diameter, more easily laid network directly pressurized by the washer or effluent pump.

The Ground on Your Site Needs to Slope at Least ¼" per Foot (2%)

The steeper your lot and the higher your house plumbing above ground level, the less painstaking to lay the pipe. If your ground slopes 1" per foot (8%) or more, you can pretty much just dig a trench, throw the pipe in, and throw the dirt in after it. (However, with very long pipe runs the water may run ahead of solids, leading to clogging.) If it slopes ¼–½" per foot (2–4%), it is a tedious multistep process to level the pipe. If your lot slopes less than ¼" per foot—wow, it's going to be rough. In this case, the farther from the house you go, the deeper your lines end up, so you can't irrigate very far from the house. You have to double the design effort and redouble the installation precision. If you have a lot of water to get rid of and low-perk soil...it may not be feasible at all.

The Pipes Must Be Sloped to Exact Tolerances

The tricky part of Branched Drain systems is designing and installing them so the pipes slope continuously and correctly downhill, within close tolerances of ¼" or less (6 mm). Hiring a plumber to get the inside pipes right is a good idea, but keep the plumber out of the

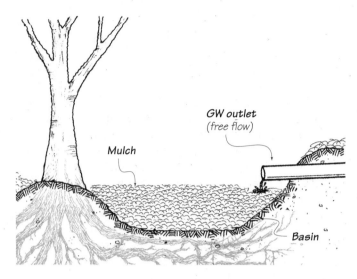

FIGURE 9.2: GREYWATER CONTAINED AND COVERED IN A BRANCHED DRAIN-FED MULCH BASIN (ELEVATION VIEW)

FIGURE 9.3: FLOWS SPLIT BY BRANCHED DRAIN NETWORKS (PLAN VIEW)

TABLE 9.1: ADVANTAGES AND DISADVANTAGES OF BRANCHED DRAIN GREYWATER SYSTEMS

Parameter	Most commercial GW systems	Drain Out Back	Branched Drain with free-flow outlets	Branched Drain to subsoil infiltration chambers
Filtration	Needed	Not needed	Not needed	Not needed
Pumping	Needed	Not needed	Not needed	Not needed
Surge tank	Needed	Not needed	Not needed	Not needed
Amount of plastic	High	Low/zero	High	Higher
Maintenance	High	Low/zero	Very low	Low
Economic cost	High	Very low/zero	Low	Medium
Ecological cost	High	Low	Low	Pretty low
Ease of building	Moderately difficult	Very easy	Requires careful pipe leveling and design	Requires very careful pipe leveling and design
Failure rate/ *failure mode*	High/*filter clogs, pump fails*	Almost never/*smells, runs off*	Rare/*greywater comes out fewer outlets*	Very good so far/*chambers tend to fill with debris, adding maintenance, or w/o maintenance, possible failure*
Life expectancy	Low	Forever	Decades	Decades, but with more maintenance
Reuse efficiency	30–80%	Can be 80% but usually zero!	30–60%	10–50%
Sanitation	Variable	Poor	Excellent	Impeccable
Soil loading	Variable	Poor	Good	Fair
Aesthetics	Variable	Poor	Good	Excellent; all is hidden
Legal?	Variable	Potentially	In AZ, NM, TX, etc.[4]	Yes
Flexible?	Varies	No	With difficulty	With more difficulty; chamber must be moved as well as pipe
Maintenance	14–90 days	Never	Yearly	Yearly

yard. First, they are expensive. Second, they are easily disoriented in the landscape. Third, plumbers tend to be conservative and tradition bound, and you might have a hard time coaxing them to adhere to your design. A landscaper or a jack-of-all-trades is a better bet, but you are likely to have to do much of the work yourself, or at least supervise it, unless they specialize in greywater. Unless you are naturally detail oriented, you may have a hard time warming to the painstaking task of getting those darn floppy pipes to slope just right in the shifting and settling soil.

Exception: If you have lots of well-situated fall, getting slopes right is a breeze.

The Pipes Must Slope Downhill Continuously

The pipes cannot drop down and then go back up again: for example, plunge to exit under the foundation and then pop up to the surface, or dip to cross a gully.

Possible exception: If the line has a large, unvented elevation drop (10–20', *3–6 m*) to build up pressure before a U-shaped section, greywater should blast through clogs. But, water pooling in the U goes septic after a while, and when fresh greywater pushes it through, it comes out stinking. Set a system up this way only if there *truly is no alternative*. Don't even think of it if you don't have a lot of pressure—it is sure to clog.

Impractical for Lawns or Small Plants

Beside the other reasons not to greywater lawns (see A Note on Lawns, Chapter 2), the Branched Drain system, with only a few dozen outlets maximum, is poorly suited to irrigating thousands of tiny individual plants. It works best with trees.

Exception: If your only goal is to get rid of the water, it may be appropriate to use plants whose claim to fame is sucking up water, regardless of their size.

Switching high-pressure gravity flow between three zones with ball valves. The pressure will clear any clog in the dead zone in front of a shut valve. (Also...these European couplings make leak-free joints in 40 mm HDPE tubing with hand tightening only.)

Poorly Suited to High Flows

There may be an elegant way to reuse more than a few hundred gallons a day through a Branched Drain network, but I haven't thought of it. The amount of pipe and the area required to deal with a single large source soon seems overwhelming. This limitation is shared by all but a few greywater system types. The average, mildly conservative, industrialized world household generates 35 gpd/person *(130 Lpd/person)*, which is well within the comfortable range for the Branched Drain system (there is no lower limit).

If you are faced with a huge water flow and a similarly huge irrigation need, the economics of other, more elaborate systems become more attractive.

Difficult to Alter

With this system, there is no easy way to supply a small amount of water to a young tree and then several times more water once that tree is large, or to shift from watering deciduous trees to evergreens when the deciduous trees drop their leaves. You make your best approximation when you design the system, and that's pretty much it.

Exceptions: It is easy to add to the ends of lines, or shorten outlet extensions. For example, you can design a system to accommodate tree growth by putting the flow splitter some distance from the trunk. An outlet extension from the flow splitter to a young tree can be removed when the roots have grown out farther, or an additional split can be added to send the water to two places in the (now) extensive root zone.

If one side of a flow splitter is the final outlet (as in the photo on p. 9 5), you can plug it and the water will continue on unsplit. This could be used to bypass a deciduous fruit tree that has lost its leaves and send the water on to a thirsty evergreen. When the deciduous tree leafs out, remove the plug and clear the opening.

Unproven for More than 16 Outlets from One Source

It is certainly possible that more outlets could be served, but it hasn't been tried to my knowledge. With ordinary flows, 16 is a reasonable limit. With pulsing output from a dipper box, 64 outlets would likely work (see Branched Drain Variations, Improvements, and Unknowns, end of Chapter 10).

Branched Drain System Design

After you've figured out what plants you want to irrigate with a Branched Drain distribution system, you're ready for the next steps: determining how to split the flow, designing the branching geometry, choosing the outlet types, and designing the mulch basins.

Ways to Split the Flow

There are several ways to split the flow (Figure 9.4). Let's consider them in turn:

1. **With a "flow splitter"** (double ell or other tee pipe fitting that splits the flow in two)— By then splitting it again, and again, and again, you can end up with as many as 16 outlet streams from one flow, in a branching network. This is the best way to split the flow in most cases.

2. **With a dipper distribution box**—These normally split the flow in four in one pass, but could possibly be used to split the flow into as many as eight outlets.

3. **By manually moving a flexible outlet extension from place to place**—This is excellent to use after the collection plumbing is done, while you're thinking about a permanent distribution system. (See Movable Drain, Chapter 7. Flexible PVC is also useful for transporting rainwater from downspouts to your greywater system to flush salts from the soil.)

4. **By not combining the flows in the first place**—Each fixture or set waters its own area.

5. **By any combination of 1, 2, 3, and 4.**

The first design decision is whether to go with one combined line, or separate the flows first by not combining them. This decision determines the layout of the collection plumbing in the house and is not easy to change. The pros and cons of each approach are described in Lump or Separate the Greywater Flow, Chapter 3. *(Note: if you want Multiple Greywater Zones—the topic that follows Lump or Separate in Chapter 3—you'll probably want to lump the flow.)*

Branched Drain for 2,700 gpd at 4,600' *(10 m³/day, 1,402 m)* **in the Sierra Nevada.** *Each cabin at Evergreen Lodge has its own system—55 of them. A lot of work and expense, but still less than a conventional system.*

FIGURE 9.4: WAYS TO SPLIT THE FLOW
(PLAN VIEWS)

Darker shaded areas have greater irrigation need. Unshaded areas are irrigated occasionally or not at all. (Septic/sewer lines not shown for clarity. GW= greywater.)

━━━ 2" GW distribution pipe   2" GW collection pipe ▬▬
━━━ 1½" GW distribution pipe   1½" GW collection pipe ▬▬
○ 3-way diverter valve
🌢 GW outlet

A: FLOWS "SPLIT" BY NOT COMBINING THEM IN THE FIRST PLACE, THEN BY FLOW SPLITTERS

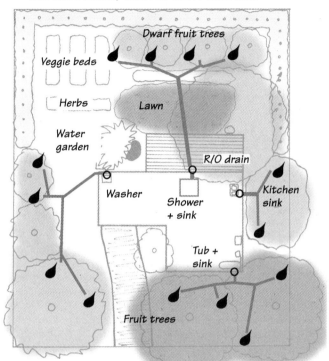

Dwarf fruit trees
Veggie beds
Herbs
Lawn
Water garden
R/O drain
Washer
Shower + sink
Kitchen sink
Tub + sink
Fruit trees

B: COMBINED FLOW SPLIT INITIALLY BY A DIPPER BOX, THEN BY FLOW SPLITTERS

Collection plumbing brings water to this point

Dipper box splits flow in four, reduces from 2" to 1½"

Diverter valves

C: COMBINED FLOWS, SPLIT WITH FLOW SPLITTERS ONLY

Diverter between irrigation zones

Diverters between sewer and yard

D: UNCOMBINED FLOWS "SPLIT" BY MANUALLY MOVING AN OUTLET EXTENSION

Flexible PVC outlet extension (these usually don't get moved much once enthusiasm wanes after first year)

Parts for Splitting the Flow

Flow splitters and wastewater bends are not available in sizes smaller than 1½", so that is the lower size limit, at least until the last split. Some plastic is saved by reducing to 1" PVC or HDPE pipe for the final outlet extension after the flow splitter (photo on p. 94 shows a reduction to 1"; see also Smaller Pipes or Other Types of Pipes, in Chapter 10).

A system uses more pipe and more fittings than you'd expect. Branched Drain networks also require large quantities of rarely used fittings such as:

❖ street bends of every angle: ¹⁄₁₆, ⅛, ⅙, and ¼ bends (22.5°, 45°, 60°, and 90°, respectively)
❖ double ells

You'll have to go to the best-equipped plumbing supply house around, and even they may not have the most exotic fittings listed in Table 9.2.

Double Ell Flow Splitters

Double ells are the best available flow-splitting coupling at this time. You'll find them only at the best-stocked plumbing supply houses, or by mail order. Modifying flow splitters to gain inspection access will vastly simplify maintenance. If you don't want to hassle with it yourself, we sell them online already drilled and tapped, with inspection plugs installed (see photo near right).[s9]

I have a strong aversion to building anything that cannot easily be serviced. I've never made a Branched Drain network that didn't incorporate some means of simplified access to the splitters. I've rarely seen a splitter clogged by anything that came down the pipe*—more often, dirt, rocks, and leaves fall in when I open the access to confirm that it isn't clogged! However, when you notice all the flow coming out one side of the splitter and none out the other, do you want to dig up the pipes and saw them in half, perhaps only to find that a banana slug was just passing through, making a temporary dam?

Although it is possible to make an installation with no way to inspect the inside of the flow splitter, I don't think it's a good idea. Installing your own threaded inspection plugs is a hassle. An alternative possibility is drilling a plain 1¼" *(3 cm)* hole and plugging it with a rubber stopper. If your flow splitters are protected in mulch shields or infiltration chambers, you don't need to plug the inspection hole at all, though a bit of water might slop out.

Cutaway view of a double ell, *a flow-splitting fitting that is largely self-cleaning with no filtration. This one is part of the first known Branched Drain network. I valiantly tried to clog it with pure kitchen sink water—took the sink strainer out and pushed bowls of soggy granola and pot scrapings down the pipe for half a year. The P-trap clogged every other day, but the Branched Drain network never did.*

1" threaded plug

*A **double ell retrofitted with inspection access**. The access is sealed with a threaded plug.*[s9]

PVC Sanitario

PVC sanitario is an eggshell-thin system of drainpipe with a small variety of loose fittings, found in Mexico and elsewhere. To make up for lack of fittings other than 90° and 45°, resourceful plumbers heat the pipe, creating clean bends, as well as bell ends in lieu of couplings. Instead of double ells for flow splitters, we successfully used sanitary tees, which in this system are almost as straight as a vent tee. These are definitely not optimal but they're working. To compensate for thinness and consequent tendency to break (under a path, for example), the pipes are protected with concrete where needed. See photos of systems made with this material in Real World Example #3. If you're working in the nonindustrialized world, consider Landscape Direct, Greywater Furrows, and Radical Plumbing before PVC sanitario.

Regular 90°   Sanitary tee   Mulch shield

½ flow

Flow

½ flow   Concrete holds weak pipe steady

*A **Branched Drain of PVC sanitario**. The flow splits inside a mulch shield; half dumps out and the rest flows on. (Note: a mulch shield is far too small to serve as a subsoil infiltration chamber; it must be surrounded by mulch.)*

Double ells from at least one manufacturer have ragged injection-molding ridges right on the smooth face where the flow is supposed to split. If you get stuck with these, grind down the ridges with a rotary file.

Component/Photos	Application/Material	Typical cost[+]	Quantity used	Sizes used	Normally used for/available from (DWV = drain-waste-vent)
Diverter valves			0–3		
3-way valve	Divert water between zones in yard/PVC	$60	0–3	1½" + 2" 2" + 2½"	Pools and spas/pool suppliers and oasisdesign.net/catalog
Pair of RV dump valves	Alternative to 3-way valve/PVC	$15	0–6	1½–2"	Recreational vehicles/RV shops
Backflow prevention valves					
Backwater valve	An unpopular CPC/UPC legal requirement to keep blackwater from backing up and going out into greywater systems*/PVC, brass	$25	0–1	2"	Backwater/well-stocked plumbing supply house
Swing check valve	A cheaper substitute for a backwater valve/PVC	$15		2"	Swing check valve is used for potable water/plumbing supply house
Dosing devices			0–1		
Dipper box	The dipper box can serve as dosing device, flow splitter, pipe size reducer, and greywater meter[28] (see Dipper Box, p. 92)	$150 + transport		2–4" in, 1½–2" out	Dosing septic tank leachfields. Must be customized to accept small pipe/call manufacturer[s20]
See Figure 4.5 Dosing siphon	Dosing device			2"	Dosing septic tank leachfields. Must be customized to accept small pipe/call manufacturer[s3,s4]
Flow splitters			1–15	1½", 2"	
Double ell	Best way to split flow in two/ABS	$5.50			DWV/order prefitted with cleanout plug from oasisdesign.net[s9] or make them from parts from a well-stocked plumbing supply house
Vent tee	Best substitute if double ell is not available/ABS	$7			DWV/well-stocked plumbing supply house
PVC sanitario tee	Workable flow splitter available in Mexico/PVC				DWV/any hardware store in Mexico
Sanitary tee	Possible but not recommended flow splitter/ABS	$4			DWV/most hardware stores
1" threaded plug	Plugs access to flow splitters/PVC	$2			DWV/most hardware stores
Reducers					
Reducing bushing	Reduce from 2" to 1½" pipe/ABS	$2	2	1½" × 2"	DWV/most hardware stores
Reducing bushing	Adapt from ABS to 1" flexible PVC/PVC	$2		1" × 1½"	
Reducing coupling	Reduce from 2" to 1½" pipe/ABS	$2			DWV/well-stocked plumbing supply house
Bends			10–20	1½", 2"	
¼ bend 90° street elbow	Turn at flow splitter/ABS	$3			DWV/most hardware stores
¼ bend 90° extra-long elbow	Horizontal 90° turn mid-pipe/ABS	$4.25			DWV/well-stocked plumbing supply house
¹⁄₁₆ bend 22½° street elbow	Slight turn at flow splitter/ABS	$3			DWV/well-stocked plumbing supply house
¼ bend 90° elbow	Turn at flow splitter/ABS	$2.75			DWV/most hardware stores
¼ bend 90° extra-long street elbow	Deluxe way to make 90° turn out of flow splitter in installation with very little fall/ABS	$2.25			DWV/well-stocked plumbing supply house
⅛ bend street elbow	Turn at flow splitter/ABS	$7.25			DWV/well-stocked plumbing supply house
⅛ bend 45° elbow	Turn in mid-pipe/ABS	$2.75			DWV/most hardware stores
⅛ bend 45° street elbow	Turn at flow splitter/ABS	$3			DWV/most hardware stores
Cleanouts, flow joining			1–4	1½", 2"	
Cleanout wye w/plug	Cleanout flow join/ABS	$2.75			DWV/well-stocked plumbing supply house
Fitting cleanout w/plug	Cleanout/ABS	$1			DWV/most hardware stores
Long-turn tee wye	Cleanout, flow join in horizontal pipe/ABS	$4			DWV/most hardware stores
Pipe, etc.				1", 1½", 2"	
Pipe	Piping/ABS	$1			DWV/most hardware stores
Coupling	Joining straight pipes/ABS	$1.25			DWV/most hardware stores
Repair slip coupling	Splicing into already-glued system/ABS				DWV/well-stocked plumbing supply house
No-hub connector	To join pipe, street fittings without glue so they can be removed/Stainless steel, rubber	$4			DWV/well-stocked plumbing supply house
Brown or green Spa-flex	Movable outlets/temporary systems/PVC	$2.25			Hot tubs/pool and spa supply house

[+]Costs are for 1.5" pipe and fittings. Fittings for 2" pipe typically cost 50% more.
*But not required to keep blackwater from backing out your shower drain! Likely to clog, so install it only if you must, with no-hub connectors and/or a cleanout.

Dipper Box or Dosing Siphon *(Optional)*

Most greywater systems use surge tanks to flatten peaks out of the flow. But Branched Drains do well with flow spikes—so much so that a device is sometimes added to transform a low flow into strong, intermittent pulses. Do you need such a thing? You do if:

❖ **A large percentage of your greywater dribbles out at a very low flow rate**—The dipper is designed for the slow drool that accounts for much of the flow out of a septic tank.

❖ **Daily flow is high**—The dipper splits the flow in four (or more) in one step, while adding such a peak to the flow that, even cut in quarters, the rate is higher than what you started with. This is one way you could cut a flow into more than 16 streams (see More than Four Levels of Splitting, Chapter 10).

My favorite "surge creator" is a custom version of the Polylok dipper.[s20] It comes standard with flexible plastic knockouts well suited for 3–4" leachfield pipes held in place by earth in the septic tank installations it was designed for. Unfortunately, these connections don't hold small pipe steady and are especially awkward in the aboveground installations preferred for greywater. Dipper boxes are made one at a time. If your local supplier is cooperative, you can have your dipper made with a 2" inlet and overflow, and multiple 1½" outlets, in the form of PVC or ABS couplings. This makes a much cleaner installation. You can use one or all of the outlets. An overflow line is a good idea if the dipper is someplace where it would make a mess if greywater overflowed out the top. If it is outside, an overflow line isn't necessary. Theoretically you could have a dipper made with just about any number of outlets, including outlets of different sizes to obtain controlled splits into different-sized flows. Figure 9.4b shows a sample layout using a dipper box to split the flow into four in one step. You can also get a standard dipper and adapt the pipes yourself with cement.

If you have to measure your greywater flow, you can use a dipper to do so.[28] The dipper uses 8" *(20 cm)* of fall. It is a few feet on a side and weighs 360 lbs *(160 kg)*—uff!

Close-up of dipper for Green Septic on p. 77.

Dosing siphons[s4] are a related technology. They are not generally designed to split the flow, only to collect a lot of water and then distribute it all at once. The water can easily sit in them long enough to become anaerobic, and unlike the dipper, dosing siphons collect crud, which must be cleaned out periodically. They also cost more fall: the height difference between inlet and outlet is typically a few feet. Dosing siphons are described in Surge Capacity, Chapter 4.

A Polylok dipper box.
When the tray fills, it dumps all the water and solids, and then pops back up, as shown in the sequence below. Have your outlet couplings installed so the bottom quarter of the pipe is below the floor of the dipper (as at left). This will provide a stronger flow to downstream flow splitters at the end of the cycle.

FIGURE 9.5: DIPPER DISTRIBUTION BOX DIPPING CYCLE

Branching Geometry Options

Even with the greywater coming from a known point and going to other known points, there are still a few different options for setting up the geometry of the branching network:

FIGURE 9.6: BRANCHING GEOMETRY OPTIONS

*The same outlet points receiving the same amount of water from the same source point using five different branching options: A) **branches with one short leg**, and all turns at the flow splitters (most recommended); B) **dipper box** makes the split; C) **manually moved flexible outlet extension** serves four points (if someone remembers to move it); D) **"Twisted Tees"** (high maintenance, unpredictable, difficult to tune. For a really long line of trees, it is tempting to try to peel off small fractions of the flow for each tree, rather than branch. This uses about half the material and is easier to install. But...the only way to manage it is to put buckets under the outlets and measure how much flow comes out of each outlet, and then tune it. Each outlet you change will change all the others. Every change in the rate of flow also changes the splitting ratios. Once you get it right you can mark the exact amount of downward twist to each tee so you can get that adjustment back later); and E) **branches of somewhat equal length** with turns mid-pipe (not recommended, as it uses more pipe and the buried pieces are harder to find and service).*

The options in Figure 9.6 are in descending order of desirability. Instead of e do a instead, with all the turns at the flow splitters, and straight runs of pipe otherwise. This approach is attractive for a few reasons:

❖ **It takes fewer glue joints**—By connecting the bends at the flow splitters, you can use <u>street</u> <u>fittings</u> (instead of a hub at each end, they have one hub end and one pipe-sized end; see Figure 9.7). This cuts the number of glue joints in half. Fewer glue joints means less use of noxious glue and a smoother water path.*

❖ **It's easier to find and fix clogs**—Clogging is most likely in bends and connections. If the bend is right by the flow splitter, you can find and most likely unclog it via the access plug in the flow splitter. (The figure Sample Plot Plan for Permit in our *Builder's Greywater Guide*[6] shows how *not* to do it: a plan for a Branched Drain network with numerous 90° bends mid-pipe. Fortunately, it wasn't actually built this way.)

❖ **It's easier to locate the piping**—If the pipe runs are straight from flow splitter to outlet, locate the flow splitters (on a site map, and/or by digging), and you know where the pipe runs are.

❖ **It takes less plastic**—This layout usually yields the most pipe- and coupling-efficient, least expensive system.

Unless the flow is very small, there will be several splits. First, work these out on paper. Next, check out your plan on the ground by marking where you want the water to come out of the house and where you think the outlets should be. Then, lay out the pipes on the surface and connect them with fittings—don't glue or cut anything yet!

Now, repeat the paper and physical layout steps above, trying different approaches and refinements until you feel you've optimized everything. Don't try to do *all* the fitting-by-fitting detail or to locate the pipes to the *inch*. Get a representative fraction of the fittings worked out and locate the pipes and outlets to within a foot or two. During installation (Chapter 10), as you lay the pipe from top to bottom, the pipe and fittings themselves lead you to the resolution of that last bit of detail.

FIGURE 9.7: "STREET"
VS NORMAL FITTINGS

¼ bend 90° elbow

Hub

¼ bend 90° street elbow

No-hub, pipe-sized end

Street fittings *have one pipe-sized end and one coupling-sized end*

---

*On the downside, street fittings are harder to find and more expensive than their symmetrical counterparts.

Reductions

Reductions in Branched Drain distribution systems require special treatment to prevent clogging:

Steeper pipe angle at reduction
helps crud get through and eliminates pockets of standing water

Side view

Reduction 2" to 1½"

Less optimal but still successful; angle reduces **pocket of standing water and crud**, *and water falls harder, helping to keep it clean*

End view

Angle fittings so reduction from 2" to 1½" pipe does not create pocket of standing water and crud at this point

Reduction 1½" to 1"; never glue joint between 1½" fitting and 1½" x 1" reducing bushing, to allow removal and cleaning

Reduction 2" to 1½"

Cleanouts, Inspection Access, and Rainwater Inlets

As with collection plumbing, you want to make it easy to inspect/unclog every part of the greywater distribution network.

A cleanout right after the line exits the house is convenient and can double as a means of bringing rainwater from downspouts into the system. After that, you need a cleanout every 100' *(30 m)* and 135° of aggregate bend (see Provide Cleanouts and Inspection Access, Chapter 4). 3-way valves provide inspection access in all directions. A dipper box provides excellent access to every pipe connected to it. Long runs of pipe may require cleanouts at intervals, particularly if their slope deviates from ¼" per foot *(2%)*.

The flow splitter inspection ports and the outlets provide inspection and cleanout access to the irrigation piping. Though the 1" *(2.5 cm)* openings are small, they are adequate. The 1" access hole at the flow splitters is not big enough to run a snake through, at least not without ruining the plastic threads holding the access plug. Blasting water from a garden hose at the flow splitter access has been effective for unclogging.

If your cleanouts/inspection access aren't convenient for admitting rainwater, be sure to include some dedicated rainwater inlets. You can include a spur from the main greywater line to a convenient downspout or filtered run-on catchment (photo p. 106). The best arrangement in most contexts is to have rainwater go to its own mulch basin by default, but make it easy to manually reroute it to the greywater system for supplemental irrigation and flushing salts. In all but the driest climates it is inadvisable to plumb rainwater into a greywater system without an easy way of diverting it elsewhere. You don't want to overwhelm the system. Some greywater codes prohibit plumbing rainwater to a greywater system for this reason.

Branched Drain Outlet Design

The options for Branched Drain outlets present a trade-off: low cost, simplicity, and durability on one hand, hiddenness on the other. We'll consider them in order of simple to hidden.

Free-Flow Outlets

From a free-flow outlet, the greywater daylights for a few inches in midair after it flows out of the pipe and before it disappears into several inches of mulch (Figure 9.8a). The free fall space is vital. If the pipe is resting on the surface, the water flows on but the solids stop just outside the outlet. This can eventually dam the flow back to the flow splitter. Stuff falls away from free-flow outlets rather than toward them. They never clog, they accommodate high surges, and they are easy to inspect—you'll note the functional status of the system just by spending time in your garden.

Free-flow outlets require 3–10" *(7–25 cm)* more fall than the subsurface options, to create

FIGURE 9.8: BRANCHED DRAIN OUTLET OPTIONS
(ELEVATION VIEW)

A: FREE-FLOW OUTLET (PREFERRED OPTION)

Greywater discharges at least 2" above the mulch surface and quickly disappears; requires most fall, but **much simpler to maintain, with minimal added health risk**

Optional plastic shield of CPC compliance

Mulch basin volume = several times design surge

C: SUB-MULCH OUTLET WITH MULCH SHIELD

Outlet/chamber allows greywater to flow, but keeps mulch out, so clogging does not occur

Flow splitter register (optional)

Flow splitter on brick for easy leveling

Access covers

Outlet must be 4" or more above shield floor to prevent obstruction

Mulch

Mulch shield 5 gal bucket, bottom cut out, holes drilled in sides

≥4"

B: OUTLET SHIELD

Outlet shielded with rocks, piece of plastic or metal is intermediate between sub-mulch and free-flow options (CA legal)

D: SUBSOIL INFILTRATION CHAMBER

Most sanitary and most costly; all surge capacity must be met in chambers; subsurface distribution preferred for kitchen sink water to prevent vermin from using as food source

Access covers/markers

Access lid

Infiltrator or plastic drum cut in half lengthwise

2" is optimum; more may be required

2" min: more is better

Louver depth = shallowest discharge level

Metric: 2" = 5 cm;
4" = 10 cm; 5 gal = 20 L

enough grade difference for the buried pipe to surface above the mulch. Leave the outlet visible or shield it with rocks, a piece of plastic, or metal.

Free-flow outlets are allowed in Arizona, New Mexico, and Texas. In other areas, it takes either a visionary or inattentive inspector to approve them.

Outlet Shield

In California, free-flow outlets above ground and mulch are legal if shielded from contact. Ideally for maintenance, you can still *hear* the greywater. Outlet shields could also be appropriate for, say, public facilities. Outlet shields, mulch shields, and infiltration chambers are collectively referred to here as outlet chambers.

Sub-Mulch Outlets, with Mulch Shield

Sub-mulch outlets emit greywater inside mulch shields made from stout plastic pots, buckets, sawn-in-half drums, or infiltrators (see Figures 9.8c, 9.9, 9.10). These chambers create voids under the mulch where solids can fall clear of the outlet, preventing clogging. Sub*soil* infiltration chambers are sized to accommodate the entire peak surge, which then soaks slowly into soil. They need to be huge. Sub-*mulch*

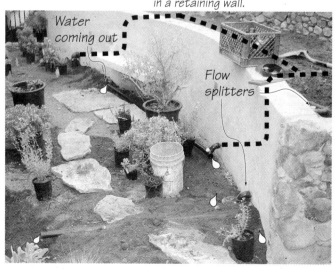

Free-flow Branched Drain outlets in a retaining wall.

Water coming out

Flow splitters

outlet shields can be smaller, provided they are permeable enough that greywater can run out rapidly into the surrounding mulch basin, where most of the surge capacity is. A 3 gal *(12 L)* bucket is the minimum size.

Mulch does degrade and must be replaced, usually annually, for the greywater to stay subsurface. Don't use gravel if a gardener might ever live in the house. Gravel is the last thing you want in your garden, and a legally sized system would use a big truckload of it.

Nature abhors a void, so sub-mulch outlet shields tend to fill with crud—mulch and greywater solids—that needs to be mucked out. Outlet shields can trap small critters such as lizards, etc.; one system owner suggests putting sticks in the shields as escape ladders.

Many codes require that greywater be distributed below the surface, but they don't specify *which* surface: soil or mulch. Mulch is preferable and has passed muster in permitted systems in many jurisdictions (e.g., Real World Example #1). Sub-mulch distribution is the best compromise for a permitted system. It yields improved sanitation at the cost of more complex design, installation, and maintenance. Go this route to satisfy code, or if you think vermin might use kitchen greywater outlets as soup kitchens. (If you have separate flows, consider making the kitchen outlets subsoil.)

Overloaded infiltration chamber. *A common error is to use mulch-shield-sized buckets as subsoil infiltrators. 3 gal works as a mulch shield, but 30–100 gal are more like the volumes needed for subsoil infiltration. (20 L, 12 L, 113–378 L)*

FIGURE 9.9: HALF BARREL MULCH SHIELD

FIGURE 9.10: BUCKET MULCH SHIELD

(ELEVATION VIEW)

(PLAN VIEW)

Half barrel of HDPE plastic; cut in half lengthwise, for more infiltration area and surge capacity

Bricks support barrel

Access port cut in barrel and covered with block of wood, plastic, etc.

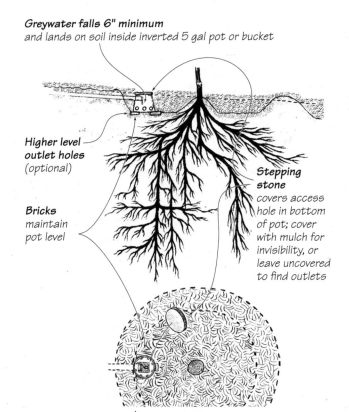

Greywater falls 6" minimum and lands on soil inside inverted 5 gal pot or bucket

Higher level outlet holes (optional)

Bricks maintain pot level

Stepping stone covers access hole in bottom of pot; cover with mulch for invisibility, or leave uncovered to find outlets

Metric: 6" = 15 cm; 5 gal bucket = 20 L

Subsoil Infiltration Chambers

It is possible to design a system with completely sub*soil* distribution. In the previously mentioned options, the outlet is just the gateway to a large surge capacity and infiltration area in a mulch basin, which in turn can overflow safely under the mulch between basins. In the subsoil case, *all* the surge capacity and infiltration area is within the infiltrator itself (Figure 9.8d). Unless the surges are small and the perk rate high, you're going to need much bigger chambers than you might think to get adequate infiltration area (see Table 2.3, Dispersal Loading Rates). It may be completely unfeasible for an inspected system. Not only is the code-specified area ultraconservative, but the greywater quantity estimates are high. If you're lucky they might let you use the area of the overlying tree canopy and mulch basin as

Infiltrator, inside view.

A: YOUNG TREE,
SANDY SOIL

3'
(1 m)
diameter,
outlet near trunk

the treatment area, since it actually is. Infiltrators (see photos) are the easiest way to provide a lot of square feet of subsoil infiltration.[s13]

Subsoil infiltration chambers are so sanitary there's no health reason not to run septic effluent through them. In fact, they may last longer due to the filtration by the septic tank. (See also Green Septic, Chapter 8, for more info and photos.)

Note: Infiltration chambers are a proven technology for dispersal of septic tank effluent, which is nearly free of clogging solids. Though promising, there is relatively little track record for application of raw, unfiltered greywater inside completely earth-covered chambers. Place them as high as possible in the soil profile (where perk and worm activity are greatest). Don't skimp on the size of the chambers. The success or failure of this design hinges mostly on distribution evenness and loading rate. Be sure to provide access for inspection/mucking out. Don't try a highly loaded subsoil chamber without an alternative, backup infiltration area such as a mulch basin or mulch-covered area. If gophers are an issue, underlay the chambers with ½" (13 mm) welded wire mesh.

B: MEDIUM-SIZED TREE OR
YOUNG TREE IN CLAY SOIL

6'
(2 m)
diameter,
outlet far from trunk

Infiltrators fed by a Branched Drain network. *Each of the eight infiltrators gets one outlet (not all are shown; two outlets visible here).*

C: LARGE TREE

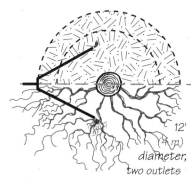

12'
(4 m)
diameter,
two outlets

Outlet Positioning

Where exactly do you put these outlets? You want the tree roots to reach the water, but not get suffocated—see examples of outlet geometry at right. To avoid root suffocation from lots of greywater and/or low-perk soil:

❖ Keep the outlets closer to the drip edge than the trunk.
❖ Provide multiple outlets per tree for large trees.
❖ Plant the tree on a high island in the mulch basin (Figure 5.7).

Except for a newly planted tree, the roots extend farther than you'd expect: 50% beyond the canopy or more. If you have a young tree, arrange the pipes so outlet geometry can be changed and/or greywater quantity increased as the tree, roots, and mulch basin grow. If your young tree needs supplemental irrigation until its roots grow out to the greywater source, burying an unfired clay pot next to the trunk is a great trick—you fill it with freshwater and the water slowly seeps into the soil. (It would clog if filled with greywater.)

D: VERY LARGE TREE

24'
(7 m)
diameter,
four outlets

Mulch Basin Surge Capacity

This section is included primarily to help you ease any fears your inspectors might have. In practice, surge capacity is rarely an issue unless the system is absurdly undersized and the overflow is to a problem area such as a public sidewalk. (For details, see Greywater System Calculations in our Builder's Greywater Guide.[6])

Branched Drain systems do not include a surge tank. The basins, and soil provide voluminous surge capacity.

This is how you calculate the required surge capacity. First, determine the peak design surge using Table 4.2. For example, if a washing machine discharges while a bathtub is draining, this yields a surge of 75 gal in 10 minutes: 15 gal for the wash cycle, 15 gal for the rinse cycle, and 45 gal for the tub.[m] Four small mulch basins or one large one can hold 75 gal. The volume that counts is the volume below the basin walls or the outlet spill point, whichever is lower in height. When making this calculation, assume that the earthen basin walls will eventually wear down to half their original height.

If the outlets are free-flow above the mulch, there is no impediment to the water quickly spreading in the basin. Still, the basin volume should be a few to several times the maximum expected surge if possible, to account for the volume of mulch, and for the walls wearing down.

If the greywater has to pass through mulch shields, surge handling is trickier. The chambers may drain slowly into the rest of the basin. The tendency is to undersize the shield volume. Beside low surge capacity, a small shield has much less infiltration area, and tends to clog. The most conservative approach is to include enough volume inside the shields to accept the entire surge (see Figure 9.12). (Generally less than 10% of the surge can soak into the small area under the shield in the few minutes the surge lasts.)

For subsoil infiltration chambers, a day's flow should be accommodated in the chambers, if the soils drain slowly.

If the flow splitter preceding a chamber is higher than the top of the chamber, the entire chamber volume counts toward the surge capacity. If it is lower, only the volume below the split counts. This is because as soon as the chamber fills to the level of the splitter, that branch stops accepting water and all subsequent flow goes to the other branch. For certain geometries, this could result in nearly all of the excess flow going to the lowest chamber after the others fill, severely overflowing it alone.

The reliability and safety of a system designed conservatively, as described above, far exceeds that of the typical sewage treatment plant. Perspective: greywater surfacing once in a blue moon is not a big deal when you consider that toilet water from failing septic leachfields across the country is pooling on the surface, and that in hard rain, municipal treatment plants abandon all pretense of treatment and discharge raw sewage into natural waters where people fish, swim, and extract drinking water.

FIGURE 9.12: MULCH SHIELD OPTIONS AND SURGE CAPACITIES (PLAN VIEW)

32 gal surge in

Half 30 gal drum/25 gal

½ = 16 gal out

½ = 16 gal/12 gal

¼ = 8 gal out

Half 15 gal drum/5–7 gal

⅛ = 4 gal out

5 gal bucket/ 3–5 gal

¹⁄₁₆ = 2 gal out

5 gal flowerpot/ 3–4 gal

Only the capacity below the outlet counts. Numbers for surge capacity of mulch shields shown are: {volume below the outlet} — {entire chamber volume} Note: Subsoil infiltration Chambers require several times this volume!

METRIC

120 L surge in

Half 120 L drum/ 40–56 L

60 L out

30 L out

15 L out

20 L bucket/ 11–20 L

8 L out

"20 L" pot/8–11 L

---

[m]**Metric:** *284 L surge in 10 min: 57 L for wash cycle, 57 L for rinse cycle, 170 L for tub.*

Branched Drain System Mental Check-Out

If you are shooting from the hip you can skip this step. Otherwise, take a moment to look over your design and consider what will happen when/if:

❖ **Ten years go by**—Can the system be adapted to foreseeable plant growth and/or changes in the house's greywater production? Flow changes when kids leave home, etc.? Will you be able to locate buried parts of the system to check up on them? (See Map the System, Chapter 10.)

❖ **More efficient fixtures are installed**—and the amount of greywater plummets?

❖ **You sell the house**—Will the new owners be able to change the system to suit their habits and preferences? Will *they* be able to locate buried parts of the system to check up on them?

❖ **There is a very large, sustained flow of water from the house**—Will it all end up at the lowest basin when the others fill and back up to the flow splitters? Or will it overflow from all the basins? The latter is preferable.

❖ **The whole site floods with rain or rising water**—Conceivably, during a flood, a Branched Drain network could transport runoff water down, or floodwater up, from one part of the yard to another, where it could be harmful.

Taking these considerations to heart, adjust your design if necessary.

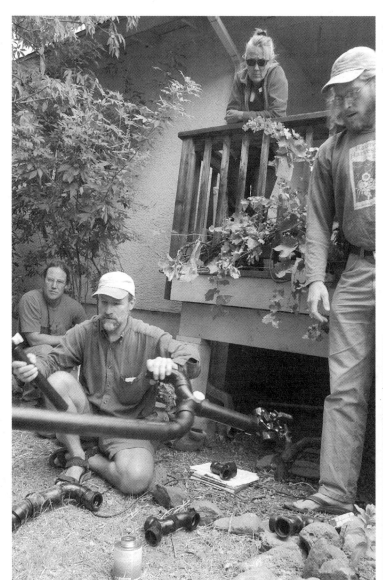

Branched Drain system installation *during a greywater workshop in Cottonwood, Arizona, with Brad Lancaster and Karen Taylor.*

3-way valve installed. *The wye on the right is kitchen sink water joining the line downstream of the diverter. It may not look like it from this perspective, but all the pipes slope down 2% in the direction of flow.*

KAREN TAYLOR SISKIYOU PERMACULTURE

Chapter 10: Branched Drain Installation

Even if you're not installing a Branched Drain system, reading the detailed tips and tricks in this chapter will help you do better greywater collection plumbing and installations of other system types.

At this point, you should have your greywater and irrigation needs connected on paper. Now it is time to connect them with pipe. Branched Drain systems are best designed from bottom to top, to ensure that there is enough fall and that the collection plumbing ends high enough; then, built from top to bottom along the water flow. Check ahead repeatedly to confirm that there is enough fall left for the outlets to come out at the desired height—the importance of slope cannot be overstated.

Install your **collection plumbing** (covered in Chapter 4). Then install the Branched Drain **irrigation piping** and **receiving landscape** as follows...

Double-Check Your Design

Obstacles such as concrete walkways, large roots, or buried pipes can block your way, forcing you to give up fall to go under them, or replumb the whole system higher to go over them. You may be able to burrow under a walkway by digging and/or boring with a garden hose (a nozzle at the end raises the pressure). You can cross over a walkway, especially next to a step, by snuggling the pipe in the corner of the step and covering it with cement, or pipe-strapping it to the riser. As a last resort, you can break a trench through a walkway, then patch it. A pipe can cross over a sunken dirt pathway in a long, gentle "speed bump" of dirt added on top. Some buried pipes can be raised or lowered to go over or under them at the height you want, by uncovering a long enough run that the obstructing pipe can be bent out of the way. This could possibly be done with a large root as well. Ditches can be bridged by a wooden plank with the pipe attached under it, or bridged by a larger metal pipe with the active pipe inside it. Make sure the pipes are out of the sun and harm's way and are not liable to settle or sag. Double-check the overall slope from beginning to end of the trench to establish that you can get where you want to without the outlets being too deep (see Appendix B: Measuring Elevation and Slope).

Check for Buried Utilities

Check for underground utilities before any digging project. Greywater systems are generally not much trouble, because their lines typically run shallower than buried gas, water, electric, and phone lines, but it doesn't hurt to check. Often utility companies will come out and mark the location of buried utilities for free.

Dipper Installation

Skip this if you aren't using a dipper.

If there's a dipper box in your design, you want to install it early on. It consumes about 8" *(20 cm)* of fall—make sure there is enough. You want permanent access, as the dipper is a great place to access the system for flushing, snaking, changing irrigation zones, etc. Finally, you need good access to install it; it is heavy, and needs to end up exactly level (photos at right; there's also more on dippers in Chapter 9).

Once your spot is established, dig a few inches deeper than the dipper's height, compact the soil well, and make a pad for it out of concrete. Rebar or other reinforcement is unnecessary. Use a stiff (low water) mix and put temporary bricks or boards on the sides to keep the concrete from squirting out under the dipper's weight (upper photo). Position bricks so they take the impact when you drop the dipper in, then pull them out so you can settle it into place. The concrete should be about 1½" *(4 cm)* higher than the final dipper height, so the dipper is still about ½" *(1 cm)* higher after it initially squishes into the concrete. You can lower the dipper, but you can't raise it without taking it off and adding more concrete. Wiggle the dipper, tap on it, and if necessary jump on it so it slowly squishes down into place, checking the levels

A pad of stiff concrete mix held in place by bricks awaits the dipper.

Leveling a dipper: Stand on it and wiggle it down into the concrete while checking levels in both directions.

continually (lower photo). Remove the bricks and scoop away the concrete as it squishes out to allow the dipper to sink farther. Push it down by smaller and smaller increments as you get close—you don't want to screw it up now. You're done when it has sunk to the right height and is level from front to back and side to side. Don't touch it again until the next morning.

Connect Pipes and Fittings on the Surface without Glue

Make any adjustments needed and confirm that the layout is basically sound, the network flows from high to low, and the outlets are situated reasonably well. Lay the pipe on the surface without glue. You can cut the more certain lengths. Deburr the cut ends so crud doesn't hang up on them. Also, tip the pipes vertical and let any stones or dirt they've collected fall out before joining them.

Dipper distribution box with a brick enclosure *around individually valved outlets.*

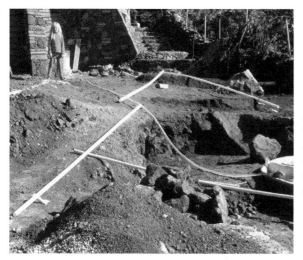

Laying pipes on the ground without fittings to help visualize the layout. *We moved them around until it seemed like the right trees would get the right amounts of water. I then drew the system, and laid out the pipes with fittings. Finally, we dug trenches, glued it all together, and buried it.*

Dig Trenches

Dig the trench to the first flow splitter. How deep? Optimal is 9" and more than 1' is certainly not necessary.[m] In most soils, this is deep enough that a truck could drive over without breaking the pipe. The greywater itself is released at this depth or shallower, so there is no health reason to dig deeper. In permitted installations you may be required to adhere to a minimum depth

In practice, it is often necessary to take the pipe all the way to the surface in problem spots (a low area on the way to a high area, for example). Considering that dumping raw greywater right on the surface is fairly common, it is hard to get too upset about greywater being *inside a pipe* at the surface. In a permitted installation you might get away with passing the plastic pipe through a steel pipe, using cast iron pipe, or covering the pipe with concrete. After all, these measures are allowed for pipes containing raw sewage.

The amount of work required to lay pipes depends greatly on their slope, as described next.

Curve marked with ashes shaken over pipe

Marking trenches. *Use string lines just to the side of the trench for straight runs, and powder (ashes, lime, whatever) over the actual pipe for curves. Straight lines are easy to map for posterity, but curved pipe is preferable to mid-run bends using couplings.*

String to side of trench

---

[m]***Metric:*** *8" = 20 cm; 9" = 23 cm; 1' = 30 cm*

Laying Pipe with Plenty of Slope

Even when the ground slopes steeply, if your pipes *traverse* (cut across) the slope at any point they may end up with the bare minimum of slope to get where they need to. But if all your pipes have plenty of slope (more than 1" per foot *(8%)*), you can throw the pipes and fittings in without glue, check the layout, spot check with a level to ensure they don't slope less than 2% anywhere, glue them, cover them, and you're done. You probably should include extra cleanouts in case the steeper slope results in solids getting left behind the water, *but you can skip all the extra steps below for Laying Pipe with Marginal Slope*—hallelujah!

Laying Pipe with Marginal Slope

If your installation requires you to conserve fall, as most do, it is an involved, multistep process to get bendy plastic pipe to slope precisely in dirt. You should never have *less than* 2% slope. The less fall you have to work with, the less you can afford to *exceed* 2% in any given portion. The smaller the range of acceptable slope becomes, the more fanatically you have to follow the steps below.

Dig the Trenches Slightly Deeper than the Pipe

Dig your trenches to a tolerance of +1", -0" *(+2.5 cm, -0 cm)*. It is easier to backfill under the pipe with sand or compacted earth where the trench is too deep than to dig dirt, rocks, and roots out from under the pipe in dozens of places where it isn't *quite* low enough.

Giant tree roots—hopefully you'll be lucky enough to pass underneath without losing any fall, as we were able to do here. Root growth can cause pipe levels to heave or sink in the future—try to design with this in mind to the extent possible.

Assemble Pipe and Fittings in the Trenches without Glue and Check Elevations

Assembling pipe inside the trenches without glue, and checking levels.

Level and assemble the system from top to bottom, occasionally jumping downstream to confirm that there is enough fall left to make it to the outlets with proper slope.

First assemble the plumbing as far as the first splitter without glue. Tip pipe segments vertical so any rocks and dirt fall out. Level plumbing coarsely to check that trench bottoms are deep enough everywhere to allow final levels to be achieved without more digging, and that you've chosen the right fittings and assembled them correctly. *Note: Pipes seat deeper and easier into couplings with glue than without; when they slide in all the way, the geometry changes slightly. Also, plastic pipe is almost always bowed. So it doesn't wreak havoc with your leveling, sight down the pipe and orient it so the bow is to the left or right, not up and down. Mark the up side of the pipe so you know which way to glue it.*

Glue the Pipes Section by Section

Gluing is not strictly necessary. I've installed a couple of Branched Drain networks entirely "friction fit" (not glued). One joint in each system has come apart in five years. If you're unsure of what you're doing, or prone to changing your mind, you may wish to leave part or all of the irrigation piping unglued. Thrifty master tinkerers do greywater plumbing unglued, to allow 100% reuse of parts when reconfiguring.

On the other hand, gluing helps ensure that proper levels will be maintained and the system won't fall apart as soil shifts and settles, roots sneak in, and plants grow. In reality, it is easy to change plastic pipe around, even after it is glued, albeit with waste. The optimal method is to glue/not glue intelligently and strategically. The things I most often leave unglued are:

❖ **Outlet extensions to trees**—When the plants have grown, pull the extensions out and the water discharges where the new feeder roots are, farther from the trunks.

❖ **Expensive fittings such as 3-way valves**—If there is pipe going into them, I often glue it (you can cut the pipe and still reuse the valve). But if there are <u>street fittings</u> coming out of the $50 valve, I glue with silicone sealer so the plumbing around the valve can be changed without having to chuck it. (See Build for Future Flexibility, Chapter 4, for other no-glue connection options.)

Load the glue applicator with just enough glue to cover the female coupling first and then the male coupling. Too much glue squirts out inside the pipe in gobs or strings, which harden and catch solids. Once the glue goes on, you've got just a few seconds to get the fittings lined up right before it grabs. Drain fittings such as <u>sanitary tees</u> have a 2% downward angle built into them so properly sloped pipe slides straight in. This angle is visible if you look for it. For fittings that lack this angle, such as flow splitters and diverter valves, it is a nice touch to tweak the fitting or pipe as you glue it into the hub so it slopes downward a bit (photo at right).

Pipes tweaked to 2% slope

A 2% downward tweak on pipes ensures smooth downward flow of water and solids.

On the whole, you want to glue the system in sequence from top to bottom. However, it is convenient to first glue subassemblies such as the one below, then glue them onto the end of the pipe and level them.

A mark shows how couplings line up—a reference for gluing this sub-assembly correctly.

Subassembly is then glued into the system and leveled as a unit.

Glued pipes ready for support/burial.

You'll notice that some joints "matter": if they are not rotated correctly, the slope won't be right. Other joints don't "matter": the pipe can go in any rotation and the slope will still be right. Paying attention to this distinction can help smooth your work flow.

Make a mark to show how the couplings should be rotated to line up together. If the pipes and fittings are all pretty much in the same plane, you can rotate the fitting to be just barely past level on the side of the flow splitter (judged by the center lines from the molds, visible on the sides of the fittings). This ensures enough slope to facilitate flow from the pipe into the fitting. Once you've glued as far as a flow splitter, you can start friction fitting the next branch, or finish all the steps through burying the pipe before starting the next branch. The advantage of leaving the glued pipe leveled but uncovered is that you can easily change its level if necessary. The advantage of covering leveled pipe is that it stays still.

Sometimes you find the pipe is too low at the end where you're working. The solution is usually to measure slopes back up the pipe you've laid, find the stretch that's sloping the steepest, and flatten its slope. This enables all the downstream pipe to be raised in elevation. For example, changing 4' of pipe from ½" per foot to ¼" per foot slope gains 1" of elevation *(changing 1 m of pipe from 4% slope to 2% gets you 2.5 cm)*.

More ecological but less rigid LDPE tubing can be held level by wire-tying it to a taut, perfectly sloped light steel cable. Each of these lines carries a portion of the flow from a 30-person kitchen in Spain.

Level and Support the Pipe at Intervals

Level and support the pipe at intervals of 2–4' *(0.5–1 m)* or as needed. Added sand is ideal for supporting and leveling pipe, and can also help alert you to the presence of pipes when digging in the future. But, compacted dirt works too. Use dirt tightly wedged underneath to raise the pipe, heavy objects placed on it to lower it, checking the levels continuously as you do so (photo at right). After this step, your pipe is like a bridge supported by pylons.

Support the Pipe along Its Entire Length

Now pack dirt under the pipe along its entire length, between the pylons. Walking barefoot on either side of the pipe to squish the dirt in with your toes works well. Wet the dirt just right to maximize compaction—wet dirt compacts much more, but if too wet it will squish out. Make sure this supporting dirt does not have leaves in it—when they decompose, the pipe will settle. Also make sure squishing the dirt underneath isn't raising the pipe, just supporting it. Check the levels of the pipe again. When the level is good and the bottom of the pipe completely supported with compact earth, fill in the trench to the top of the pipe. Leave the very top of the pipe clear. Wipe the top of the pipe clean to check the slope yet again (a pebble between the level and the pipe wrecks the measurement). Fix any place that's off. When you've done that, compact the earth again and recheck the levels one last time.

Supporting dirt mounds

Weighing upward-bowed pipe down with a heavy paving stone to level it

4' level

Pipe leveling
Pipe is supported at 4' (1.3 m) intervals with dirt mounds, pushed down to level as needed with weights.

Bury the Pipe

At last you can bury the pipe. *Don't bury the flow splitters or valves yet,* for easy access for the system test later. It doesn't matter if there are leaves in the fill on *top* of the pipe. Compact the backfill and leave it mounded up so when it settles it comes out even. Now trench the next section, and repeat the steps above.

Form Mulch Basins, Install Outlet Shields, and Plant Trees

This end of things is well out of the range of plumbers—it's landscaper's work. Once again, it's up to you to either do it right yourself or bend your gardener's work conventions to meet special greywater requirements. Compared to regular mulch basins for fruit trees:

❖ Basins should be deeper.
❖ Basins should be wider.
❖ Walls should be compacted watertight by stomping or tamping.
❖ Mulch should be a thicker layer of woodier (i.e., more durable) material.
❖ Trees should be planted in taller islands.

Mulch basin construction is especially critical for greywatered trees, as the trees will often get too much or too little water, due to the vagaries of greywater production.

It is generally best to wait until you have installed the pipe to finalize the *exact* position of the outlets and trees, because it's easier, for example, to move the outlet a bit than to turn 38° with a 45° fitting.

Once the pipes are in, it's time to construct the receiving landscape.

Dig Basins

Rake any leaf litter to the side and dig the mulch basins plenty deep. They only get shallower over time (review Mulch Basin Design, Chapter 5, for fine points; also Branched Drain Outlet Design, Chapter 9, and Real World Example #1).

Install Mulch Shields and/or Infiltration Chambers (if Any) and Plant Trees

Whether you use the 5 gal pots the trees came in, 5 gal *(20 L)* buckets, half drums, infiltrators, or something else for mulch shields, a hole saw cuts very nice pipe passages. Thinner-walled chambers can be cut with a knife. Support the chambers in the mulch basins with stones or bricks so they don't sink into the wet ground. This is especially critical for those that contain both a flow splitter and an outlet. The flow splitter is supported by the pipe coming into its inlet and the pipe going out one side. The tendency is for the splitter to list toward the unsupported outlet side, which is just hanging in space in the mulch shield.

System Test

This is optional but fun. Offering to demonstrate that greywater does not surface is a card you can play with an inspector. Try it without the inspector first, to avoid surprises (see Builder's Greywater Guide).

Take the access plugs out of the flow splitters and blast a hose into each one from top to bottom to flush through any rocks that fell in during installation. Rocks are tough to flush with normal flows. Now try out the system at a low flow rate and confirm that the flow splits correctly. With a very low flow, the water might all go to one outlet. See which one it is. If it is a water-sensitive tree, consider fine-tuning the flow splitter levels so it goes somewhere else. Now run the hose full blast into a 5 gal *(20 L)* bucket, timing how long it takes to fill. Then run the hose full blast into a cleanout above all the splitters, timing how long it takes for the greywater to overflow a mulch basin. Multiply the minutes by the measured flow rate and you have the maximum surge capacity for your system. The measured surge capacity on installation day should be at least double the design's estimated surge, as actual surge capacity lessens between maintenance intervals.

For the inspector demo, you could fill your bathtub and sinks to the brim with stoppers in place, fill the washer and turn it off just before it pumps the water out, then turn on the shower full blast and let everything rip. *Voila*: no daylighting, no problem!

Map the System

You may be tempted to skip this step, but if you're like most people, the day after you've buried the system and raked the leaves back, you'd be hard pressed to locate the pipes.

The perfect cover for outlet chambers and valve boxes is a flat stepping stone, which hides their inner workings while *marking their location*. In case these markers get moved or buried, it is a good idea to record some measurements from stable reference points (buildings, large trees, concrete walkways, big rocks, whatever you think isn't going to move in the coming decades).

To map the system, note distances to each important point—flow splitters, registers, outlets, diverter valves, cleanouts, and dipper box—from two stable reference points on your biggest-scale site map. Ideally these points form a right triangle with the thing you're locating. Using three points is more work but improves mapping accuracy (see Figure 10.1).

Take snapshots of every part of the system. Number them and then note them by number on the site map where you were standing when you took them, with an arrow for the direction you were facing (Figure 10.1, and Real World Example #3). Put this site map and the photos in your house files. Low maintenance has a flip side: because the system will work without even looking at it for years at a time, it is very easy to forget where the parts are.

To find these buried treasures, hook your tape measure on the reference point (the corner of the house, say), then scribe an arc on the ground at the recorded distance. Now move the tape to the next reference point, and scribe an arc from there. Where the arcs cross, you'll find your treasure.

Cover Up

Now you can cover the mapped flow splitters and outlets with dirt and/or stepping stones, and fill the mulch basins with mulch.

FIGURE 10.1: LOCATING SYSTEM COMPONENTS ON A MAP

Measurements from two stable reference points at approximately right angles can be used to locate these buried flow splitters in the future.

Branched Drain Maintenance

These systems have held up very well for the years they've been in existence (since 1998). They are so dead simple it is likely that they will not be affected much by the passage of a few more years, or possibly decades. The required maintenance is minimal.

Service Mulch Basins

Mulch basins need fertilizer and new mulch annually. When that's all they need, just toss it on top, fertilizer first; it will bind to the mulch and time-release. Each few years, the basins need to be emptied of mulch and reformed, larger if the trees are growing. You may also wish to extend outlets or add more splits. Stomp in the roofs of any burrowing animal holes, as these could drain water out of the basin and cause erosion. Refill the basins with fertilizer and mulch, putting clippings on the bottom to facilitate spreading of water, then wood chips, then yard waste, then the most attractive mulch on top. This normal garden maintenance is more important for greywatered trees, as it keeps the greywater covered.

Clear Outlets

Check the outlets. Are the outlet chambers (if any) filling with dirt or getting buried so the water can't get out? Remove the dirt with a rubber-gloved hand and trowel. "Rough mulch" (twiggy, woody clippings or chips) around the chamber enables free passage of water for much longer than materials like leaves, straw, or grass clippings. Don't replace the covers on the chambers until after the flow-splitting test, below.

Check Flow Splitting

Turn on an inside fixture to feed the system, or stick a garden hose in a cleanout, and confirm that water comes out all the outlets and splits more or less as it should. (It takes surprisingly long for the water to reach the outlets—longer than it takes to walk to them after turning the tap on.) Are the outlets that are supposed to discharge, say, ⅛ of the flow, all flowing at about the same rate? With lower flow, the test is more stringent. If the flow seems uneven, flush the system by opening the flow splitter access plugs and blasting a garden hose into each split. Now put the plugs back in and check again. If the splitting is still not correct, check each splitter in turn to isolate the problem. If there is a clog that can't be flushed from a splitter's inspection access, blast water up from an outlet, using a rag or adapters to make a semi-pressure-tight connection to the garden hose. Once the blockage is dislodged, flushing through the accesses should be sufficient to clean out the system.

Flush Salts

In a rainy climate with free-draining soil, this step is unnecessary.

Once a year or so it is a good idea to flush the system with copious freshwater or rain to wash accumulated salts in the soil down below the root zone (see Preserving Soil Quality, Chapter 5). The easiest way to get rainwater into the greywater system is via a hose or flexible PVC from a roof gutter into a cleanout above all the splits. In one existing Branched Drain system, about 100,000 gal/year *(300 m³)* of clean rain run-on from an uphill driveway and a few acres of wild watershed is routed into the system at about 1–100 gpm *(4–400 Lpm)*.

Branched Drain Troubleshooting

Here are some known problems, with suggested solutions:

Mulch Shields Overflow or Won't Accept More Water

If this happens, the flow between chambers and mulch basins is too restricted, or the surge capacity in the mulch basins is not adequate. With some layouts, if the upstream outlets are full and won't take any more water, the lowest outlet is overwhelmed. Try the outlet maintenance procedure described above, but you probably need to put in bigger shields or switch to the free-flow type of outlet.

Whole Basin Overflows or Fills Up Past Outlet Level in Rainy Season

If the whole basin overflows, you need a wider, deeper basin, or to divide the flow among more basins. If this occurs due to rain, first make sure no runoff is getting in. If the problem persists, you may need to switch to long, sloped, open-ended basins (described in Real World Example #4).

Free wood chips are often available from tree trimmers. *Through a recommendation from Oasis Design, the City of Santa Barbara Water Conservation Program pays for mulch deliveries for customers to reduce evaporation loss and promote groundwater recharge. Water customers can receive two large truck loads per year.*

Run-on inlet inside curb cut *routes filtered stormwater into two Branched Drain systems (inlets at left) and one infiltration basin (right corner). This unassuming bit of infrastructure effectively flushes salts from the greywater basins and totally changes the hydrology of the property: it infiltrates 50–300,000 gal/yr, doubling the water to the property (200–1,000 m³/yr).*

Animal Burrows Drain Water from Basins

Although this has not been problematic to my knowledge, gopher or mole tunnels could transport greywater out the bottom of the basin and off to who knows where.

The potential for this problem is greatly reduced by good design and installation. With a flow split into eight or more, then slowed and absorbed by mulch, the flow rate is so low that even if some water does escape through a gopher tunnel, it is unlikely to cause erosion or even get out of the tree's root zone before it soaks in.

If burrowing-animal-induced drainage would be disastrous, the entire basin could conceivably be armored above and below with ½" (13 mm) wire mesh before planting.

Flow Does Not Come Out One or More Outlets

It may just be a leaf or a piece of lettuce forming a temporary dam. Such blockages resolve themselves on their own. Another possibility (in an unglued system) is that a friction-fit joint has come loose.

See Check Flow Splitting as described on previous page. If blasting downstream with a hose doesn't work, stuff the hose in the end with a rag wrapped around it to tighten the connection and blast upstream from below (or use one of the techniques at right). If there isn't a clog, part of the system may have shifted out of level, so the flow is not going to one side. The only solution for this is to dig the blocked section up, re-level it carefully, and backfill around it carefully.

Outlet Chambers Become Slug Nurseries

Most systems have a few resident slugs. One had 30–50 in each outlet chamber. The owner of this system pointed out that intentionally creating slug lounges is a known organic control technique; you can go to the lounge and wipe them out, if you so desire. Pouring a huge pot of boiling water down the pipes might be a low-effort way to knock them back.

Grease

Pouring the occasional pot of boiling water through the system is also effective to prevent grease buildup. The grease melts and moves on to congeal on the surface of the soil. If the quantity is not overwhelming, soil creatures will consume the grease. If you expect a lot of grease, upsize the infiltration area, or install a grease trap. A grease trap is a *small* inline tank in which grease cools, coagulates, and floats to the top. They are available commercially or you can make your own. They tend to get gross and stinky, especially if too big or if water sits in them for more than 24 hours.

Foul Smell

One of the attractions of a properly constructed Branched Drain system is the absence of anaerobic conditions. This is because every part of the system slopes down, so it drains completely each time water comes in, so there is no pooled water to turn anaerobic—well, almost none. There is a bit of water in each fixture trap, and if the system incorporates a dipper box there is up to 1½ gal (6 L) in the tray. If no water goes through for 24 hours or more, this water can start to stink. The stink will go out through the vent system to the roof, so you won't notice it until you use some new water, which pushes the old stinky water out to the yard. Any odor thus generated should be minor and transient.

If you have a persistent foul smell, it is probably due to a temporary dam of crud creating a long wedge-shaped lake inside a pipe; incorrect levels in the pipes, creating anaerobic U-shaped lakes; or an undersized, waterlogged infiltration area. Here's what to do:

❖ **To fix crud dams**—Do the flushing procedure under Branched Drain Maintenance, above.
❖ **To fix U-shaped pipes**—Dig up the U-shaped sections and re-level them.
❖ **If the infiltration area is too small for the amount of water it is receiving**—Use less water, make the infiltration area bigger, add provision to alternate between irrigation zones, add another zone, or divert greywater to another dispersal option. Kitchen sink water is the most effective to divert, as the compost in it sucks a lot of oxygen from the soil. Prefiltering kitchen sink water will drastically lower the stink potential (and attractiveness to vermin).

*A **water-pressure drain opener** can be inserted in the flow splitter inspection hole to one side of the split then the other. When it expands, all the pressurized flow will go to that side, blasting through clogs and scouring out solids.*

Prefiltration on kitchen sink in 30-person kitchen in Spain dramatically reduces kitchen water solids...before they get nasty.

❖ **Add a trap**—If your Radical Plumbing stinks, add an S-trap or P-trap. One installation had a long slope of pipes exposed to the sun. In the summer, air in the pipes would heat up, wafting warm, moist drain ambiance into the kitchen.

Branched Drain Variations, Improvements, and Unknowns

Caution: Try at your own risk. None of these designs are proven...

Supplying Box Troughs in a Solar Greywater Greenhouse

The many reasons to send greywater to a greenhouse in a cold climate are summarized in Solar Greywater Greenhouse, Chapter 8. Greywater has been supplied to 3'-wide *(1 m)* raised beds through box troughs. The unproven variation—which could prove simpler and easier to maintain—is to supply box troughs by gravity through a Branched Drain network instead of with a flooding dose from a Drum with Effluent Pump or a dosing siphon. The pipes inside the box trough could possibly be cut in half, reducing the plastic use and simplifying maintenance.

Green Septic System

A Branched Drain can distribute clarified septic effluent to subsoil infiltration chambers. See Green Septic, Chapter 8.

Automatic Alternation Between Irrigation Zones

Automated switching between irrigation zones gives the soil a chance to rest, without someone having to remember to switch a valve manually. Manual switching tends to happen sporadically until the novelty wears off, and then not at all—certainly not at the optimum frequency of twice a week or so.

Automated switching could be done with a timer-controlled motor drive on a 3-way valve.[s2] (This is a common configuration for this valve in its intended use: pool and spa installations.) Similarly controlled valves could send a portion of the greywater to the septic/sewer when only some of it is needed, or, admit freshwater when the amount of greywater is insufficient, or send water to different places based on readings from moisture sensors in various zones… The more you delve into it, the more possibilities you'll dream up. (But, before embarking too far on this course, see Error: Overly Complex, Delicate, and/or Expensive System, Chapter 11.) Perhaps someday someone will think of a simple, non-electric solution for switching greywater automatically between two zones...

Supplying Bogs

Branched Drain networks have not been used to supply wetlands or bogs to my knowledge, so there could be some unforeseen difficulty. However, the means of getting the water to a wetland should have little effect on the proven ability of wetland plants to treat water. Clogging at the inlet is the most likely issue. Clogging by unfiltered greywater has successfully been avoided in wetlands by using a 3' x 6' *(1 m × 2 m)* infiltrator surrounded below and to the sides by rocks a few inches in diameter, and above by gravel.

The multiple outlet feature of Branched Drain networks serves little purpose when supplying one pond. The water attains the same level and extent whether it has one inlet or 16. I could see Branched Drains supplying a sort of self-equilibrating bog, which might occasionally be a pond but is otherwise just really wet soil. Multiple inlets would distribute the water over a wider area, so there would be standing water for shorter periods of time or not at all. The bog would equilibrate by plant growth or death as the water needs of the plants varied. As long as there was any greywater at all, the plants around the outlets would live to recolonize the bog when the balance shifted in their favor.

Be sure the bog does not intercept surface runoff, or it could easily be overwhelmed.

More than Four Levels of Splitting

More than four levels of splits (i.e., 16 outlets from one inlet) might work well using double ells; however, this hasn't been tested yet. The difficulty is that the water flow gets too low to push individual crud particles along (see Figure 4.7). A dipper or dosing siphon, which introduces peaks into the flow, would help a great deal to achieve finer splitting.

Smaller Pipes or Other Types of Pipes

It is preferable to use smaller- and smaller-sized pipes as the flow is halved and then halved again. This saves plastic and improves flow (Figure 4.7, again). It might be possible to make the finest branches with ½" class 200 PVC pipe; so far, the smallest I've heard of being used was 1".

Also, it may be possible to make Branched Drain networks out of welded HDPE (see Radical Plumbing, end of Chapter 4).

Double ells, 3-way valves, dipper boxes—none of the most important components of Branched Drain networks are specifically designed to be used the way they are in this system. If you own a factory for making plumbing fittings, contact me and we'll get some more optimally designed fittings made.

Two novel options for 1½" x 1" x 1" reducing wyes in HDPE.

Climate with Very Hard Freezes

This will probably work, but to my knowledge, a Branched Drain has not been tried outdoors in a climate colder than high altitude New Mexico, where temperatures drop to -10°F *(-23°C)*. As every part of the system drains completely, there are no pools of water to freeze. Greywater is probably warm enough to melt a film of ice inside the buried pipes with each use, so ice buildup would not occur.

Free-flow outlets might get blocked by ice buildup, as drips freeze at the outlet. Oversized outlet chambers under a thick, insulating blanket of mulch and snow are oases of microbial activity warmed by the heat in greywater. These should work in all but the most extreme climates, in which case a Solar Greywater Greenhouse is indicated. (See also Appendix C: Cold-Climate Adaptations.)

Very Low-Perk Soil

The logical adaptations are free-flow outlets, oversized mulch basins, and trees planted on high islands (Figure 5.7). If you must use infiltration chambers, they should be sized with exceptional generosity. It would be helpful to have two or more alternating infiltration zones, so they could each rest and have aerobic conditions restored. If someone dreamed up a simple system that automatically switched zones at intervals of time or after a specified amount of water was delivered, that would help.

Grease-Laden Water

We don't have much information about the long-term result of hard-core carnivores running their kitchen sink water through a Branched Drain network. It may be that grease will congeal inside, giving the pipes arterial sclerosis (narrowing of the pipes) as occurs in regular collection plumbing (and blood vessels). Grease may also clump in such a way that the flows split unevenly or not at all. If you expect a lot of grease, follow the recommendations mentioned in this chapter under Branched Drain Troubleshooting/Grease.

Chapter 11: Common Greywater Errors

Every reader should scan this chapter for applicable pearls of wisdom. Don't, however, let it scare you. Even the most pathetically misguided greywater systems rarely cause actual harm. For the few that do, it's not much (see p. 114). The pitfalls are easy to avoid, and even if you fall into one, odds are your system will still be beneficial relative to the alternatives.

Though our readers do way better than average, they are not totally immune to the siren song of the popular greywater mistakes. Around 1995 we implemented a two-pronged approach: warning people about mistakes as well as steering them toward preferred practices. Over time, we've accumulated quite a compendium of common errors. A few of the issues:

❖ Many complex greywater reuse systems are abandoned, and many simple ones achieve less than 10% irrigation efficiency within five years.
❖ Some greywater systems consume a lot of energy and materials to save only a little water.
❖ Economic payback time for some systems is longer than the system's life.
❖ Claims made for packaged systems are often inflated.
❖ The majority of successful systems are so simple that it is difficult for regulators, manufacturers, consultants, and salespeople to appreciate them.
❖ Hundreds of websites illustrate and promote the errors that follow. Some of the content is reproduced from manuals of the early 1970s, despite having been discredited years ago.
❖ Greywater best practices remain underpublicized. *2015 update: Best practices are now way more common. We hope 50,000 of our books in circulation and millions of website views helped.*

Of the greywater systems in the US, probably 15% are achieving most of the benefit they should, 80%+ could easily do better, and a few have overall negative net benefit.

Pondering the failings led our design path further and further from mainstream greywater thought. The more realistic we get, the lower we aim—and the more often we hit the target. Our designs hold up well in the field. In more than a dozen book revisions we've had to take back very little we've said.

This collection of mistakes took many intelligent people many years to make, recognize, and fix. Each error description includes exceptions and preferred practices. We update this compendium constantly and post it to the Web, as a public service (oasisdesign.net/greywater/misinfo). We hope you benefit from it. To help others benefit from your perspectives and experience, please share them with us, especially if you see a mistake that isn't in our collection. If you contribute an outstanding mistake, we'll send you a free book.

Error: Assuming It's Simple

Most of the errors that follow stem from this fundamental error, which in turn stems from:

1. the instinctive recognition that in most cases the resource potential of the greywater (water, nutrients, embodied heat) is not worth very much in the scheme of things, and the costs of poor management (smells, etc.) are not very high either
2. failure to realize that a greywater system which achieves *high water reuse efficiency* is a highly site- and user-specific design challenge that forces you to improve almost every other system in the home: water supply, water efficiency, rainwater harvesting, ecological landscaping, solid waste management, food production, etc.

In other words, greywater seems like it *should* be simple, so people often don't allocate greywater system design the effort required to achieve the performance they expect.

Preferred practice: Either lower your goals or put more thought/energy/money into the design. Upside: if you have to improve every other system...they will be improved, too. Reading this book is a great start. If your site is difficult, your goals high, or your time short, consider a design consultation as well (oasisdesign.net/design/consult).

Exceptions: If the performance goals are low enough for the context, a greywater system is simple. The Drain Out Back is a very common example of a "system" that doesn't require any effort at all and still offers benefits.

Error: Out-of-Context Design

Constructed Wetlands in the desert. Irrigation of a swamp. Sand filtration, ozonation, and pumping for flushing toilets in a residence. These are valid designs but applied in the wrong contexts.

In a culture where standardized solutions are the norm, we must remind ourselves constantly to pay attention to the context. Once context is seen clearly, the steps to deal with it come out of the mist.

Preferred practice: All appropriate technologies are context-specific—that is a big part of what makes them appropriate. However, greywater reuse is the most context-specific and interconnected of any green home technology. *The one universally applicable principle for all greywater system design is that there are no universally applicable principles.* The final section within each error description notes the inevitable exceptions when it isn't a mistake. Reuse or treatment, new construction or retrofit, soil and climate conditions, legal considerations: each of these variables in particular has the potential to change the design completely. Carefully check the list of design variables (Appendix A). General background on context-specific design can be found in our book *Principles of Ecological Design*, from which the sidebar at right is excerpted.

Exceptions: There are no exceptions to the "no universal principles" rule.

Error: Overly Complex, Delicate, and/or Expensive System with Negative Net Benefit

This class of systems misses the big picture and results in negative net benefit. A typical residential greywater system saves $100–$600 of freshwater a year. If the system costs more than a several thousand dollars it is probably overbuilt. The owner would have been better off paying for the extra water. The Earth would be less impacted by the wasted water than the wasted pumps, valves, piping, filters, and electricity used by the overbuilt system.

Achieving "actual net benefit" can be a challenge. This constraint more than any other makes good greywater system design a challenge. Systems are often built despite the absence of net benefit, with vague allusions to a "demonstration project." This justification should be used sparingly...or we'll end up with lots of demonstrations of resource waste.

In a residential context, any system that uses a pump and/or filter or costs more than you'd spend on water in several years is suspect. Disinfection is extremely suspect. Systems that entail massive, permanent disturbance to the planted area (e.g., burying truckloads of gravel in your garden) are also missing the point. Unfortunately, strict interpretation of the greywater codes which are still works in progress frequently runs counter to economic, ecological, or community benefit.

Preferred practice: *Choose the **simplest** possible design, and build it as well as you possibly can.* Keep one eye on your original goals and the big picture throughout. Ask yourself what the system is likely to do in flood, in drought, or in 20 years after four owners. What is most likely to fail or be abandoned? How is it likely to be "patched"? Often, the way systems get modified later to comply with reality is the way they should have been built in the first place. If no future "patch" seems acceptable, perhaps the system should not be built that way at all.

Exceptions:

❖ **New construction** economics can justify much more complex systems.

❖ **Drought emergency** causes greywater to skyrocket in value. If greywater is the only way to save a $50,000 landscape during a drought, an expensive system that falls apart in a year may be justifiable. On the other hand, a very well-built, simple system that lasts for decades could possibly be made for the same price, if the design resources are available.

Context-Specific Design

There are no solutions that apply universally—there are a variety of approaches and patterns that can be applied to generate the optimum solution for any need in any context.

This is a vitally important principle of ecological design. In all cases the greatest efficiency—and quality as well—is achieved when the tool is well matched to the task at hand. Frequent technological overkill is one of the saddest sources of waste in our society. Elimination of overkill does not involve real sacrifice. The resources saved by using simple tools for easy tasks can be applied toward performing more difficult tasks. Using transportation as an example, walking would be used for the tasks for which it is adequate, bicycles for distances too long to walk, busses and trains for distances too long to bike or in bad weather, planes for speed or great distances, and cars for special applications such as ambulances, mobile homes, or workshops. Among countless other benefits, getting superfluous cars off the road would enable the necessary ones to get around without being choked by traffic.

Cleverly matching the power of the tool to the task at hand is cheaper, healthier, has lower environmental impact, and is more enjoyable—but ultimately more powerful—than any single solution. Though uniform solutions appeal to centralized bureaucracies, attempting to implement a single solution across the board, without regard to context, will generate a host of new problems. Bare sufficiency produces optimal growth; deficiency is stunting, excess is unbalancing.

Those readers who are used to single solutions will be quick to point out situations where, for example, a composting toilet is unsuitable. No solution is applicable across the board; few technologies should be eliminated completely. What is suggested is that a range of solutions be matched to the range of contexts using common sense.

—From Principles of Ecological Design[15]

❖ **Chronic water shortage** has the same effect. I designed a greywater system for a house where the only water supply is rain, stored for the eight-month dry season in giant cisterns (Real World Example #3). The greywater system costs several thousand dollars, but provides the same amount of water as a $20,000 cistern, uses a fraction of the material, and solves the problem of disposition of greywater.

❖ **Acute dispersal problems** change the picture as well. I got a call from an Alaskan oil camp where the greywater from several hundred people was boiled down to ash, and the drums of ash shipped to a toxic waste dump in Texas (got to love oil company engineers, who prove the adage, "if you are a hammer, every problem looks like a nail"). Compared to this, any other system would be cheaper, simpler, and more ecological. In another case, a hotel in Big Sur was sending out the laundry at a cost of a few thousand dollars a month because they could not make a conventional onsite dispersal system that could handle the volume. A large, complicated, but well-built greywater system enabled the hotel to do laundry onsite and pay off the investment in less than a year.

❖ **Well-designed, proven systems that last decades** can pay for themselves even if complex. The US EPA State Revolving Fund program qualified the ReWater system[s5] for loans that had previously only been available to cities for conventional centralized sewer systems, primarily because the system lasts long enough to pay for itself.

❖ **Sheer volume** shifts the economics drastically. Institutions with several thousand gallons a day of greywater production and a similar amount of irrigation need often find that a complex treatment system enabling efficient distribution can be paid off quickly.

❖ **Regulatory necessity.** Regulators are generally more comfortable with complex, expensive, engineered systems than with biological systems that rely on the mysterious workings of nature. An overly complex greywater system may be the best alternative to an even more overbuilt conventional system, if that's all they'll let you do.

Note: One manufacturer's website claims that our 20-plus years of info about pumps and complex systems does not account for recent technological improvements. It's important to us that our info be accurate; we update it all the time. We hoped we were wrong— but based on more than a year of testing their system, we were right. We applaud their efforts; it's certainly getting closer, and we look forward to the day when we can confidently, broadly recommend this type of system for residential-scale flows. As we go to press we're negotiating with that manufacturer to test an improved version of their system. Someday...

Error: Mansion with a Greywater System

This is a specific case of the general problem described above. A greywater system for a large house with acres of irrigated area and just a handful of inhabitants is more likely to have negative net benefit. In this situation, the value of the greywater is literally a drop in the bucket compared to all the other waste going on—and attempting to capture it costs more waste. A one-bathroom house might require 30' of extra pipe to be dual plumbed, a mansion could easily require hundreds. When you add the level of construction perfection and use convenience required to fit in with the rest of the house, the resource cost of the system compared to its conservation value can become ludicrously out of balance.

Preferred practice: *Build a smaller house.* In the US in the 1950s the average house was nearly half as big as today's, and had almost twice as many people in it. A house half as big built with completely conventional materials and systems is almost certainly more ecological than a "green" mansion. Focus money and energy on a good, space-efficient design, and you'll have lots left over for state-of-the-art green materials and systems.[29] Think like a boat builder; utilize not just each square foot, but each cubic foot well. A smaller space with more concentrated design and craftsmanship is more soulful to live in.

If you must have a huge house, rather than spend plastic and money on dual plumbing, consider *reusing combined greywater and blackwater,* in a system that can handle it (see the System Selection Chart). You drastically reduce plumbing cost, get significantly more water and nutrient volume, and in drip irrigation systems, get much higher reuse efficiency.

Exceptions: None, really.

System spotted at the Los Angeles Eco Expo that demonstrates a number of mistakes.

First, there's overkill. For several thousand dollars it does what a $500 Drum with Effluent Pump does. Second, the pictures on the poster show filtered but unsterilized greywater coming out at high pressure through sprinklers and inundating a concrete walkway from both sides. That violates three health principles (at least it didn't show kids dashing through the sprinklers). The tank is also too big, so that violates a fourth...probably a record for one system.

The argument is frequently advanced that giant green custom homes nourish providers of green technologies with huge infusions of money. As one of the affected professionals I am not immune to this logic. My personal standard for taking on a job of this sort is that if the owners are willing to commit themselves and other users to significant lifestyle accommodation for the Earth and take the risk of pioneering new designs, then I'll do it. Redefining comfort and convenience standards (lifestyle accommodation) can easily cut the project's environmental impact in half. Furthermore, this raises awareness and effects culture change in an influential class of people. The benefits of pioneering are obvious. Still, these goals can be accomplished even better in fewer square feet. One of the most powerful lifestyle statements I've witnessed is an exceedingly successful attorney and his wife living happily for several years in a tasteful 120 ft² *(12 m²)* cottage on a multimillion-dollar lot in Santa Barbara. That's the size of the master bedroom closet of the house you'd expect these people to live in!

Error: Pump Zeal

Many people reflexively reach for a pump when they want to move greywater around. There is no denying that in the initial demo, it is very cool to see greywater squirting out where you want thanks to a pump. But, a pump is the first step on the slippery slope toward an Overly Complex System quagmire. It won't work very long without filtration, and filtration is a big hassle (see Error: Inexpensive Greywater-to-Drip Irrigation for a typical filtration story). Your house will still be generating greywater in 30 years, but pumps are not a long-term solution. Odds are that if your greywater system uses a pump, within five years the system won't be working. If the pump hasn't been killed by long hairs which worked their way through the 75 micron filter and wrapped around the rotor, or by you when the float switch hung up at 3:00 AM and stayed on noisily yet again, that's about the time it will die of old age. Unless you're still eager to clean fetid filters after doing it hundreds of times (often during parties, when use peaks), you probably won't buy a replacement.

Even if everything works perfectly, a pump can suck a lot of electricity, particularly if it strains for hours against a filter that should have been cleaned months ago. For all your effort and expense, you may have simply substituted electricity waste for water waste.

Preferred practice: Use a system that doesn't need a pump (see the System Selection Chart).

Exceptions: If all your potential irrigation area is at higher elevation than your greywater sources, you have to either forget about reuse or get a pump. In this case, bite the bullet and get a good one that doesn't require filtration (Appendix E). In institutional contexts with more than 300 gpd *(1 m³/day)* of greywater generation and a similar irrigation need, the water can easily be worth more than the fancy filtration and pumping hardware needed to manage the large volume, even if it all has to be replaced every five years. At present, volume greywater reuse hardware and support are weakly developed, but this is a legitimate application for a pump. And... there is always the hope that one of the "systems that really work" which crop up each drought will—unlike all its predecessors—actually work

Beautifully made but ill-conceived greywater storage tank. *This 250 gal (1 m³) tank is the final of a four-chamber system that converts greywater to blackwater over the week it takes to get through the system. It smells wicked, and generates hydrogen sulfide, which has eaten through the steel lid.*

Error: Storage of Greywater

The word "storage" should immediately sound an alarm, as should any residential system that includes a tank bigger than 55 gal *(200 L)*. Storage rapidly turns greywater into blackwater (see photos, above). If you doubt this, fill a bucket with greywater and observe as it progressively darkens and reeks. Bacteria multiply to blackwater levels as well, at least indicator bacteria. In Mexico the *trampa de grasa* (grease trap) often included in greywater systems is a popular way to commit this error; omitting, bypassing, or downsizing the *trampa* would be much better.

Emptying "black mayonnaise" out of a greywater wetland. *This wetland was undersized by a factor of 10; the sludge was black as tar. It was replaced with mulch basins.*

Greywater Basics · Greywater Basics · Greywater Basics · Greywater Basics · Greywater Basics

Preferred practice: 24 hours is generally considered the prudent maximum time for storage. Since this is not enough time to, for example, store greywater from a week when irrigation is not needed to a week in which it is, it is better to eliminate pooled greywater anywhere it occurs—send it straight to the soil. The fewer anaerobic corners and pockets the better. My latest designs drain *completely*. The collection and irrigation piping, and surge tanks (if any), slope at least 2% across their bottom surfaces.

Exceptions: Temporary "storage" in surge tanks, which moderate peak flows, is okay. *1) Greywater intended for manual distribution can be stored for the day to allow for its distribution all in one session.* Tanks for this purpose should drain completely (not leave a bit of fetid greywater at the bottom to inoculate the next batch) and *not be too big* as this invites misuse in the form of letting the water sit too long. *2) Greywater can be filtered by settling in a septic tank,* but then it must be dispersed subsoil, like blackwater. In this case, the longer it sits in the tank the better (lower suspended solids and BOD; see Settling (Septic) Tank, Appendix E). *3) Highly treated greywater* (for example, from a Constructed Wetland) can be stored for up to a month before it goes septic, depending on the BOD and temperature. *4) Really cold greywater* takes longer than 24 hours to stink, though I'd need a really persuasive reason to rely on this factor in system design.

Error: Paranoia about Negligible Health Concerns and/or Cavalier Disregard for Legitimate Public Health Concerns

Some people advocate irrigating lettuce and carrots with untreated greywater. Others fret about distributing greywater under soil without disinfection. Some worry about eating fruit that contains molecules from biodegraded dish soap, forgetting that they imbibe traces of dish soap directly with every glass of water and plate of food. Greywater reuse poses a fantastically low health threat in industrialized countries. Proper handling can eliminate the small health threat (see Health Considerations, p. 18, and our *Builder's Greywater Guide*).

Preferred practice: Each user and community has to find his/her comfort point on the paranoia-vs-recklessness continuum, and each community has to determine what mix of hazards to aim toward. In many cases reducing one hazard will increase another. For example, forcing low-hazard greywater into overloaded septic/sewer systems increases the chances of untreated blackwater getting loose in the environment.

It's poor form to construct pathways for infecting people into your design, and totally unnecessary; review the principles on page 4.

Error: Treatment Before Irrigation

Pretreatment is sometimes presented as an essential element in a greywater system. But, plants and soil, especially the upper, most biologically active layer of soil, are fantastically effective at wastewater treatment. Plants and soil are fine with funky, chunky water. It is pipes and people who may have a hard time with it. **Pretreatment is only necessary to overcome limitations of the irrigation piping.** With proper design, even straight kitchen sink water can be reliably and safely distributed with no pretreatment whatsoever (see photo on p. 90).

Preferred practice: For simple residential systems, design the distribution system/ plumbing to handle funky water—particularly high levels of solids—and to make human (or animal) contact with greywater unlikely to occur before the water has passed slowly through healthy topsoil. The Branched Drain and other systems fulfill these requirements.

Exception: For several hundred gallons a day of greywater with a similar irrigation need, it can be economical to pretreat greywater so it can be distributed by more efficient irrigation hardware.

Error: Discharge of Greywater Directly to Natural Waters or Hardscapes

You'd think this would be more rare, because it is so obviously wrong. These systems come in two categories: legacy systems, from places built 50–100 years ago before they knew any better and/or before it mattered, and new systems, which are generally more furtive and criminal-feeling, or just so unconscious it is beyond belief (photo).

How Dangerous Is Greywater?

There are 8 million greywater systems in the US, with 21,000,000 users. From 1950 to 2010, there have been more than a billion user-years of exposure.

There have been zero documented cases of greywater-transmitted illness.[1]

Soapy creek from a legacy system at a hot springs resort constructed in pristine wilderness around the turn of the century.

A laundry pipe runs out the formal drive of an estate in the foothills above Los Angeles, into the public street. It flows untreated for blocks before running into a gulch.

Preferred practice: Almost anything is preferable. Dumping greywater on the soil surface is a big improvement over dumping it in natural waters or impermeable surfaces. Dumping it into a mulch-filled basin where it is contained and covered is a huge improvement.

Exception: When the receiving body of water has sufficient capacity to purify the water, and there is no other reasonable alternative. Sailboats on the open ocean are the only example which comes to mind. Even if you are in the middle of a vast wilderness next to a large river, you can just take a few steps back and rinse your shampoo onto soil, which will purify it before it goes into the river.

Error: Greywatering Lawns

This is awkward. Do I denounce thousands of greywater users who see no harm in what they are doing (and in most cases are causing no harm), or condone a marginal activity?

Applying greywater to the surface of a lawn short-circuits the purification step. If the lawn receives traffic, it invites direct contact with untreated greywater. The likelihood of transmitting pathogens is small, but it exists.

Greywatering a lawn is also a pain in the rear (see A Note on Lawns, p. 15). The system almost universally used is a hose from the washing machine or house plumbing that is moved all around the lawn. The effort to greywater a large fruit tree is much less, as the target is one big root system instead of thousands of tiny ones.

Preferred practice: Replace most of your turf with something else; replace what's left with a water-conserving grass such as Tall Fescue, watered with the freshwater you save from using greywater elsewhere; or just let your lawn go dormant when there's not enough rain to sustain it.

Exceptions: Subsurface drip irrigates lawns safely and well. Greywater generation/irrigation need of 100–300 gpd *(0.4–1 m³/day)* is the break-even point where such a system, at $2,000 or more, could start to make sense (see Automated Sand Filtration to Subsurface Emitters and Advanced Treatment System to Subsurface Drip, Chapter 8). Every dryland school should irrigate their playing fields with water from showers and towel laundering.

Error: Irrigating Vegetables

The concern with greywater on vegetables is the possibility of transmitting disease. Some people greywater veggies anyway. Why? See Exceptions, below.

Preferred practice: If your goal is to get rid of your greywater responsibly and not to irrigate, there is no reason to put greywater on food crops. If your goals are both to grow food and lower overall water consumption, chances are you'll have more irrigation demand than greywater generation. In this case, use greywater first on ornamentals, then on fruit trees, and use the freshwater you saved to water your veggies.

Veggies irrigated sub-surface with greywater in a greenhouse—a probable exception to the "no greywater on vegetables" principle. Most greenhouse greywater irrigation is subsoil.

Exceptions: In the past I have categorically recommended against greywatering vegetable gardens, but I've decided to write more about the boundary between responsible resource reuse and reckless public health threat in this area, because I understand the attraction. Drip irrigation does not adapt well to home veggie gardens. The hardware is not great, coverage is uneven, water goes on top of mulch instead of under, and wind blows the water off course. Lines with inline emitters are super-expensive, and clog rapidly even from filtered potable water. During weeding, seeding, transplanting, growth, and harvest, irrigation need varies tremendously in a way that is hard to match with an irrigation controller. Veggies are more sensitive than fruit trees to daily (even hourly) weather changes. In short, home-grown veggies are a poor fit to automated irrigation. The efficiency is likely less than 30%, vs 80% for fruit trees. Hand watering is the obvious alternative. If you're hand watering anyway, why not use hoses or buckets of free greywater, instead of freshwater costing nearly a penny a gallon? Hand watering with greywater can yield 80% efficiency, and you're much more tuned into the plants.

The greywater systems recommended in the rest of this book include several layers of protection, each capable of preventing the spread of infectious microorganisms. When irrigating veggies with greywater, the tenuous protection is only from:

1. not happening to have anything nasty in the water
2. only getting nasties back that came from you in the first place
3. not splashing greywater on the edible portions
4. washing the veggies
5. cooking the veggies
6. not getting sick even if you eat something nasty, because your immune system is robust

Additionally, greywatering vegetables is typically manual, which inevitably results in direct contact with greywater. If you engage in this reckless practice, pay attention to what you're doing, because your margin of safety is slim. If anyone in the house has an infectious disease, protections #1 and #2 above are not operative and you should stop using greywater on veggies. For protection #3, exercise care in applying greywater, and give crops that are splashable and/or eaten raw (e.g., carrots, salad greens) a wide berth, even more so near harvest time. Try not to splash, and wash your hands afterward. For #4, always wash greywatered raw veggies with soap, iodine, or equivalent. (I'm reluctant even to mention #6, but it seems to work in much of the nonindustrialized world.)

Error: Irrigating Plants That Can't Take It or Don't Need It

Certain plants cannot take greywater, and certain plants can't take too much of any kind of water. Acid-loving plants tend to have a hard time with greywater. Certain plants native to dry areas have a hard time with any dry season irrigation. Also, some plants have problems with soggy conditions.

Preferred practice: Avoid irrigating plants that don't want it and design your system so it doesn't create sogginess for plants that can't handle it.

Error: Garden Hose Directly from the Washer

This works until any of these problems occur:

1. The hose kinks, and, with the flow stopped, the washer pump burns out.
2. The pump, after months of working too hard to push water through a long, skinny hose, burns out.
3. A flood of scalding hot water boils your prized plant.
4. The machine tries to refill itself, and the hose (with its end lower than the washer) continues to siphon freshwater out until someone shuts off the washer.
5. The pump doesn't get all of the water out, so clothes stay soggy.
6. You lift the hose to move it, and weeks-old, fetid greywater rushes backward into the machine and onto your clothes.

Preferred practice: The Laundry to Landscape system solves these problems (see Chapter 7: Simple Greywater Systems).

Exceptions: A percentage of installations which perfectly embody the errors listed here are used for years without any of these problems manifesting. The percentage of people who get away with this hose "error" because of a favorable confluence of characteristics of washing machine internal plumbing, site geometry, and use habits is fairly high, as the incidence of each individual problem is fairly low. If you have an installation like this which has been working for years, why rock the boat? On the other hand, if you're installing a new system or replacing your old one, why not choose a design which protects against these unhappy possibilities?

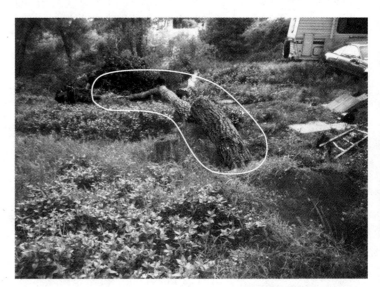

Dry season greywater application is suspected of toppling these two giant oak trees in the most dramatic case I've ever seen of this problem. (Dry season irrigation promotes root disease in these trees.) Mysteriously, oaks across the street seem unaffected by their greywatering, perhaps because the trees had nearly a century to get used to it, while the greywatering of these trees was new.

Error: Distribution of Greywater through Perforated Pipe or Other System Where You Can't Tell or Control Where the Water Is Going

There are two problems with distribution of greywater through perforated pipe:

1. It will clog—Perforated pipes don't clog in septic tank leachfields because a septic tank effectively removes suspended solids. Suspended solids are plentiful in greywater, even after the crude filtration sometimes attempted in home-brewed systems. If solids don't eventually clog the pipe, root infiltration will. If the pipe is big enough, and the greywater clean enough, it may take so long to clog that the durability is acceptable, but this is rare. A seldom-used bathroom sink draining into 10' of 4" *(3 m of 10 cm)* perforated pipe in gravelly soil might last several years before failing. Laundry water, however, will quickly clog perforated pipe of almost any capacity.

2. It is unmanageable for irrigation—Any system where you don't know where the water is going is all but unmanageable for irrigation (only a problem for water reuse). The problem with any system where emitters are lined up in series (like holes in perforated pipe) is that the majority of the water will dump out the first few holes, or the lowest few holes, depending if the flow is low or high. Then these holes will clog, and the water will all go out the adjacent holes. To actualize irrigation water savings, you have to coordinate with freshwater irrigation so all the plants get enough but not too much. This is all but impossible with perforated pipe, which invariably waters one small area too much and the rest hardly at all, in a pattern that is constantly changing and, if the pipe is buried, invisible—except in the form of distressed plants.

3. Gravel is nasty in the garden—Most perforated pipe systems have gravel around them. Most greywater users are keen gardeners. Gravel is the last thing you want in your garden; it degrades soil and makes digging really difficult. If you wrap the gravel with filter fabric to contain it, that will clog, as well as turn to lots of bits of plastic trash over time.

You may be able to fine-tune the pipe slope, hole spacing, and size so each hole spits out the same amount of water along the entire length. Attempted by numerous greywaterers before you, this perfection is very fragile. If you alter the slope 1% or the flow a few percent, or if lint blocks some holes, distribution evenness is shot.

A series of garden beds with water flowing in gravel underneath is another example. Will the first bed get 90% of the water because the plants suck it up before it can move on, or will the last bed get the most because water rushes down to it? Who knows?

Preferred practice: *1) For subsoil dispersal* use gravelless infiltration chambers or subsurface drip. If you must have perforated pipe, add it as an extension to your leachfield and filter the greywater through the septic system first so the pipe doesn't clog. *2) For separate dispersal* of residential greywater, use mulch-filled basins supplied by a Drain Out Back or a Branched Drain, with pipes a few inches above mulch or in good-sized underground chambers. *3) For reuse,* plumb in such a way that you know with certainty where the water is going and can adjust supplemental irrigation accordingly. This typically means a parallel system, or one with only one outlet. Examples are a Drain Out Back, Movable Drain Out Back, Branched Drain, well-made and regularly serviced distribution boxes, Bucketing, etc. Crude but effective parallel splitting of greywater flow can be achieved by not combining fixtures, keeping flows separate in the first place. This is difficult to manage if fixture use is highly variable and/or unknown, but works in some applications (see Lump or Separate the Greywater Flow, Chapter 3). *4) For large flows,* high-level treatment and underground drip irrigation are preferred (p. 81).

Exceptions: Effluent with suspended solids removed, for example, by septic tank or sand filtration, *can* be distributed evenly through perforated pipe. For even irrigation, pressurized perforated 1" pipes with ⅟₁₆" holes on 1" centers up to 50' long have been used (see photo on p. 82).[m]

As with many of these cautions, some folks seem inexplicably to get perforated pipes to work well. I've heard reliable accounts of a few gravel pit or trench systems that have worked for ten years or more with shower water only. Perhaps there is something magical about these installations, or shower greywater in general?

Laundry water is normally the worst. However, I have seen an old-fashioned clay drain

An exception: This "Twisted Tees" system in Santa Fe, New Mexico, has been successfully tuned so that the same amount of laundry water comes out each outlet, each of which branches off at progressively lower angles toward the end. If you can put buckets under the outlets, that shows how much water comes out each outlet and facilitates tuning.

GREYWATER BASICS ❖ GREYWATER BASICS ❖ GREYWATER BASICS ❖ GREYWATER BASICS

---

[m]*Metric: 25 mm pipes with 1.5 mm holes on 25 mm centers up to 15 m long.*

tile line that handled laundry greywater for 30 years in clay soil without clogging. Although it was not failing, it was replaced with modern perforated pipe as part of a remodel. The replacement clogged completely in less than a year and was abandoned—go figure.

Error: Combined Wastewater Designs Used for Greywater

Most plumbers have more experience with combined wastewater (greywater + blackwater) than with dedicated greywater plumbing, and sometimes misapply principles of one to the other. Here are some common pitfalls:

Pipe Too Big—Combined wastewater in residences generally requires 3" or 4" pipe. This is too big for greywater. If you just ask your plumber to run greywater and blackwater separately until outside the house, you'll likely end up with a 3" or 4" greywater stub-out. How can a pipe be too big? First, it is more awkward, more expensive, and burns up valuable elevation faster. Second, crud in small flows doesn't flow down it as well (see Figure 4.7).

Preferred practice: Use 1½" or 2" pipe.

Exceptions: Huge multifamily or institutional flows.

Pipes Too Low—Combined wastewater in residences generally is on its way to sewer or septic lines deep underground. This is too low for greywater.

Preferred practice: Plumb pipes as high as possible—see Squander No Fall, Chapter 4.

Error: Freshwater Designs and Hardware Used for Greywater

Although it is natural to expect greywater to follow the same laws of physics as water...it doesn't. Here are some common pitfalls:

U-Shaped Pipe—Greywater should pass through a U-shaped pipe section, seeking its level just like freshwater, right? Wrong! Crud in greywater settles at the bottom of a U, clogging it.

Preferred practice: Continuous slope of 2% in rigid lines. This prevents airlocks as well, which plague all low-pressure inverted U-pipes, for freshwater and greywater alike.

Exceptions: *1) Flexible lines* won't develop this problem if moved once in a while; *2) Pressurized greywater lines* blast the crud through U's; *3) Traps* are short U's at the bottom of vertical drops that (usually) blast crud through.

Cheap Electric Valves—Greywater distribution can be controlled elegantly and automatically using $20 drip irrigation electric valves, right? Wrong! Crud in greywater prevents the valves from closing, greywater quickly corrodes them, and greywater rarely has enough pressure to make this type of valve (powered by water pressure) work right, even on the first day.

Preferred practice: Forget automated valves, use one of the handful that work with greywater (see Valves, Chapter 4), or buy super-expensive electric sewage valves.

Filters—This nifty sand/gravel/carbon/reverse osmosis/fill-in-the-blank filter will filter my greywater just like it does my freshwater so I can... Wrong! Crud in greywater clogs that filter in the blink of an eye.

Preferred practice/Exceptions: Don't filter greywater, or see Appendix E for proven greywater filtration options.

Soaker Hose—I'll just run my greywater through this soaker hose... Wrong! Soaker hoses are such a poor technology that they typically have 30% variation in flow when brand new and used with freshwater, and soon clog with all but the cleanest freshwater, let alone greywater.

Corrugated Flexible French Drain Tubing—Corrugated flexible drainpipe has small, rapidly clogged outlet holes and collects festering crud in all its ups and downs, as well as the corrugations, which are likely to elevate bacteria and smell levels.

Error: Inexpensive Greywater-to-Drip Irrigation

This subset of the error above deserves special mention. Backyard tinkerers naturally converge on the idea of distributing greywater through drip irrigation hardware. How else to achieve 80% irrigation efficiency, short of manually bucketing water plant by plant? The problem is that it doesn't work. Of the hundreds of such systems built during the California drought of the 1990s, every one I know of was shortly abandoned. (The systems going in during the 2015 California drought seem likely to last maybe 50% longer.) The most common configuration was a surge tank with an inlet filter and a float-actuated sump pump (see Drum with Effluent Pump, Chapter 8). It works great for a few weeks, then the filter clogs…

At first, the drains are just slow, then not draining at all. Finally, there's no denying it's time to clean that filter. When you remove it (wearing rubber gloves, of course), you realize too late that the upstream pipes are brim-full. A deluge of chunky, days-old greywater pours into the surge tank. Fortunately, you are quick on your feet and only lightly spattered. Not more than a third of the solids caught in the filter has spilled into the surge tank. As you struggle to get your rubber gloves off to wipe the flecks from around your lips and eyes, the sump pump cycles on. Horrified, you stand paralyzed as $500 of dripline is pressurized with last week's split pea soup. By the time you wiggle under the crawl space and pull the pump's plug, the dripline is history and the pump is already stopped by hair wound around its rotor anyway.

Preferred practice: Do something simpler and more robust with less efficiency, like a Laundry to Landscape or Branched Drain system; choose a more labor-intensive, less sanitary system like Bucketing; or bite the bullet and pay several thousand dollars for a greywater-to-drip system that works (see Automated Sand Filtration to Subsurface Emitters, Advanced Treatment System to Subsurface Drip, Chapter 8).

Exceptions: None.

Error: Low-Volume Automated Greywater Toilet-Flushing Systems

Flushing with untreated greywater fouls the tank and produces fetid smells (see Error: Storage of Greywater). Automated treatment is fabulously expensive and complex. The cost for one greywater-to-toilet-flushing system is $10,000. Even at the punitive water rate of $0.01 a gallon, that's five years of 325 flushes a day to recoup your investment, not counting lost interest, electricity, or system maintenance. The cheapest system I've heard of ($650 in 2007 dollars)[s21] would take 23 flushes a day. It is doubtful a cheap greywater-to-toilet-flush system would work well or long given the poor track record of low-budget greywater-to-drip systems, a less demanding application. Economic infeasibility can indicate ecological infeasibility; the Earth could be much better off if you just wasted the water than if you wasted all the plumbing, pumps, tanks, filters, and electricity needed to make this sort of system work. Residential greywater-to-toilet systems are an area rife with hucksterism. It is a shame to see companies taking advantage of well-meaning homeowners. These companies keep cropping up, though on the plus side they don't seem to last long. If you are evaluating claims, check the assumptions. The amounts of water saved are often based on false or misleading assumptions, such as a high number of flushes with old high-flow toilets.

Preferred practice: *1) Put in an ultra-low-flush toilet (or a waterless composting toilet).* Old toilets use 3.5 gallons per flush (gpf), 1.6 gpf is currently common, and the lowest-use toilets at the moment use 0.8 gpf. If you have a low-flow toilet, you can reduce your toilet water usage by half just by switching to the lowest-flow-available toilet. *2) "If it's yellow let it mellow, if it's brown flush it down."* That can save another 50%. *3) Toilets can be flushed with greywater by simply bucketing* it directly from the bathtub/shower into the toilet bowl (*not* the tank, where it will fester). An added plus of reusing bathtub water in this way is having the flush volume under intelligent control, so you can use just the amount of water needed to get the job done. Also, in cold climates, you get a primitive but highly effective greywater heat recovery as the bathwater heat escapes into the home. *4) Use rainwater to flush toilets.* This makes way more sense; *5) Install a "lid" that flushes the bowl with cascaded handwash water* (see photo on p. 145).[s7]

Exceptions: If you have highly treated water already, say from a Constructed Wetland, and don't know what to do with it, it may be worth supplying it to the toilet. An advantage is that toilets need flushing every day, whereas irrigation need is usually seasonal.

Clearwater such as air-conditioner drip, reverse osmosis water purifier drain water, and fixture warmup water is a natural for flushing toilets. It needs no treatment and can be stored indefinitely. Steven Coles of Phoenix, Arizona, suggests that supplying the toilet from the reservoir of an evaporative cooler also keeps the mineral concentration in the cooler water from rising.

Multifamily, institutional, or any other high-use installations can benefit from flushing toilets with highly treated greywater, especially when incorporated in the original design of the building.

Error: Use of Government Agencies, Engineering Firms, or Salespeople for Greywater Design

There is very little overlap between the set of practical greywater systems and the set of legal greywater systems (outside of Arizona and the several other states that wisely exempt simple greywater systems from permitting[4]). This seriously hampers government's ability to give out useful information, if they had it. Because greywater reuse is a new, marginal, rapidly evolving field, it is hard for ponderous bureaucracies to keep up.

Also, there are few practical greywater systems which can be profitably installed professionally. It is likely that an established trade organization, engineer, or plumbing company would set you up with an unproven, overkill system adapted from some better-known treatment technology. Therefore, you're pretty much on your own.

Appropriately designed greywater systems are not a very sales-friendly product: way too site specific, variable, and inexpensive. The Internet features numerous generic, expensive, prepackaged greywater systems with fantastic claims, which seem to benefit the vendor more than the user.

Preferred practice: Our books and website are the most complete and up-to-date references for home greywater systems. The designs in our books promise less than in other sources…because we don't sell systems, we sell accurate information.

Exceptions: For new construction, sometimes an overengineered greywater system is less overengineered than conventional treatment. Also, a few prepackaged greywater systems are actually good[s5] (please let us know if you make or have used a good one).

Error: Guidance from Work-in-Progress Codes

The California Plumbing Code (CPC) 1992 greywater standards—the first state greywater code—was an important step and certainly as well done as was politically possible. Too bad it was a step not quite in the right direction, as it has been widely emulated in the Uniform Plumbing Code (UPC)—the International Plumbing Code (IPC) has its own issues. The Mini-Leachfield system, for example, was described in great detail as if it were a proven technology, but has been installed in no cases I know of. I can't think of any application for which I would recommend it, either. *2015 update: The CPC greywater standards got a lot better in 2009 and continue to improve. The terribly misleading drawings are gone, Mini-Leachfields are gone, laundry-only standards are nearly there. This error in the CPC case is not as severe as it was…but the whole proscriptive model is a bad fit to greywater. Arizona's performance code is a* much *better model.*

Unrealistic codes have poor participation rates. Santa Barbara, for example, issued approximately ten permits for greywater systems in 1989–2009. Yet there is evidence that during this time, which included several years of severe drought, more than 50,000 Santa Barbarans used greywater! There are so many obviously overkill requirements that the entire code, including the sensible provisions, is dismissed as a source of design guidance.

Preferred practice: If you're a homeowner in a place with a backward greywater code, don't follow it unless you can get a favorable interpretation from your inspector or have no choice.

If you're an inspector, sections of the code grant you nearly total discretion to approve whatever you want. Please exercise this discretion to discount the more pointless sections of the code and allow genuinely well-designed and well-executed systems. (There's more on this code in our *Greywater Policy Center*[4] and it is discussed line by line in our *Builder's Greywater Guide*.)

If you're making policy, don't blindly follow the CPC/UPC's lead when writing your own administrative authorities' greywater regulations—instead, follow Arizona, New Mexico, and the growing roster of states that exempt simple greywater systems from permitting.[4] A reasonable regulatory stance leads to a greater compliance rate, a much higher proportion of professional installations, and a reduced risk from perpetuation of unregulated systems.

That's it for greywater basics. Fill out the Site Assessment on p. 131 if you want, or just get your system going…

Chapter 12: Real World Examples

We suggest you scan through these and read at least the ones that are similar to your context in some respect...though something can be learned from all of these examples.

So far we've started with general principles and explored their application in different contexts. Now we'll go in the opposite direction: starting with specific contexts and seeing how the principles get applied. Some of the examples below are exotic and extreme, all are real. There's something to learn from each of them. Their titles give the most salient site feature, the location, and the greywater system type. *(Costs have been adjusted to 2015 dollars.)*

Example #1: Town—City of Santa Barbara (Branched Drain)

A classic residential Branched Drain system on a small lot in town with a really nice garden.

System: Branched Drain with dipper, to sub-mulch emitters.

Context: Part of a State of California study.[30] (See *Builder's Greywater Guide*,[6] Getting a Permit, for a copy of the permit and site map.)

Goals: To enable yet more extensive gardening without raising the water bill (the original owners were keen organic gardeners), to send the greywater somewhere other than the ocean (a recent spate of beach closures had raised public awareness about this cost of sewer systems), to gather data for a greywater study, and to demonstrate feasibility of Branched Drain system design in an officially monitored and permitted installation.

Under these fruit trees are inverted 5 gal pot mulch shields in large, deep basins. Basins are filled completely with wood chips. The system is completely invisible in the landscape, yet easily serviced by pulling mulch back. (Flowerpots are not turning out to be that durable.)

Branched Drain to Mulch Basins that I installed in Santa Barbara as part of a State of California study.[30] (There's a bigger picture on the front cover.) The study showed that greywater systems save water and do not adversely affect soil quality. This system has received only occasional inspection since installation, and reliably distributes greywater to about a dozen fruit trees.

Greywatered bananas with outlet under clay pot.

Dipper installed.

- Cleanout
- Diverter valve: greywater/sewer
- Dipper tray
- Backwater valve on sewer line
- One of two RV dump valves for zones
- Overflow to sewer (required but unnecessary in this outdoor installation...and you won't know if system overflows)

- Mulch shield
- Greywater splitter access chamber

Design and installation issues: Conserving fall was especially arduous on this site, which has an average slope of 2%. Because greywater pipes need a 2% slope, this sounds great...until you realize that when you go at an angle across the slope, the pipes slope less. Maintaining adequate slope was greatly complicated because we threw away perfectly good fall at many points to comply with the 8" *(20 cm)* legal burial depth requirement for the pipes (I don't think the inspector even noticed...thankfully, this requirement was removed in 2009).

The basin area is way oversized, as per California greywater code.

Costs and benefits: The study reported favorably on the economics of this system—despite the fact that its cost was nearly doubled by the legal requirement to plumb twice as much area as there was water to irrigate with, and nearly doubled again by the requirement that the flow be measured. It cost about $1,000 in parts and $400 for a plumber to help replumb the entire underneath of the house to gain the 8" *(20 cm)* fall needed to run a dipper box with a counter. The other two systems in the study handled similar amounts of water but cost $5,000 each and had an estimated five-year life expectancy. The life of the Branched Drain system was estimated at 20 years. The study also showed that greywater systems saved water and did not adversely affect soil quality.

The system has received only zone switching and slug control since installation, and reliably distributes greywater to about a dozen fruit trees.

User's view: The house's new owners are maintaining the beautiful garden nicely. They were very concerned about the greywater system before buying the house and are pleased to have had no problems, or hardly anything to do about the system, in the years since. They said: *"We never saw water surface. Not even from the lowest outlet, during a deluge of rain when we turned on all the fixtures in the house for a few hours to test the surge capacity of the system."*

Example #2: Suburbia—Southern California (Branched Drain)

Another classic Branched Drain system on a relatively small, intensively planted lot.

System: Branched Drain to free-flow, sub-mulch, and subsoil emitters (see facing page).

Context: Three separate Branched Drain networks irrigate an existing, extensive orchard. Mostly owner-installed one at a time starting in the kitchen, with some hired labor for trenching. Supplemental irrigation by automated drip.

Goals: To enable the orchard to grow without using even more water from a limited supply, and to stave off replacing the septic tank leachfield.

Costs and benefits: Costs are summarized in Table 12.1 (a simple cost-benefit analysis for this system can be found in Table 2.7). With 85% of the wastewater diverted from the septic, it is almost inconceivable that the leachfield will require replacement within the owner's lifetime. This saves a future expenditure of several thousand dollars. The septic tank has been monitored but has not required pumping since this system was installed. The interval between pumpings is probably doubled. One pumping at a cost of $350 has been saved thus far. Irrigation efficiency is high because the greywater goes mostly to evergreen subtropical fruit trees at a rate approximately equal to their average *wet season* irrigation demand. Thus, there is little water applied that is not useful. At an average water rate for the area of $0.003/ gal *($0.80/m³)*, the three greywater systems together save about $68 a year, total, for a simple payback time of eight years on water savings alone, or two years considering the septic savings.

User's view: *"I installed the first Branched Drain system unglued because my experience was that greywater systems were unreliable. I was skeptical that the flow splitters would work for even a day before one side clogged and all the flow went to the other. I tried very hard to clog it at first but it never clogged, not even where the flow was split into sixteenths! As the superiority of the kitchen system became evident, I put in the other Branched Drain systems one after the other. If I had done them all at once, it would have been better to join the flows before splitting them. We leased out our house for a year and the system did great without even being looked at. The only difficulty was one separated joint. I'd have glued the first system if I'd known it was going to work. The new systems are glued. The systems are low-maintenance. We add wood chips annually and extend basins as fruit trees grow—things I did before there were any greywater systems. We've got a few way-undersized subsoil outlets (5 gal pots) that I've mucked out once a year. These should be replaced with properly sized ones. Overall, I am frankly amazed at the robustness and self-cleaning of this system type."*

2015 update: The laundry Branched Drain has been changed to a Laundry to Landscape system, the shower system to a Green Septic for the toilet. The toilets were also changed to 0.8 gal/flush toilets, so this system only greywaters about 15% of the irrigation need now, with the rest made up by Laundry to Landscape.

TABLE 12.1: COST OF SUBURBAN GREYWATER SYSTEM

Subsystem	Parts	Plumber hrs/$	Laborer hrs/$	Owner labor hrs
Kitchen	$100	1 / $50	0	20
Bath	$150	3 / $150	10 / $80	15
Laundry	$150	1 / $50	10 / $80	18
Subtotal	**$400**	**5/$250**	**20/$160**	**53**
Total cost	**$810**			

Four outlets with ⅛ each of bath/shower flow. *These subsoil infiltration chambers are way undersized. The owner plans to replace them with a continuous row of several infiltrators 30' (10 m) long and 14" (35 cm) wide, like this one:*

FIGURE 12.1: GREYWATER SUPPLY, IRRIGATION NEED, AND DISTRIBUTION SYSTEMS

Bath/shower system irrigation need:
245 gpw *now,*
1,335 gpw *in 10 yrs*
254 gpw *greywater generation*

Toilet/Green Septic system irrigation need:
237 gpw *now,*
318 gpw *in 10 yrs*
254 gpw *greywater generation*

1' (30 cm) graphic contour lines

	Metric
5 gal	20 L
192 gpw	0.73 m³/w
237 gpw	0.90 m³/w
245 gpw	0.92 m³/w
254 gpw	0.96 m³/w
261 gpw	0.99 m³/w
318 gpw	1.2 m³/w
357 gpw	1.4 m³/w
799 gpw	3.0 m³/w
1,335 gpw	5.0 m³/w

Kitchen system irrigation need:
357 gpw *now,*
799 gpw *in 10 yrs*
261 gpw *greywater generation*

Deciduous tree *Evergreen tree*
Darker shaded areas = higher irrigation need; unshaded areas irrigated occasionally or not at all. Supplemental irrigation by drip irrigation on a timer.
gpw = gal/wk

Mulch shields *are upside-down 5 gal buckets with access holes in top. Square tile is lid over access hole.*

Two outlets with ¼ each of bath/shower flow.

Example #3: No Water—Highland Central Mexico (Various)

A high-class system in a nonindustrialized world context with acute water shortage.

Systems: Branched Drain to free-flow outlets, Multimode Greywater Tank, septic, and Constructed Wetland to Branched Drain.

Context: A large home in an international ecovillage at 7,000' *(2,300 m)* in central Mexico. The village has an eight-month dust-dry season followed by 4½' *(140 cm)* of rain in four months (!). The only dry season water supply is from cisterns filled during the monsoon. Freshwater irrigation during the dry season is unfeasible, as cistern storage is prohibitively expensive; enough capacity to provide one person with 5 gal *(20 L)* a day for the dry season costs $2,000—what a laborer makes in a year. Villagers without sufficient cistern capacity travel two hours round-trip by donkey to distant springs to carry back 10 gal *(40 L)* of water, collected drips at a time. As in most of Mexico, Huehuetortuga's greywater was generally dumped through Drains Out Back, or simply on the ground wherever it was used, with poor sanitation and inefficient or zero reuse.

Huehuetortuga house.

This site has a dry toilet for the owner.[31] It also has a large septic tank, and a tiny Constructed Wetland which treats the water from two low-flow toilets (see photo in Constructed Wetlands, Chapter 8). Greywater systems include a Branched Drain network for two kitchen sinks and a new hybrid design I call a Multimode Greywater Tank. It is working well, but trials have been limited. The Multimode system can be a good choice where water for gardens is precious, as long as the users are not prudish about hygiene and have energy to bucket greywater.

Goals: To pioneer/demonstrate new systems for doing more with less water in this area, enable tastier varieties of fruit trees to be grown, and create green relief in an environment where there is no water income of any kind for at least half the year.

Design and installation issues: It was not known what sort of landscape this house would have or how much the guest rooms would be used, so the systems were designed for maximum flexibility. The kitchen system—the Branched Drain network—is the only system that commits the water to one set of outlets. The trees it serves are the main irrigation commitment. The other systems can all be adjusted and adapted as needed.

The Multimode system has four use modes, depending on the irrigation efficiency desired:

❖ **Bucketing**—80% efficiency, considerable effort. Pairs of buckets are filled from four tanks spaced around the landscape and manually doled out to plants. It takes about one 5 gal bucket per square yard of irrigated area to apply 1" of water; 1" per week is a typical irrigation level.[m] A benefit of bucketing is that whoever empties the tanks is acutely aware of how much water is used indoors, which can improve indoor conservation. On average, people who carry water *to* their homes use 10% as much as people with piped water. Carrying water *out* should have a similar effect. Pipes can't distribute wastewater to plants nearly as well as they can supply potable water to the home, so if bucketing is going one way or the other, from house to plants is preferable.

Multimode Greywater Tank with enough fall to fill a bucket from a valve at the bottom. A quarter-cylinder shape, this tank fits nicely in an inside corner of the house. It holds 50 gal (190 L) and is made of ferrocement faced with stone. The floor slopes strongly toward the outlet, so it drains completely of water and is self-cleaning of solids.

❖ **Manual hose**—65% efficiency, medium effort. Water is released from the tanks once a day through a large-diameter hose with a valve at the end. The hose is moved by hand and shut off between watering areas.

❖ **Semi-automatic hose**—50% or less efficiency, low effort. The drain of each tank is left open, so it functions as a surge tank rather than as a storage tank. Water runs immediately out the hose to whatever plant is at the end of the line. The line is moved periodically among plants.

❖ **Automatic hose**—Nearly 0% efficiency, no effort. For the wet season, the hose is routed to a mulch-filled infiltration basin and left there (the soil perks very rapidly, so infiltration capacity is not an issue).

The greywater tanks are conveniently spaced around the house, near thirsty plants. The tanks are sized to accommodate one day's high average greywater flow. Tank shape depends on the amount of fall available. Where there is enough fall to fit a bucket under the drain, the tank can be any shape (a plastic drum works), and buckets are filled by placing them under the drain line (see photo at right).

---

[m]***Metric:** One 20 L bucket per 1 m² is about 2.5 cm of water.*

Where extra fall was not available, the tank was built with a special "canoe" shape, which can be emptied quickly and completely by bucket (photo at right).

We were able to make a low area next to the tank for people to stand and scoop buckets without having to bend over so far.

The Branched Drain requires only annual flushing near the end of the wet season. The use of the other systems is quite labor intensive in bucketing and manual hose modes, but labor is inexpensive here and many people need work. An excellent wage for a day's skilled work in this area is $8. It was a key design assumption that a gardener/maintenance person would be present to manage the system. Managing all the irrigation takes about a couple hours per week in the dry season—34 buckets a week, on average. (The gardener empties them all by yogurt container onto the plants to ensure the water goes exactly where he wants it to.)

Costs and benefits: All the wastewater reuse systems together cost about $5,000. This includes the septic system and wetland for treatment and reuse of blackwater. Most of the cost was for design work at industrialized world rates. In addition, the design and construction labor was increased two to four times because most of the project consisted of prototype designs invented for this site, or designs that were new to the region.

There are a number of very different ways to evaluate the economics. The least favorable is to assign zero value for treatment and compare the entire cost of pioneering all the systems against the cost of replacing the actual greywater reused so far with the cheapest short-term water source (trucked-in water). Due to low occupancy of the house this past dry season, only about 1,000 5 gal buckets *(20 m^3)* of greywater were generated and reused. (The low demand inside freed an equal amount of fresh cistern water to be used directly in the landscape.) Despite the staggering environmental costs, water trucks can be hired to haul water up from a rapidly dwindling aquifer far down in the valley for a spectacularly low sum: 1.5¢/gal *($28/7 m^3)*. By this measure, $80 worth of water/year was saved at a cost of several thousand dollars.

From a more realistic view, the very high reuse efficiency enables the maximum water consumption of the house plus yard to be nearly what it would be with double the cistern capacity. Thus, it functionally substitutes for about $4,000 worth of storage and $2,000 worth of septic system, with much lower environmental impact—90% less cement, for example. Additionally, this system provides extremely effective treatment for blackwater and greywater in a area where water quality is important (all above in 2015 dollars).

User's view: *"My system is a delight. Living in an area that has an eight-month-long dry season, reusing water is clearly the right thing to do. The four fruit trees that are watered directly from the kitchen sink via a branching greywater system are especially happy with this energy-efficient (works on gravity), simple to use, very low-maintenance arrangement."*

(More photos and figure of this system on next page. Bottom left photo p. 78 shows the mini-wetland.)

FIGURE 12.2: FERROCEMENT BUCKET-SCOOP ("CANOE") TANK

Overflow
Locate at highest point.
Overflow joins drain,
or just dumps to a nearby fruit tree

Shape and texture
Tank is ferrocement with smooth finish. Entire tank slopes ¼" per foot (min) to drain.
Bottom and end curves match lower third of a 5 gal bucket to within ¹⁄₁₆". This enables all water and crud to be scooped out very efficiently. Lid opening should be 20" × 55", with round ends to accommodate a natural bucket scoop. Depth can be varied; 20" is good. Usable volume of tank shown is 30 gal

Inlet
Locate as high as possible

Tank extension
To attain daily greywater volume, shape and location of extension are unimportant as long as it drains to low point

Drain
Locate at lowest point, in middle of bucket scoop. Plug with recessed rubber stopper in bathtub drain with metal cross removed

Metal lid

SVANTE VAN BART

Metric: ¹⁄₁₆" = 1.5 mm; ¼" = 6 mm; 20" × 55" = 0.5 m × 1.4 m; 5 gal = 20 L; 30 gal = 113 L

WARNING!
Unattended buckets with even a few inches of water are a drowning hazard for little kids

FIGURE 12.3: HUEHUETORTUGA LANDSCAPE PLAN
SHOWING IRRIGATION NEED AND FOUR OF SIX GREYWATER SYSTEMS

Cleanout registers

Kitchen sink

A

Guest shower, bathroom sink

2nd kitchen sink

Macadamia nut

Avocado gets two outlets after tree grows

Rainy season diversion

Lemon

B

Valencia orange

Constructed Wetland fed from two toilets and septic tank (not shown)

Hass avocado

C

Shaded areas = projected irrigation demand in 10 years

Strawberry guava

Tangerine

Overflow of reservoir of treated blackwater from Constructed Wetland

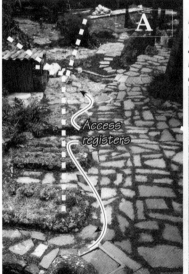

A

Access registers

Pipe locations in Huehuetortuga landscape.
Positions and orientations of photos A–C are noted on plan above. Path of pipes is shown on photos with dashed lines. It is best to take pictures of pipes before and after they are covered.

B

C

Example #4: Too Wet—Oregon (Mulch-Covered Bog)

A good example of a simple system for responsible treatment of greywater in a wet environment.

System: Drain to two long, sloping, open-ended mulch basin infiltration beds. These are designed to dispose of the water responsibly in the wet season. The water is transpired by plants in the same bed in the dry season.

FIGURE 12.4: EVAPOTRANSPIRATION / INFILTRATION MULCH BASIN IN OREGON
(PLAN VIEW)

(SECTION VIEW)

Evapotranspiration/ infiltration mulch basin in Oregon.

Context: The location is desert in the summer, rainforest in the winter. The owners had already converted to composting toilets, so the only wastewater going in the septic was greywater. However, the septic effluent was somehow leaking into a culvert and thus into a creek nearby.

Goals: To keep the septic tank water out of the creek, eliminate standing or surface runoff of untreated wastewater, and maximize reuse of the nutrients in wastewater.

Design and installation issues, owner's view:

"We varied from the original plan in a couple of ways, which I would do differently next time:

1. *We filled the basins completely with bark mulch (not "rough mulch"), and it seems to be compacting down more than I would like. I think that if we had used some rough mulch (unchipped woody sticks) at the bottom, it would have stayed looser longer.*

2. *We put a lot of effort into making the floor of the basin have exactly the right slope. In retrospect, I don't think we needed to have worried about that so much, since I doubt that the water is following the exact path we planned.*

3. *We made the mulch shields a bit smaller than originally planned, since we were using materials on hand: large planters (approximately 18–22" in diameter) with the bottoms cut off and holes drilled into the sides. We covered these with wooden caps. If I were doing it over again, I would use larger bins for the mulch shields and put bigger holes in the sides and pack larger, coarser mulch around them. Drainage out of those is a bit slow, and I suspect the water sometimes bubbles out the top, under the wooden caps. Originally, we left the wooden caps exposed on the surface, which resulted in the area smelling slightly anaerobic. The smell vanished when we covered the caps with a thin layer of mulch. I have never seen water surface above this thin mulch layer, although the area is usually very damp.*

We added the walkway and bench so that the mulch basins would look more like a garden area than a water treatment area. We put the most water-loving plants at the inlet end of the basins, since the outlet end often stays dry during the dry months. We switch beds once a week using a diverter valve. I am glad we chose to put in the diverter valve instead of having to swing an open unglued pipe from basin to basin. It makes switching beds so much easier and more pleasant, and it's nice to have the inlets all hidden away. We have the diverter valve housed in a small handmade valve box with a lid, which looks like a bench.

So far, I haven't seen any water standing in the mulch beds or being discharged from the basin drain, except for what I presume to be rain during the heaviest downpours.… We love our system. Our land is cleaner, and the system is discrete and beautiful. It's great fun on nice days to sit out on our 'observation bench' and watch the bathtub drain."

Example #5:
Big Family in New House (Automated Subsurface Emitters)

This example describes a system appropriate for new construction and moderately high flow.

System: Automated sand filter to subsurface emitters, manufactured and installed by ReWater Systems[s5] at the time the house was constructed.

Context: This permitted system is in a neighborhood of large homes with extensive landscapes. Irrigation is required year-round due to low-rainfall, semi-desert conditions (10", *(25 cm)* average annual rainfall). The family has six children and generates lots of greywater.

Goals: Irrigate landscape without excessive water use, dispose of water safely, reduce ocean pollution, save money on water bills.

Design and installation issues: The soil is heavy clay. Tap water is expensive, salty.

Costs and benefits: This system cost a few thousand dollars for the collection plumbing, and an equal amount for the irrigation piping, which is being installed piecemeal by the owners. This system qualified for a state Wastewater Recovery Facility rebate, on the strength of ReWater's detailed life cycle analysis. Unfortunately, this program was terminated before the system was completed. In my opinion, this site perfectly fits the profile for an automated system. It seems the owners see it that way, too.

Wife's view: *"I was against it at first. It seemed like a difficult system to set up. I've installed most of the emitters myself. Now that I'm through the learning curve I like it. We have a large lot—a couple acres. We have six children, so we have a lot of water to reuse. Our water bill is not bad at all compared to our neighbors'. I think we're saving a lot of money. And when my 17 year old spends 20 minutes in the shower I don't get nearly as upset as I would otherwise."*

Husband's view: *"It is a very sophisticated, well-designed system, but out of reach of most people without government assistance. The system is complex for the average guy. It takes a certain amount of maintenance, which is hard as I'm quite busy. We had to replace a pump (a fluke, apparently) and* *have had to service the filter once in five years. But I love the idea of not wasting the water, and our palm trees are growing faster than anybody's. We have expanded the system to service 25 more fruit trees. The worst thing about the system is the meddling of the water district. We have two expensive backflow valves on the makeup waterline and they need to be recertified each year at a cost of $75."*

REWATER SYSTEMS, INC.

ReWater surge tank, sand filter.

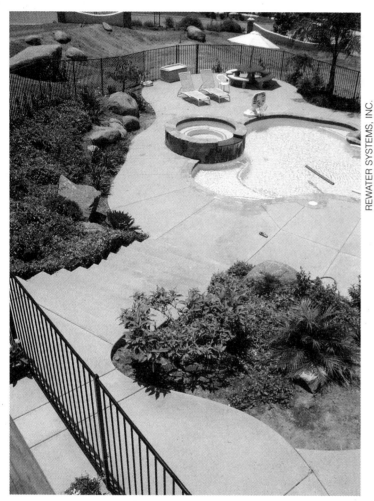

REWATER SYSTEMS, INC.

Greywater-irrigated landscape,
freshly installed.

Where to Go for More Information

This book's appendices cover:

❖ Site assessment
❖ Measuring elevations and slopes
❖ Cold-climate adaptations
❖ Systems for the nonindustrialized world
❖ Pumps, filters, and disinfection
❖ Cascading greywater to other indoor uses
❖ Sensible regulations
❖ Units and conversions

You'll find more information on the following specialized topics in our *Builder's Greywater Guide*[6]:

❖ Installation of greywater systems in new construction
❖ Conforming with the CPC/UPC
❖ Improving greywater laws
❖ Multifamily, commercial, and institutional-scale systems
❖ Greywater science and research
❖ Information for professionals: architects, landscape architects, landscapers, greywater and rainwater systems installers, contractors, plumbers, inspectors

Our website, oasisdesign.net, includes more information on:

❖ Indoor greywater reuse (for example, for flushing toilets or cooling)
❖ Greywater policy
❖ Links
❖ Water system design
❖ Greywater for camping
❖ Plants for greywater systems

There is more information and handy tools in our Oasis Greywater Extras packet: oasis-design.net/greywater/extras.[43] There's also a survey where you can provide us with feedback: oasisdesign.net/catalog/satisfaction.htm.

The Future of Greywater Use

In the future, we can look forward to greatly expanded water recycling and options for legal greywater reuse, as well as integration with stormwater. Necessity has a way of eroding the attitudes and regulations that stifle design advances and their adoption.[4]

In the US, the reclamation of treated sewage for irrigation is exploding in popularity. Commercial car washes and many industrial processes already purify and reuse their wastewater. In Europe, highly treated sewage is pumped back into the potable water system. These systems require considerably more energy, chemicals, and infrastructure than onsite systems for the reuse of untreated or partially treated greywater.

As global resource constraints tighten, home greywater systems will improve in efficiency, ease of maintenance, and popularity. I predict that such systems—widely illegal only recently—will soon be mandated for new construction in some areas.

Taking responsibility for the small part of the global water cycle that flows through your home yields great satisfaction. I hope this book enables you to benefit fully from the experiences others have had with greywater use, whether you're implementing a proven design or picking up experimentation where others left off. If you experience a notable greywater success—or failure—that you think should appear in the next edition of this book, please drop us a line, and share photos.

Art Ludwig

Oasis Design
oasisdesign.net/about/contact/feedback

Appendix A: Site Assessment Form

Site _____

Date_____

Free copies of this form may be downloaded from oasisdesign.net/design/consult/checklist.

This form serves as a reminder of the common variables to take into account when designing a residential greywater system. Many of these questions may be difficult or impossible to answer—just skip over them for now and they may become clear later. Reading the text of this book will help identify which items are most germane to your context. Also remember that the map is not the terrain...this sheet matters only to the extent that it helps things get built well on the ground.

If you are working with other people on the project, this form can serve to orient them, along with a site map and (if they can't visit in person) photos.

Reminder: Careful attention to the context will pay good dividends. Greywater systems are affected by more variables than most systems in natural building, and to a greater degree. A change in one of any number of variables can change the whole design.

Goals

General project goals

What are the guiding philosophies and aesthetic? (E.g., fancy gated subdivision, shack in hippie commune)

What perfection standard* are you aiming for?

Hygiene standard?

Greywater system goals *(check all that apply)*

- ☐ Irrigate/Save water *(don't forget conservation before reuse)*
- ☐ Dispose of water safely
- ☐ Improve sanitation
- ☐ Reduce pollution
- ☐ Save septic
- ☐ Save money
- ☐ Feel good
- ☐ Demonstration *(it should still justify itself)*
- ☐ Other _____

Landscape goals *(check all that apply)*

- ☐ Beauty
- ☐ Food production
- ☐ Erosion control
- ☐ Slope stabilization
- ☐ Fire break
- ☐ Privacy screen
- ☐ Windbreak
- ☐ Outdoor living
- ☐ Microclimate modification (e.g., windbreak, increased cooling via evapotranspiration, shade)

Water System

Prospective and existing water sources:

- ☐ Well _____ gpm
depth of water table in wet ____, dry season _____
- ☐ Spring _____ gpm (minimum)
- ☐ Meter _____ (size)
- ☐ Rainwater harvesting
- ☐ Runoff harvesting
- ☐ Other _____

How is your water supply constrained by power supply, economic, ecological, or availability considerations?

Quantity of water _____
Security of water _____
How much does water cost? _____

Volume of onsite water storage _____

What are the water security issues?
(E.g., no power = no water = dead fruit trees in a month)

To what degree do you want to or have to conserve?

Existing Wastewater Treatment Facilities

- ☐ Septic: Is it failing?
- ☐ Sewer: Where does it go?
- ☐ Greywater system: Is it functioning satisfactorily (yes/no/sort of)? If not, how?
- ☐ Composting toilet
- ☐ Constructed wetland
- ☐ Other: _____

Special wastewater dispersal constraints?

* *See definition p. 5.*

Population of Water Users

Average population _____
Minimum population _____
Peak population _____
Duration and nature of peak _____
Max continuous days unoccupied during dry season _____
Pending changes in users/use?

Landscape and Irrigation

Native vegetation type(s):

Land use(s), existing and planned:

Irrigated area: Current _____
                    Potential _____
Existing freshwater consumption?
What is the existing/planned irrigation system?

Is the landscape fenced or free of browsing animals?
Important trees to irrigate?

Slope

Is the area to be irrigated below the greywater source?
Slope % _____
*(Note a Branched Drain system on a 2% slope takes **four times** the labor to build than one on a 4% slope. If the slope is under 2%, it will be very challenging.)*
Are there erosion and/or slope stability (landslide) issues?

Slope aspect (orientation)_____

Soil and Groundwater

Soil type(s): _____
Soil fertility: _____
Digging ease: _____
Permeability (has there been a perk test?)
minutes/in _____   location_____
minutes/in _____   location_____
minutes/in _____   location_____
(Note location(s) and values of perk test on your site map)
Minimum seasonal groundwater depth, seasonal variation:

Distance to nearest year-round surface water_____

Distance to nearest seasonal surface water_____

Where does runoff go?

Greywater Sources

Fill out table, mark on your site map
with quantities of water

Source	Possible to irrigate downhill (y/n)?	Plumbing accessible (y/n)?	Quantity and variability of water, surges, conservation measures, comments
❏ Washing machine			
Bathroom 1			
❏ Bathroom sink			
❏ Bathtub			
❏ Shower			
❏ Toilet water*			
Bathroom 2			
❏ Bathroom sink			
❏ Bathtub			
❏ Shower			
❏ Toilet water*			
Green Septic only			
❏ Outdoor shower			
❏ Utility sink			
❏ Wood burning tub			
❏ *Lavadero* (washboard)			
❏ Kitchen sink			
❏ Dishwasher			
❏ R/O water purifier			
❏ Dishwasher			
❏ Water softener flush			
❏ _____			
❏ _____			
❏ _____			

Climate

Annual rainfall _____
Maximum evapotranspiration (inches or cm/week) _____
Minimum evapotranspiration (inches or cm/week) _____
Growing season (frost to frost) _____
Minimum temperatures _____
Typical max duration w/o significant rain _____
Duration of snow cover _____
Solar exposure (directions) _____
Hours lost from sunrise _____, sunset ____due to surrounding geography and trees
Greenhouse possible? _____ (especially good for cold, wet, low-perk locations)

Forces of Nature

Predictable disasters, which may affect the design:

- ☐ Flooding
- ☐ Torrential rain
- ☐ Landslide
- ☐ Fire
- ☐ Very high wind
- ☐ Extreme drought

Users and Maintenance

To what degree are the users interested in understanding/maintaining the system?

Is the system public?

Will there be a person responsible for maintenance?

What are the maintenance goals or constraints?

Regulatory and Social Climate

Will the project be permitted?

Might it be subject to later inspection as part of another project?

What is the applicable greywater code? Other legal considerations?

Neighborhood appropriateness?

Economics

Budget constraints?

Do you own the land where the project is to be built?

How long are you planning to stay there?

Is resale value a concern?

Are there time and money constraints for maintenance, repair, and system replacement?

Is it imperative that the system meet a particular economic payback timetable, or is doing the ecological thing the overriding concern?

Materials and Skilled Labor Availability

Where are plumbing parts and plants coming from?

Are biocompatible cleaners available?

Who is going to do the installation?

Site Map and System Elevations

A ⅛" = 1' scale, 1' contour map[m] **of the site and a ¼" = 1' plan of the structures involved would be ideal,** but any sort of sketch is a help. The map or other diagram ideally would show topography, property lines, septic tanks, leachlines, wells, surface waters, buildings, major vegetation, and irrigated areas, existing and planned. Aerial photos can help for some sites.

If you're sharing this information with people involved in the project off site, take snapshots showing general feeling of the site and any special features, indicating the location and the direction of each shot with a letter and arrow on the site map.

Make copies of the map and sketch the possible ways to connect the greywater sources with irrigation/treatment areas.

The elevation relationship between features such as buildings, foundations, walkways, greywater sources, septic or sewer inlet, and irrigated areas is critical.

For all Branched Drain system installations, I strongly suggest making an elevation view drawing as well.

---

[m] *Metric: 1:50 site map, with 25 cm contours, 1:25 house plan.*

Appendix B: Measuring Elevation and Slope

Naked Eye

The unaided eye is good for determining the direction of a slope. It is, however, *amazingly inaccurate* for judging the height difference between two points, especially if there is anything but an uninterrupted, dead flat between them.

Water Level

To measure elevations across short distances up to 30' *(10 m)*, use a simple water level (upper photo). This can be a length of ⅜" *(10 mm)* transparent plastic tubing, or a garden hose with clear plastic extensions. Both are available at hardware stores. Make sure your tubing does not leak. To ensure it is 100% bubble-free, fill it by siphoning water through the tubing until you see no more bubbles zipping through. When moving it, put thumbs over the ends. Raise or lower the line until the water surface at your end is at the elevation of the first point. (If this point is too close to the ground, use a reference point a measured distance above it.) Then have a partner at the other end measure from the water height (which is the same as at your end) to the second point. The difference between the two measurements is the elevation difference between the two points. (There is another version of the water level called the reservoir level, which can be used by one person but is more awkward for greywater work; see figure at right.)

Water Transit

For long distances (as far as you can see), you can use a homemade <u>water transit</u>—a 3' *(1 m)* length of transparent tubing filled with water. Hold it in a U-shape with one end near your eye and the other at arm's length, and you can accurately transfer the elevation of your eye to a measuring tape above a distant point or points (lower photo).

There are lots of scenarios for how to measure using this technique. I suggest you make a drawing showing the heights to keep the accounting straight. Here are a few examples:

Sight along the near and far water surfaces in the level to the first point (or to a reference point a measured distance above or below it). Take your time to get the two water levels, your eye, and the point exactly in line. Have a partner mark the reference point. Now turn, keeping your eye at the same height, and look out toward the prospective outlet or obstacle or whatever is at the second point. Have your partner hold a tape measure with the end on the point, and the tape extending up from it vertically. Have them move a finger up and down until it is in line with your eye and the two water levels (lower photo). The difference between your measured eye heights above the two points is their elevation difference.

Checking levels with a water level. *Person at right adjusts tube until water level is at her reference mark. Person at left measures from water level in tube to ground with a tape measure.*

Reservoir water level. *Can be used by one person—water level in stationary bucket barely changes as you move around checking levels in different places. You have to start over if you spill any water, though.*

Checking levels with a water transit. *Person at right adjusts tubing height until her eye and the near and far water levels are exactly in line (don't drink coffee before doing this!) while person at left moves his finger up and down tape measure until his finger is exactly in line as well. Reading on tape measure minus distance from her eyes to ground is height difference between locations.*

Checking levels with a water transit, *person's eye view. The near and far water levels are exactly in line with the eye and the point up the canyon that has the same elevation as the eye.*

You can also stand on one of the points and look to the other. Subtract the distance between your eye and the ground from the height of your partner's finger above the second point to get the height difference between the two points.

These measurements can be chained together to go great distances and around visual obstacles with amazing accuracy, if you are careful. Using this technique, I surveyed across a canyon and through trees for the freshwater supply line at the house in Real World Example #3 to within 4" in 1,000' (99.97% accuracy).

Tubing ends joined with smaller piece of tubing

+2%
Water level
-2%

Water transit variation that can be used to measure slopes *as well as horizontal plane, by sighting to marks above or below water level.*

Abney Level

The Abney level is a scope with a split view that shows your distant point on one side and a bubble level on the other. It can measure steep slopes as well as a flat plane. It is especially handy for laying out Branched Drain distribution plumbing, with the slope just set at 2% (though you have to be careful not to space out and sight upstream with the slope set to downstream).

Transit

A modern transit does just about everything: measure a flat or sloping plane, and even distance (by bouncing a laser off a distant object). For this, expect to pay upward of $700. An old-school, non-electronic transit costs a few hundred dollars.

Abney level

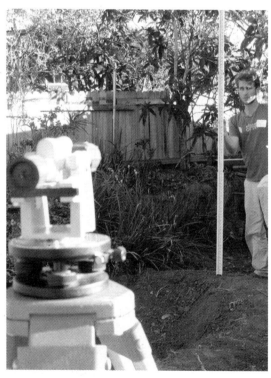

Using a transit *to establish the minimum height for a mulch basin rim for run-on from the adjoining public road.*

FLT GEOSYSTEMS

Transit

Appendix C: Cold-Climate Adaptations

If you live where it gets cold, you must evaluate all greywater system designs in light of possible freezing. Knowledgeable local contractors can ensure that proper precautions are taken. For example, all plumbing should drain between uses, be below frost line in the soil, be insulated, or be in a heated space.

The heat in fresh greywater, plus the microbial activity it fuels as it biodegrades, make freezing rare in distribution systems such as box troughs and infiltration chambers, even in very cold climates. Heaping leaves or other insulating material over the treatment area helps a great deal. To switch distribution from a shallow, freezing-prone zone to a deeper, frost-free one, use a manual valve, or a passive, automatic bypass (Figure C.1). (In remote applications where human contact is not a concern, frozen greywater has been successfully accumulated on the surface of the soil and treated when it thaws.[3])

FIGURE C.2: GREYWATER HEAT EXCHANGER

Falling film heat exchanger *extracts up to 60% of heat from greywater and uses it to preheat incoming shower water.*

FIGURE C.1: AUTOMATIC SWITCHES FROM SHALLOW TO FROST-FREE ZONES/LEVELS

PUMP VERSION

When shallow trench freezes, water will back up and spill over into deeper trench

GRAVITY-FEED VERSION

In cold climates, the **heat in greywater may be its most valuable attribute.** To reclaim it, you can make or buy a heat exchanger,[33,s22] or just wait to drain the bathtub until the heat has escaped into the house.

Here is a list of design suggestions for greywater systems in cold conditions:

❖ **Continuous downhill slope in collection and irrigation piping**—No standing water = nothing to freeze. Greywater is warm enough to melt a film of ice in irrigation piping each time it drains, without buildup. Branched Drains are a distribution system with continuous downhill slope; see photo, p. 70.

❖ **Free-flow surface outlets**—At least 6" *(15 cm)* of fall from the greywater outlet to the surface the water lands on will prevent the outlet from plugging with ice. The ground should slope away steeply from the outlet at first, then may gradually flatten—transitioning from, say, 4% slope to 1–2% within a couple paces of the outlet.

❖ **Insulate the system**—Continuously downhill-sloping pipes may not require any insulation. However, burying them in the soil and covering them with mulch certainly provides some. Mulch basins generally stay unfrozen well above the frost line, because the heat from applied greywater and internal composting is held in by insulating mulch and snow. Composting heat can be cranked up by adding plenty of carbonaceous yard waste (leaves, for example) in the fall, then adding nitrogen via greywater (by peeing in the shower, for example) throughout the winter.

❖ **Apply greywater in a warm microclimate**—The south and west sides of a house, within a windbreak to the north, are significantly less frosty.

❖ **Apply greywater in a Solar Greenhouse**—A Solar Greywater Greenhouse is the ultimate in favorable microclimates, and the best option for year-round treatment. The treatment capacity per square foot in a greenhouse can easily be many multiples of the capacity outdoors. (Each 18°F *(10°C)* increase in temperature doubles the rate of most biological reactions.)

A snowbound greywater greenhouse *in Massachusetts, filled with fresh veggies.*

Appendix D: Greywater in the Nonindustrialized World

There are special considerations to take into account when working with greywater in the nonindustrialized settings in which most of the world's population lives:

- **Water is often scarcer**—Especially where carried in by hand. For this reason, greywater is much more valuable.
- **Greywater-irrigated produce can contribute significant nutrition**—Especially when nearby water sources dry up and direct irrigation with freshwater doesn't make sense.
- **Money is often scarce to nonexistent**—So *any* purchase can be a barrier to implementing a greywater system.
- **Infection rates can be high and sanitation norms low.**
- **It is not unusual to have greywater flowing on public streets and in surface waters**—Where it is a health threat.
- **Many villagers prefer to have washing and bathing occur outdoors or in structures separate from living quarters.**
- **Shade in the tropics is a life necessity**—This can be provided by greywater-fed trees, making outside tasks such as hand laundering much more pleasant.
- **People's immune systems are generally stronger**—So a moderate level of pathogen exposure is sustainable.
- **Cleaning products**—Can be better (home-made soap) or worse (commercial powdered laundry detergent with high levels of fillers and non-biodegradable detergents).
- **The concentration of solids in greywater is often higher**—Due to lower per capita water use.
- **Laws are rarely a consideration.**

Landscape Direct, Dishpan Dump/Bucketing, and Drain Out Back systems are all adaptable to these conditions. However, in many circumstances, the system that follows is ideal...

Greywater Furrow Irrigation

Furrow Irrigation is an ideal system for the nonindustrialized world. A greywater system reduced to its most elemental form, it consists entirely of soil and plants. It can be owner-built and maintained with nothing more than a shovel and a hoe or rake. This description is based on my experience designing and installing nearly a hundred of these systems over several years with a cooperative of village women in Maruata, Michoacán. After this work, greywater in the public streets was rare, irrigation in place for approximately 1000 new fruit trees, and about 100,000 lbs/yr of fruit added to the local economy and nutrition.

The genesis of this system (for me—I've no doubt it has been independently invented countless times) was the resistance of villagers I worked with in Mexico to using mulch.

Traditionally, yards in this coastal village are bare swept earth. With the movement of greywater unimpeded by mulch, furrows in the earth eventually suggested themselves as an option for delivering greywater to plants. Utilizing greywater to irrigate home orchards provides multiple benefits: it eliminates fetid black puddles that otherwise provide habitat for mosquitoes that carry dengue fever, and it can irrigate trees that give fruit and shade, improving nutrition, health, and the economy.

Greywater "main" running down a Tijuana street—a bona fide health threat. In theory, this water could produce fruit and green relief in a sanitary way. Unfortunately, low rainfall, clay soil, and high salt concentration from handwashing with small amounts of hand-carried water and generous amounts of "Fab One-Shot" renders this greywater unusable. Though it is year-round water in a desert, not even weeds grow from it. An enlightened soap factory with a line of biocompatible cleaners and a suitable marketing plan could dramatically change neighborhoods like this all over Mexico, transforming fetid, mucky streets with thriving shade- and fruit-providing trees.

Shallow hand-dug well next to a flooding, feces-filled river.

Washwater from a home feeds a black puddle. This can be rerouted into irrigation furrows (next page) which water and feed about 20 fruit trees. Because the water is spread over a wide area, it never stays on the surface long, so it doesn't stink or breed vermin.

Characteristics and Advantages

❖ **The materials are simple and cheap, and little equipment is necessary**—Soil, trees, a shovel, and a rake or hoe to make the furrows.
❖ **The system requires only ten minutes of maintenance per week.**
❖ **It is necessary to take a multitude of considerations into account to build them optimally**—The design depends on the owners, soil, slope of the land, water sources, sun, existing trees, and more.

Principles of the Design

❖ **Water supply located above**—Water storage and water use should be above the areas to be irrigated.
❖ **The slope and width of the furrows is varied to release more or less water as needed**—For example, more sloped, narrower trenches near the water source and between plants infiltrate less water, whereas flatter, wider trenches over plant roots infiltrate more water.
❖ **To prevent stagnation, the water is distributed widely, to sufficient soil and plants to absorb it all**—A property with gravity-flow springwater is going to need much more dispersal area than a house where water is bucketed in.
❖ **Systems are designed so water does not puddle or soil remain saturated more than 24 hours**—Thus, the water maintains a clear grey color without an unpleasant odor (if it remains stagnant longer, it develops a black color and a nasty smell).
❖ **Each property infiltrates its own greywater**—It doesn't drain into neighboring properties or into the public road.
❖ **The furrows are to be adjusted so the water is distributed uniformly.**
❖ **Water is distributed over more area more easily if the greywater sources are separated**—For example, one spot for dishwashing, another for clothes washing, another for bathing, rather than all these activities taking place in one very wet area and the rest of the land being dry. Other factors to consider when locating water fixtures and work areas are privacy, sun, soil quality, and protecting natural waters from contamination.

Tools and Materials

❖ **Tools**—Shovel or stick, rake or hoe
❖ **Optional tools**—Wheelbarrow, pick, bucket
❖ **Materials**—Soil, fruit trees
❖ **Optional materials**—Compost (so the plants grow well), stones, bricks, cement (to pave bathing/washing areas where the water falls), clay (to line furrows to make water infiltrate more slowly)

Implementation

❖ **Pave the areas where water falls**—Sometimes falling water excavates a hole in the ground, which then forms a stagnant puddle right next to where water is used. By paving it with stone, bricks, cement, or rot-resistant wood, you can avoid this.
❖ **Raise the areas where people walk or stand to wash**—In those areas, the soil tends to compact and erode, leaving the ground lower and wetter. It is healthier and more comfortable if these places are higher and drier. This problem can be fixed by laying down extra dirt once in a while, or paving these areas.
❖ **Review the levels**—Where can the greywater flow by gravity? If necessary, this can be verified by using a water level. Normally, ⅛"/ft (1%) slope is necessary for the water to run down the furrows.
❖ **Review where runoff flows**—The ideal situation is that the furrows for rainwater drainage are not the same as those for greywater drainage. This is because heavy rain can whisk greywater off the property without treatment.

Irrigation furrows for bananas. The more sloped the land, the more sinuous the channel. Note the coconut husk that serves as a valve where the trenches divide.

Garden committee members installing a masonry floor (normally men's work) over the puddle that a neighbor used to stand in while doing laundry.

❖ **Connect the sources of greywater with irrigation need**—Once you've settled where the greywater comes from and how much there is, you can design a connecting system of furrows. The furrow routes can be scratched in the dirt as you work them out.

❖ **Decide how many furrows**—If there is a large quantity of water, make at least two systems of furrows. That way you can change sides when necessary, allowing the other side to rest. The "valve" can be a simple wye in the furrow, with a coconut shell or stone to close off the side that is not in use. Another technique is a movable channel or hose at the water source, shifted from one furrow to another. It is preferable to have this first valve very close to the water source. This is because the beginning of the furrow always has more water, and thus needs a rest more. Moreover, the watercourse before the valve never has a rest, so it should be either very short or of an impermeable material.

Form the Water Channels

If you want more water to infiltrate, for example, near the plants, or in not very permeable soil, make the channel:

❖ Wider
❖ Flatter
❖ Longer and more curvaceous
❖ More permeable
❖ With basins to one side or in the middle where water will pool; if they are in the middle, they have to fill up before the flow continues—a technique that is only useful when the land is at a steeper incline and there is a lot of water

If you want less water to infiltrate, for example, where there are no roots, in very permeable soil, or in very flat soil, make the channel:

❖ Narrower, especially in the bottom of the channel where the water actually runs
❖ Steeper
❖ Narrower and straighter
❖ Less permeable; this can be done by smearing the channel with clay, to form a half tube of clay—remember that greywater itself will lower the permeability of new furrows over time

Typically, the channels will be straighter, narrower, and steeper near the water source, and flatter, wider, and more winding farther away.

For most trees, the roots grow farther from the trunk than the branches do. It is only necessary to make channels pass near the trunk for newly planted trees.

The best situation is that the channels and basins have enough volume to absorb all of the water.

If the volume of water changes dramatically, as it does in tourist lodging sites, the trench cross section can be narrow at the very bottom, and wide above.

Plant the Plants

Plant the trees where they can take best advantage of the greywater and provide greatest benefits of shade,

A giant papaya from greywater-irrigated tree at a house with only hand-carried water for domestic use. The papayas which weren't near greywater trenches didn't bear fruit at all.

privacy, windbreak, etc. Typically, plants that require a lot of water, such as bananas, will be near the water source, and plants that need little water will be nearer the end of the furrows.

Plant intensively right around areas used for washing/bathing. These plants will form a dense network of roots below these constantly wet areas, helping to dry them, as well as providing shade and privacy above. In the tropics most work areas require shade. This system creates low-cost, fresh green shade that gives fruit and deepens over time, instead of costly, high maintenance shade roofs made from cut trees that deteriorate and provide less shade with time. Also, as the water evapotranspires, it cools the air, making the microclimate more comfortable.

Test the System

Pour water into the channels to see where it goes. Adjust anything that needs adjusting.

Explain the System and Its Maintenance

Explain to the owners how to maintain the system. Explain to the children that it is fine to play with the flow of water as it is being sent to the plants, but that they should use a stick, hoe, rake, or their feet, not their hands, because the water is dirty. Also, it is necessary to wash their hands immediately afterward if they do touch the water.

Review How the System Works over Time and the Change of Seasons

Return to the system in a week, a month, and with the change of seasons (dry to wet or wet to dry) to see how the plants are growing and how the maintenance is going.

Planting coconuts for shower runoff. Hiring women gets around the problem that men often spend most of the money they earn on beer. Paying women the same as men (instead of the going rate of about half) helps advance social equality.

Jardineras Co-op replacing dead shade (plastic tarp) over a dishwash station with live shade *(coconut trees from their cooperative nursery, in back of the bicycle). In five years the trees were twice as tall as the rock. They give deep, cool shade—not to mention building material, coconuts, and protection against erosion.*

Team of albanilas (female masons) making a cement channel *to route greywater from a washing area to the first split between Greywater Furrows.*

Appendix E: Pumps, Filters, and Disinfection

Pumping, filtration, or disinfection are complications you're better off without unless there is no way around them. Gravity-driven systems are much simpler, cheaper, and less failure prone. In certain contexts, however, these things make sense—primarily high-flow systems. This section explains how to do them with minimal trouble.

Pumps

The ecological cost of pumps—their manufacture and power consumption—is considerable. There are only two justifications for pumping:

1. When greywater *must* go uphill (e.g., failing septic, no downhill dispersal option).
2. When the improved irrigation efficiency from distributing greywater more widely and evenly is worth more than the materials and electricity involved in pumping. The more greywater and irrigation need you have, the more likely this is.

A pump will likely be the most expensive part of the system. But don't be tempted to buy a cheap pump. You will end up buying the good one anyway, after the cheap one fails. Don't buy a pump unless it is rated to handle at least the lift and volume your system requires.

An effluent pump that is rated to pump a ¾" solid won't choke on unfiltered greywater and is thus the most reliable. These are not cheap: $150 for a low-pressure one, $500 for a high-pressure one. They can be used to pump unfiltered greywater to the landscape through plumbing that has orifices ½" *(12 mm)* or larger, or through a rapid sand filter to drip irrigation. They live submerged in a surge tank and require a float switch to turn them on and off at the appropriate water levels.

Throwaway, cheap, submersible sump pumps are, unfortunately, the most commonly used greywater pumps. They require a pre-pump filter and a backup filter. Experience has shown that filters are not maintained for long, so the pumps are doomed to fail (see Filters, following). They are only appropriate for temporary, drought emergency systems...if that.

A mercury float switch at the end of an electric cord controls many pumps. An advantage of mercury float switches is that the water level at which they turn on and off can be adjusted by tethering them with a different length of free cord. They can also be used with any pump. The disadvantage of this type of float switch is that it can hang up on the pump or the side of the tank and fail to turn on or, worse, fail to turn off. If not held in place by stiff outlet plumbing or such, the pump tends to migrate around the bottom of the tank until it finds the spot that keeps the float switch from shutting off. Sump pumps require submersion for cooling, so running dry will fry them. They are relatively unaffected by pushing for hours against a clogged distribution line, as long as they are submerged—they just turn into electric water heaters.

An integral float switch such as the ones on the top and bottom pumps pictured at right has the advantage that it is relatively unlikely to hang up on anything. It turns on in 7–10" of water and shuts off in 2–4". This can lead to a small amount of water being pumped out frequently, which could mean that only the first plant or two gets watered, if the volume of the distribution lines is large.

Pressure sensors and other schemes for turning pumps on and off often clog with greywater.

Beside being expensive and a maintenance hassle, pumps use electricity. In an average home, *a greywater pump can easily be in the top ten energy-consuming appliances, accounting for 3–10% of total household consumption.* To maximize efficiency:

❖ **Minimize the distance that water drops in collection plumbing and surge tanks before reaching the pump**—A wide, flat surge tank wastes half the fall of a tall, narrow one. Reducing the drop by half may not be that hard and significantly reduces electricity consumption.

❖ **Don't pump water any higher than necessary**—If you only have enough greywater to water half of your landscape, greywater the lower half. Unlike freshwater systems, it rarely makes sense to pump greywater to an elevated tank and gravity feed from there.

*An **effluent pump** that doesn't need filtration and will last for many years is the way to go (a $300 Zabel p-se-12t pictured).[95]*

*A **cheaper effluent pump** doesn't provide quite the longevity or pressure (a $160 Little Giant Model 8E CIA RFS pictured; now discontinued).[88]*

Integral float switch

*One of the **better throwaway pumps** that require a filter (a $273 Little Giant Model 5.5-ASP pictured).*

Mercury float switch

❖ **Use adequate-sized distribution pipe to minimize friction loss**—1" pipe should be adequate for a home system's pressurized greywater main.

❖ **Size your distribution system for adequate flow, and don't pressurize it any more than necessary**—If all the distribution orifices together can only handle half the flow the pump puts out, the pump has to run twice as long. Likewise with pressure; more than 10–15 psi *(70–100 kPa)* is not necessary for most systems, so a pump that maintains 30 psi *(200 kPa)* uses two to three times the necessary energy.

Filters

Filtration is the biggest problem in the systems that require it. Hair and bacterial slime are particularly difficult to handle. Yard-long hairs can work their way through a fine-mesh filter and then wrap around the pump rotor. Bacterial slime can grow on the "filtered" side of the filter, then slough off in large chunks. Filter cleaning is a disgusting task. This is the #1 cause of abandonment for any system that requires filter cleaning. A cheap pump won't work without a pre-pump filter, followed by a net filter around the pump itself. The occasional extremist will clean pre-pump filters, but *no one* cleans the around-the-pump backup filter... with the result that the cheap pump dies.

Filtration is definitely an area for more research. Here are the current options:

No Filtration

If at all possible, no filtration is definitely the way to go.

Solids are easily handled by collection plumbing and are not a problem for soil—they're just compost. A system without a pump or any passages smaller than 1" *(2.5 cm)* doesn't require filtration. Expensive effluent pumps can handle solids, but even these may occasionally have problems with hair. It is all but impossible to achieve automated, even distribution of greywater without filtration (except to a limited extent with a Branched Drain system or an effluent pump to open outlets); but the absence of filter maintenance weighs heavily in the trade-off.

Pre-Drain Filtration

If your system requires only minimal filtration, **catch the solids before they get into the pipes** and get grosser. A simple mesh screen over the kitchen sink drain, for example, filters out a large proportion of solids.

Net Bag

The net bag is the most common, but not especially recommended, greywater filter (see Figure 8.2, photo at right).

The net can be pantyhose or a fine-mesh filter bag for airless paint sprayers (available in hardware stores). 75 micron mesh bags were used as prefiltration in drip irrigation, but this technology fell into disfavor due to an excessively short filter-cleaning interval. Net bags are disgusting to clean. Pantyhose are readily available and cheap enough to throw away when full, especially if already worn. They also stretch to shed the aforementioned bacterial slime.

Net bag filter in a *Drum with Pump.*

Net bags are notorious for dumping gallons of backed-up crud irretrievably into the surge tank when removed for cleaning (see story under Error: Inexpensive Greywater-to-DripIrrigation, Chapter 11). A second filter around the pump is recommended to catch this crud, and a filter on the outlet side is essential with medium-sized emitters. Small-orifice emitters would be a mistake.

Pressure Sand Filtration

Successful greywater-to-drip-irrigation systems have employed a swimming-pool-type pressure sand filter that automatically backflushes, providing a high level of "hands-off" filtration. These can work well, but are expensive and require lots of electricity to push the water through the filter at 40 psi or so, or the energy equivalent of raising the water 100 vertical feet *(3 atm, or 30 m)*.

Note: a non-backflushing, unpressurized sand filter clogs too quickly with greywater.

Settling (Septic) Tank

These are excellent filters, and the required maintenance interval is measured in years or decades instead of days or weeks.

In a septic tank, water sits still long enough for scum to float to the top and sludge to settle to the bottom, leaving smelly, infectious, but clear water in between. The settling tank should have capacity for 1–30 days' flow. More is better, within reason.

Most greywater systems avoid the worst odor and bacteria proliferation problems by distributing water as it's generated, eliminating settling as an option. If effluent dispersal is completely subsurface, storage is not an issue, and this shouldn't matter. Perhaps settling will become more popular in the future, due to its infrequent maintenance. Sludge can be pumped out of small settling tanks with a wet/dry vac.

Septic Tank and Media Filter

This is another proven technique for getting greywater clean enough to use in subsurface drip irrigation (see end of Chapter 8).

Constructed Wetland as Filter

A Constructed Wetland with successively smaller media in the direction of water flow (rocks to gravel) could be a good filter, if sized adequately (see end of Chapter 8).

Caution: unproven design; Constructed Wetlands are experimental as filters.

Disinfection

Ozone and UV disinfection have both been used successfully. I'd trust ozone more. But like filtration, disinfection is best avoided. Unless the greywater is sprayed in sprinklers (illegal except in Wyoming), used in a pond, or returned to fixtures for reuse, disinfection should not be necessary. Plus, disinfection won't accomplish much unless the water is finely filtered first. Indoor reuse in fixtures is the most legitimate application for disinfection (see The Household Water Cascade in Appendix F, and Resources[34,35]).

Ozonators *provide sterilization with far fewer environmental and health side effects than chlorine and may be more reliable than UV due to low water clarity in greywater.*

Appendix F:
Related Aspects of Sustainable Water Use

Natural Purification

Ideally, all water should cascade through the house and yard by gravity, from the highest vertical level and degree of purity to biological treatment in the soil at the lowest level.[34,35] The result is a house surrounded by an oasis of biological productivity nourished by the flow of water and nutrients from the home.

In the natural water cycle, water is purified in two ways: 1) distillation, where evaporation from the ocean leaves particles and dissolved salts behind; and 2) biological land treatment, where microorganisms in topsoil degrade biological contaminants into nutrients, which are removed by plant roots before groundwater recharge (see p. 18 for effectiveness factors).

Both natural distillation and biological land treatment compare favorably in effectiveness with artificial options such as activated sludge treatment. Conventional water use and artificial treatment, by ignoring the structure and logic of the natural water cycle, encourages excess, depletes and contaminates aquifers, contaminates aquatic ecosystems, and bleeds the land of nutrients.

Natural Purification by Soil Bacteria and Plant Roots

In one cubic foot[m] of rich topsoil there are:

* *One and a half million square feet of treatment area*
* *Three trillion beneficial bacteria*
* *Enough root hairs to wrap around the perimeter of the US*
* *Countless specialized proteins which pump specific nutrient molecules (e.g., nitrate) through root hair cell walls*

Effectiveness:

* *Slow passage through one foot of soil removes about 90% of pathogens*
* *Code allows untreated drinking water well one hundred feet from a septic leachfield*

FIGURE F.1: A HOUSEHOLD WATER CASCADE
(THE WIDTH OF THE LINES CORRESPONDS APPROXIMATELY TO THE VOLUME OF WATER FLOWING THROUGH THAT PATH)

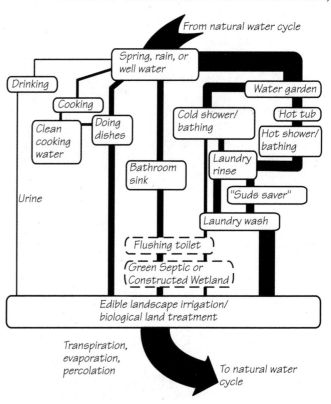

The Household Water Cascade

Water conservation is popular during a water shortage. However, there are more reasons to cascade water and use it ultimately for irrigation: conserving nutrients, conserving the energy used to heat water, and reducing dispersal problems. Keep these factors in mind when designing the water flow through a living environment in which water is plentiful.

Elevation relationships are a major consideration in the siting of different elements of the water cascade, such as water tanks, gardens, solar heaters, buildings, cooking areas, kitchen gardens, washing areas, bathing gardens, and edible landscaping. Within the home, drinking is the highest use, followed by cooking, bathing, handwashing, dishwashing, and clothes washing, in descending order of both water quality required and elevation. Ecologically, it only makes sense to dump feces into water when dry feces dispersal is infeasible. If so, this use comes last in the cascade.

---

[m]*Metric: 1 ft³ = 28 L; 1.5 million ft² = 14 hectare; 1 ft = 30 cm; 100' = 30 m.*

Even if you're not building your own radical eco-home, cascading can still be employed in simple ways. For instance, water used to steam vegetables or boil pasta can be substituted for some of the hot water for doing dishes. The water might be a little cloudy, but no more than it would be after washing a few dishes in clean water. "Suds saver" washing machines are a classic example of cascading; laundry rinse water is pumped to a sink or tank, then drawn back into the machine for use as wash water in the next load.

When showering in bathrooms with a shower / tub combination, save the shower water in the tub for handwashing clothes. The water will already be hot, so just add a little detergent. When finished, siphon the water outside.

Rainwater Harvesting

Even in dry climates, quite a bit of water falls from the sky. In industrialized nations the propensity is to seal the surface of the soil with pavement, roofing, plastic sheeting, and compaction—transforming groundwater recharge zones into flash flood generation zones. (Los Angeles supposedly absorbs only 10% of the water it used to.) In arid lands, water is best stored in covered tanks or in groundwater. Groundwater can be supplemented in wet decades and drawn upon in dry ones, a practice called "conjunctive use." To capture runoff and get it to seep quickly into the ground, spread mulch, add plants, and shape catchment basins and swales in the surface of the soil (see Mulch Basin Design, end of Chapter 5).

More significant than rainwater quantity is its quality. When irrigation greywater evaporates, salt is left behind in ever-increasing concentrations. Rain has virtually no dissolved salts and is effective for flushing excess salts from the root zone (see Preserving Soil Quality, Chapter 5). Our book *Water Storage*[10] describes how to store rainwater in soil and groundwater and how to collect it in ponds or tanks.

Composting Toilets

Used in conjunction with greywater systems, composting toilets promise a household that uses little water, recycles all of its nutrients and water, and employs no conventional treatment systems at all. Proceed with caution in pursuit of this lofty ideal. Though some composting toilets have worked well for decades, we have collected mixed reviews of their function. Carefully research your toilet decision[36,37,38,s15] (and please share your experiences, as we are researching books on flush toilet alternatives and rainwater harvesting[39,40]).

The "lid": a super-easy, inexpensive cascade retrofit *that enables hands to be washed in the flow of freshwater on its way to the toilet bowl.[s7]*

Rainwater harvesting *provides all domestic water by gravity for a house near Hilo, Hawaii.*

There are dozens of waterless toilet technologies to choose from for different population densities and contexts.
The Chesapeake Bay Foundation's 32,000 ft² (3,000 m²) headquarters (above) features capacity for 160,000 toilet uses a year, right on the bay. This is the first LEED Platinum-Certified building. It uses photovoltaics, solar hot water, rainwater collection, natural lighting/ventilation, and ground-source heating/cooling. Its water conservation technologies include waterless Clivus composting toilets (seat and basement treatment units at right). The use of composting toilets demonstrates a key technology for eliminating nutrient pollution of water resources.

Appendix G:
Greywater Regulation Revolution

A move is afoot toward sensible greywater codes in the US. The greywater code in Arizona, the pioneer, is reproduced here. New Mexico has a similar code, Texas has one that needs some work, and Nevada is about to introduce one like Arizona's. In Arizona your greywater system is automatically permitted if it meets this handful of (mostly) reasonable requirements. If only all jurisdictions were so levelheaded! For dealing with greywater codes anywhere else, see our *Builder's Greywater Guide.*[6] It has much more information about greywater codes (including how to improve them) as well as other aspects of incorporating greywater systems in new construction and remodeling. (There is also information on greywater laws in our Greywater Policy Center, oasisdesign.net/greywater/law.)

Arizona Greywater Standards

R18-9-711. Type 1 Reclaimed Water General Permit for Gray Water

A. A Type 1 Reclaimed Water General Permit allows private residential direct reuse of gray water for a flow of less than 400 gallons per day if all the following conditions are met:

1. Human contact with gray water and soil irrigated by gray water is avoided;
2. Gray water originating from the residence is used and contained within the property boundary for household gardening, composting, lawn watering, or landscape irrigation;
3. Surface application of gray water is not used for irrigation of food plants, except for citrus and nut trees; [*This is a funny provision; it should prohibit direct contact between greywater and consumable portions of food plants.*]
4. The gray water does not contain hazardous chemicals derived from activities such as cleaning car parts, washing greasy or oily rags, or disposing of waste solutions from home photo labs or similar hobbyist or home occupational activities;
5. The application of gray water is managed to minimize standing water on the surface;
6. The gray water system is constructed so that if blockage, plugging, or backup of the system occurs, gray water can be directed into the sewage collection system or onsite wastewater treatment and disposal system, as applicable. The gray water system may include a means of filtration to reduce plugging and extend system lifetime;
7. Any gray water storage tank is covered to restrict access and to eliminate habitat for mosquitoes or other vectors;
8. The gray water system is sited outside of a floodway;
9. The gray water system is operated to maintain a minimum vertical separation distance of at least five feet from the point of gray water application to the top of the seasonally high groundwater table;
10. For residences using an onsite wastewater treatment facility for black water treatment and disposal, the use of a gray water system does not change the design, capacity, or reserve area requirements for the onsite wastewater treatment facility at the residence, and ensures that the facility can handle the combined black water and gray water flow if the gray water system fails or is not fully used;
11. Any pressure piping used in a gray water system that may be susceptible to cross connection with a potable water system clearly indicates that the piping does not carry potable water;
12. Gray water applied by surface irrigation does not contain water used to wash diapers or similarly soiled or infectious garments unless the gray water is disinfected before irrigation; and
13. Surface irrigation by gray water is only by flood or drip irrigation.

B. Prohibitions. The following are prohibited:
1. Gray water use for purposes other than irrigation, and
2. Spray irrigation.

C. Towns, cities, or counties may further limit the use of gray water described in this Section by rule or ordinance.

Appendix H: Measurements and Conversions

How units are dealt with in this book:

Any measurement clearly expressible without numbers or units is expressed without them (e.g., "an arm's length").

Where the text flow is too chopped up by non-essential numbers, they are relegated to footnotes or this page. Metric conversions of pipe sizes are here, only.

Units that are approximations or don't really matter are given to the nearest round number or conventional expression. Thus, a photo of a surge tank might be captioned "55 gal *(200 L)* tank" rather than "55 gal *(206.8 L)* tank."

Using the tables:

Everything in the same row is equal. For example: 1' = 12" = 0.3 m = 30 cm.

LENGTH / HEIGHT

Feet ft'	Inches in"	Meters m	Centimeters cm	*<to* *From*
1	12	0.30	30	**ft**—*Long as…your foot*
0.08	1	0.025	2.5	**in**—*Long as 1st knuckle of the thumb*
3.28	39.37	1	100	**m**—*A long stride*

AREA

Square meters m²	Square feet ft²	Acres ac	Hectares ha	*<to* *From*
1	10.76			**m²**
0.093	1			**ft²**
4,047	43,560	1	0.405	**ac**
10,000	107,639	2.47	1	**ha**

VOLUME

Cubic meters m³	Liters L	Gallons gal	Cubic feet ft³	*<to* *From*
1	1000	264.17	35.3	**m³** *A cube 40" on a side*
0.001	1	0.26	0.0353	**L**
0.00387	3.78	1	0.134	**gal** *1 US gal = 0.833 imperial gal*
0.0283	28.3	7.481	1	**ft³**
0.2	200	55	7.06	*Big plastic or steel drum*
113	113,562	30,000	4,010	*Standard suburban swimming pool*
1,233	1,233,482	325,851	43,560	*1 acre-foot (af)*
0.00235	2.35	0.62	0.0829	*1" of water on 1 ft²*
	1			*1 mm of water on 1 m²*

FLOW

Abbreviations: gallons per minute (**gpm**), gallons per day (**gpd**), liters per minute (**Lpm**), cubic meters per day (**m³/day**), acre-feet per year (**afy**)

From to>	gpm	gpd	Lpm	m³/day	afy
1 gpm	1	1440	3.79	5.45	1.61
1 gpd	0.0007	1	0.0026	0.0038	0.0011
Lpm	0.264	360	1	1.44	0.43
m³/day	0.183	264	0.694	1	0.296
afy	0.620	892	2.34	3.38	1

More abbreviations not converted above: liters per day (**Lpd**), gallons per week (**gpw**), gallons per year (**gpy**), liters per week (**Lpw**), cubic meters per year (**m³/yr**)

*An industrialized world household of four uses roughly **1 m³** a day of water.*
*A nonindustrialized world household of ten uses roughly **1 m³** a day of water.*
*A healthy stream of urine is a bit over **1 Lpm**, a bit under **0.3 gpm**.*

PRESSURE

Abbreviations: atmospheres (**atm**), pounds per square inch (**psi**), kilopascals (**kPa**)

atm	psi	kPa	Feet	Meters	*<to* *From*
1	14.70	101	33.9	10.3	**atm** = *A 1"x1" column of air from the Earth to space in height weighs 14.7 pounds.*
0.0680	1	6.89	2.31	0.703	**psi**
0.0099	0.145	1	0.334	0.102	**kPa**
0.0295	0.433	2.99	1	0.305	**Feet**
0.0978	1.42	9.80	3.28	1	**Meters**
6.80	100	689	231	70.3	*Max pressure for household plumbing, ideal pressure for fire hoses*
1.70	25	172	57.7	17.6	*Min pressure typical for washer, demand heater, toilet valves*

PIPE SIZES

US	Metric
½"	15 mm
¾"	20 mm
1"	25 mm
1¼"	32 mm
1½"	40 mm
2"	50 mm
2½"	65 mm
3"	80 mm
4"	100 mm
6"	150 mm
12"	300 mm

Resources

Further Reading and Resources

Note: Oasis Greywater Extras[43] includes a PDF of resources and suppliers with clickable links and email addresses. Electronic extras packets for each book are included free with books purchased from our online store, oasisdesign.net/catalog

[1] **Relative Health Hazard of Different Waters** oasisdesign.net/water/quality/coliform.htm *Understanding and converting bacteriological water quality measurements to real world measurements. Water Quality Testing Information Packet; How to Do Water Tests Simply, Inexpensively, and Accurately.* oasisdesign.net/greywater/law/ california/ #references *Statistical analysis of health hazard from greywater.*

[2] **Sewers, Sludge Treatment, Sludge** riles.org/library.htm *Various writings on the evils of sewers and advantages of nutrient reclamation.* oasisdesign.net/wastewater/sewer/beach.htm *A letter about misinterpretation of a study of contamination from oceanfront septics, and the inadvisability of sewering.*

[3] **Green Land—Clean Streams: The Beneficial Use of Waste Water Through Land Treatment** R. Michael Stevens, 1972. Temple University's Center for the Study of Federalism *Analysis of large-scale land treatment facilities. Out of print; copy at the library at Temple U. Summary table of treatment effectiveness (amazingly high, even for overland flow) is reprinted in our Builder's Greywater Guide.[6]*

[4] **Greywater Policy Center** oasisdesign.net/greywater/law *Includes CA, AZ, and other greywater laws, and suggested policy improvements.* **States with rational regulations that exempt simple systems with surface application of greywater from permits: AZ, NM, TX, MT, NV, and WY...as** far as we can make out. Everyone has a different way of doing it, change is rapid, and confusion rampant...even among regulators. If you are told greywater is illegal where you are, ask politely for the code reference and make sure it is current.*

[5] **Greywater Pilot Project Final Report** Los Angeles Department of Water Reclamation, 1992. Los Angeles Department of Water and Power, Los Angeles, CA. (800) 342-5397, ccenter@ladwp.com ladwp.com *First quantitative field testing of greywater health safety. Report available from* water. ca.gov/wateruseefficiency/docs/monitoringGW_Use.pdf

[6] **Builder's Greywater Guide** Art Ludwig, 2006. Oasis Design, Santa Barbara, CA. (805) 967-9956, oasis@oasisdesign.net oasisdesign.net/greywater/buildersguide *Supplement to* Create an Oasis; *of interest if your project involves permitting, inspection, building a system for someone else, writing or applying codes, or greywater research.*

[7] **National Environmental Services Center** West Virginia University, Morgantown, WV. (800) 624-8301 ext. 3, info@mail.nesc.wvu.edu nesc.wvu.edu/wastewater.cfm *Clearinghouse with a wealth of information on small- to large-scale wastewater treatment.*

[8] **The Septic System Owner's Manual** Lloyd Kahn, 2007. Shelter Publications Inc., Bolinas, CA. (415) 868-0280, shelter@shelterpub.com shelterpub.com *Everything you need to know about maintaining a septic system. Includes section on alternative systems.*

[9] **Rainwater Harvesting for Drylands and Beyond, Volume 1, 2nd Edition** Brad Lancaster, 2013. **Rainwater Harvesting for Drylands and Beyond, Volume 2, Water-Harvesting Earthworks** Brad Lancaster, 2008. Rainsource Press, Tucson, AZ. brad@harvestingrainwater.com harvestingrainwater.com *Available from* oasisdesign.net/catalog

[10] **Water Storage** Art Ludwig, 2013. Oasis Design, Santa Barbara, CA. (805) 967-9956, oasis@oasisdesign.net oasisdesign.net/water/storage *Tanks, cisterns, aquifers, and ponds for domestic supply, fire, and emergency use. Includes how to make ferrocement water tanks.*

[11] **Residential End Uses of Water Study (REUWS)** Peter W. Mayer et. al., 1999. American Water Works Association/Water Research Foundation, Denver, CO. (303) 347-6100, info@WaterRF.org waterrf.org/ PublicReportLibrary/RFR90781_1999_241A.pdf *In this study special data loggers were attached to the water meters in 1,188 homes, in 14 cities. Data obtained allowed researchers to separate water usage into individual end-use categories. 6,000 households responded to a survey about water use, and 12,000 households had their billing records incorporated into the study.*

[12] **Unless you are in Texas,** *where use of greywater to keep expansive clay soils around a foundation permanently wet is officially encouraged. Opinions vary on advisability. If your greywater system fails, your foundation is liable to crack!*

[13] **Cost-Benefit Spreadsheet** ReWater Systems[55] *has done comprehensive cost-benefit analysis of greywater systems. They have an unpublished spreadsheet you might be able to talk them into letting you use for a good cause.*

[14] **Complete Home Plumbing, 2nd edition** Scott Atkinson, editor, 2001. Sunset Books, Menlo Park, CA. Available at oxmoorhouse.com *Plumbing know-how for repairs, remodels, or building from scratch. Easy-to-follow text and photos illustrate basic and advanced projects, from simply fixing a leaky faucet to remodeling a kitchen or adding a bath. One chapter covers plumbing outdoors. A must for every homeowner's bookshelf.*

[15] **Principles of Ecological Design** Art Ludwig, 2003. Oasis Design, Santa Barbara, CA. (805) 967-9956, oasis@oasisdesign.net oasisdesign.net/design/principles.htm *Principles for redesigning our way of life to live better with less resource use (description on inside back cover).*

[16] **Cob Cottage Company** Ianto Evans, Linda Smiley. Coquille, OR. (541) 396-1825, cob@cobcottage.com cobcottage.com *Thanks to Ianto for insights about Radical Plumbing.*

[17] **Guide to Greywater-Compatible Cleaning Products** Ecology Center. Berkeley, CA. (510) 548-2220, erc@ecologycenter.org ecologycenter.org/factsheets/greywater-cleaning-products/ *Easy-to-use guide to what chemicals and products are safe to put down the drain based on your type of greywater system.*

[18] **Untried ideas for urine management in dry, clay soil environments:** *1. Constructed Wetland populated with plants that extract nutrients but not salt (assuming such plants exist). Leftover salty water could be routed to a dispersal field, and nutrient-laden wetland plants harvested and spread in the garden as fertilizing mulch.* *2. I suspect that salination could be slowed in critical environments by using less dietary salt.*

[19] **Cadillac Desert: The American West and Its Disappearing Water** Mark Reisner, 1993. Penguin Books, New York, NY penguin.com *Exceedingly well-researched history of Western water.*

[20] **Washington Toxics Coalition** Seattle, WA. (206) 632-1545 watoxics.org/ healthy-living *Alternatives to most household toxins.*

[21] **The Book of Bamboo** David Farrelly, 1984. **Bamboo World: The Growing and Use of Clumping Bamboos** Victor Cusack, Deirdre Stewart, 2000. Simon & Schuster bambooworldbook.com.au

[22] **Designing and Maintaining Your Edible Landscape Naturally** Robert Kourik, 1986 robertkourik.com *Landmark reference on edible landscaping. A phenomenal quantity of quality information. Out of print, but available used. Ideally an edible landscape is designed in "four dimensions" (i.e., time as well as 3D space). Properly selected varieties yield a steady stream of fruit throughout the growing season (could be all year), instead of an inundation for a few months. See our website for more:* oasisdesign.net/landscaping/fruittrees.htm Also **Understanding Roots** Robert Kourik, 2015 robertkourik.com *How roots work and how to best apply mulch, fertilizer, compost, and water.*

[24] **Alternative Septic System: Watson Wick** Tom Watson. P.O. Box 8, Embudo, NM. (505) 501-0949 oasisdesign.net/compostingtoilets/watsonwick.htm *Consulting.*

[25] **The Food and Heat Producing Solar Greenhouse: Design, Construction, Operation** Rick Fisher, Bill Yanda, 1980. John Muir Publications, Inc. *Excellent. Out of print but available used online.*

[26] **Earthship Sewage Treatment**. Earthship Biotecture, Taos, NM. (575) 751-0462, reception@earthship.com earthship.com/Systems/ sewagetreatment *Earthships use greenhouses to create passive comfort and year-round food production in harsh mountain climates. Greywater is used and cleaned in interior botanical cells, then toilets. After toilets, water is contained and treated, and used a fourth time in exterior botanical cells.*

[27] **Graywater Treatment Using Constructed Wetlands** Adam Jokerst et. al., 2012. US Environmental Protection Agency, Office of Research and Development, Cincinnati, OH. (513) 569-7562 nepis.epa.gov/Adobe/PDF/P100FSPJ.pdf *More reports available at* water. epa.gov/type/wetlands/restore/cwetlands.cfm

[28] **How to measure gravity flow of greywater with a dipper box:** *Get the inlet set right so it cannot pin the dipping trough in the down position (adding a double ell to the inlet helps). Then there will be one dip for every 1½ gal of flow. With a battery-powered counter and a magnetic reed switch you can count dips, thus measuring an intermittent flow of cruddy water at atmospheric pressure. This is just about impossible to do any other way.*

[29] **Can a 4,000 ft² Home Be Green?** Art Ludwig. Oasis Design, Santa Barbara, CA. (805) 967-9956, oasis@oasisdesign.net oasisdesign.net/faq/green4000ft2home.htm

30 **Monitoring Graywater Use: Three Case Studies in California** Alison Whitney et al., 1999. California Department of Water Resources, Sacramento, CA. (916) 653-1097 water.ca.gov/wateruseefficiency/docs/monitoringGW_Use.pdf

31 **Dry Toilets** Centro de Innovación en Tecnología Alternativa, A.C. Cuernavaca, Morelos, Mexico. (52-777) 382 15 82 acua@terra.com.mx esac.laneta.apc.org/citaing.htm *Well-proven designs for dry toilets.*

33 **Design and Analysis of a Residential Greywater Heat Recovery System** G. Proskiw, 1995. Available from builditsolar.com *Energy used to heat water can be recovered and stored to heat water again. Systems and installers can be found online.*

34 **Indoor Greywater Reuse** Art Ludwig. Oasis Design, Santa Barbara, CA. (805) 967-9956, oasis@oasisdesign.net oasisdesign.net/greywater/indoors *Indoors, the "receiving landscape" is plumbing fixtures. Especially noteworthy is the Toronto Healthy House, where all greywater is recycled directly to fixtures.*

35 **Residential Water Reuse** Murray Milne, 1979. California Institute for Water Resources (formerly California Water Resources Center), University of California, Davis, CA. (510) 987-9124. Available at fastonline.org/CD3WD_40/JF/424/18-401.pdf *550-page, readable goldmine of information and history of water reuse; 50-page annotated bibliography.*

36 **Excreta Disposal for Rural Areas and Small Communities** Edmund Wagner, J. N. Laniox, 1958. World Health Organization Monograph Series No. 39, Geneva, Switzerland. Available at apps.who.int/iris *Information on the effectiveness of soils for containing and processing nutrient and pathogen contamination from human feces, as well as other technologies.*

37 **Composting Toilet System Book** David Del Porto, Carol Steinfeld, 2004. Ecowaters Projects, New Bedford, MA. (978) 318-7033, info@ecowaters.org ecowaters.org *Information on composting toilets.*

38 **The Toilet Papers: Recycling Waste and Conserving Water** Sim Van Der Ryn, 1999. Chelsea Green Publishing, White River Junction, VT. (802) 295-6300, web@chelseagreen.com chelseagreen.com

39 **Toilet Alternatives** (book in progress) Art Ludwig. Oasis Design, Santa Barbara, CA. (805) 967-9956, oasis@oasisdesign.net oasisdesign.net/compostingtoilets/book *Comprehensive guide to alternatives to the flush toilet for homeowners, builders, and regulators.*

40 **Rainwater Harvesting and Runoff Management** (book in progress) Art Ludwig. Oasis Design, Santa Barbara, CA. (805) 967-9956, oasis@oasisdesign.net oasisdesign.net/water/rainharvesting

41 **Long-Term Effects of Landscape Irrigation Using Household Greywater—Literature Review and Synthesis** Larry Roesner, Yaling Qian, 2006. Water Environment Research Foundation, Alexandria, VA. (571) 384-2100, werf@werf.org. Available at www.werf.org *Excellent summary of current state of greywater science.*

42 **GreywaterAction.org** *Training for lay and professional installers, active in greywater politics.* **The Water-Wise Home** Laura Allen, 2015. Storey Press, North Adams, MA. greywateraction.org/contentpublications *How to install a greywater or rainwater catchment system, design a rain garden, and build a waterless composting toilet.*

43 **Oasis Greywater Extras** oasisdesign.net/greywater/extras *Editable home water makeover checklist, more examples/site plans/photos, PDF of resources and suppliers with clickable links and email addresses, Excel calculator for perk rate and fixture flows.*

44 **Water Storage Extras** oasisdesign.net/water/storage/extras *Excel calculator for tank construction, water pressures and flow rates, tank and pipe material information.*

45 **Laundry to Landscape Instructional DVD** oasisdesign.net/greywater/laundry *Two hours of visuals and instructions for making L2L systems in a wide variety of situations. Enough information for a homeowner to install a system or a landscaper to add L2L systems to their landscaping business.*

Suppliers (References s1-)

Caution: Unless specifically noted, we don't know anything about the suppliers' experience or the quality of their offerings. Supplier information changes rapidly; this list was last updated August 2015.

s1 **Compass Minerals (formerly North American Salt Co.)** Overland Park, KS. (913) 344-9200 nasalt.com/products-applications/water-conditioning/residential *Manufacturer of potassium chloride water softener salt. Contact for suppliers in your area.*

s2 **3-way valves** *More likely found through pool and spa places than regular plumbing supply houses. We also sell these valves through oasisdesign.net/catalog*

s3 **Orenco Systems** Sutherlin, OR. (800) 348-9843, (541) 459-4449 orenco.com *Established makers of residential and small community secondary treatment systems; sells components, gives seminars.*

s4 **Fluid Dynamic Siphons, Inc.** Colorado Springs, CO. (800) 888-5653, (719) 632-6899, info@siphons.com siphons.com *"The primary use of the Automatic Siphon is to dose leachfields, sand filters, and other soil absorption systems. They may also be used to maintain minimum water velocities to insure proper scouring action of the liquid in the pipe lines."*

s5 **ReWater Systems** Thousand Oaks, CA. (805) 716-0104, support@rewater.com rewater.com *Makers of a range of manual and automated single-family to commercial greywater systems from $1,795 and up (2015). Source for proprietary controllers and underground emitters. Active in greywater politics.*

s6 **Pacific Echo, Inc.** Torrance, CA. (310) 539-1822 pacificecho.com *Makers of flexible PVC. Call for local distributor.*

s7 **Real Goods** Hopland, CA. (800) 919-2400, (707) 472-2430 realgoods.com *Source for the "lid" hand-wash-to-toilet-flush sink*

s8 **Little Giant Pump Company** Fort Wayne, IN. (844) 250-4982, PlumbingHVAC@fele.com littlegiant.com

s9 **Oasis Design** Santa Barbara, CA. (805) 967-9956, oasis@oasisdesign.net oasisdesign.net/catalog, oasisdesign.net/about/contact. *Supplier of double ells pre-drilled with access plugs, 3-way valves, fruit tree and plant lists, books.*

s10 **Geoflow** Corte Madera, CA. (800) 828-3388, (415) 927–6000, krf@geoflow.com geoflow.com *Their premium underground drip irrigation tubing is impregnated with herbicide to keep roots out and has a good reliability record.*

s11 **Oasis Biocompatible Cleaners** Distributed by Bio-Pac, Inc., Incline Village, NV. (775) 831-9493, info@bio-pac.com www.bio-pac.com *Makers of plant and soil biocompatible cleaners.*

s12 **Clean Water Components** Oakland, CA. andrew@cleanwatercomponents.com cleanwatercomponents.com *Good source for greywater- and rainwater-specific components.*

DripWorks, Inc. Willits, CA. (800) 522-3734, support@dripworks.com dripworks.com *Good source for polyethylene and vinyl microtubing, dripline, and automatic and electrical valves. Don't buy their 1" LDPE tubing; it comes flattened and kinked.*

Aqua-Flo Supply Goleta, CA. (805) 967-2374 aquaflo.com *A storefront/UPS source for greywater system components.*

s13 **Infiltrator Water Technologies (formerly Infiltrator Systems)** Old Saybrook, CT. (800) 221-4436, (860) 577-7000, info@infiltratorwater.com infiltratorwater.com *Originator of plastic "infiltrator" gravelless infiltration chambers. Sells through local distributors.*

s14 **NutriCycle Systems** John Hanson, Jefferson, MD. (301) 371-9172, jhanson@nutricyclesystems.com www.nutricyclesystems.com *"Nutrient recycling system" composting toilet, box trough greywater systems. Leaching chamber and box trough designs are thanks to John Hanson.*

s15 **Clivus Multrum, Inc.** Lawrence, MA. (800) 425-4887, (978) 725-5591 clivusmultrum.com *Longtime manufacturer and distributor of composting toilets. Supplier of greywater systems/information. Half pipe infiltration galleys, greenhouse, and freeze switch designs are courtesy of Carl Lindstrom.*

s16 **John Todd Ecological Design, Inc.** Woods Hole, MA. (508) 548-2545, info@toddecological.com toddecological.com *Pioneer provider of site-specific, integrated wastewater solutions including greenhouse aquatics, Constructed Wetlands, stormwater management, etc.*

s17 **Tad Montgomery & Associates** Brattleboro, VT. (802) 251-0502, eco@tadmontgomery.com tadmontgomery.com *Ecological engineering and design, focus on code-approved systems in northeast US, Constructed Wetlands, composting toilets, etc.*

s18 **BioHabitats (formerly Natural Systems)** Baltimore, MD. (800) 220-0919 *An engineering firm specializing in Constructed Wetlands.*

s20 **Polylok, Inc.** Wallingford, CT. (888) 765-9565 polylok.com *Call them to find local dealers, then ask local dealers about making a custom dipper box for you, modify a standard dipper, or use the components to make one yourself.*

s21 *Surprise! The outfit that used to sell these is no more. We could put a new fly-by-night residential greywater-to-toilet system vendor here...but then we'd have to take it out in turn in the next revision when they've gone out of business... we're just going to leave this here as a symbolic placeholder for all such outfits.*

s22 **WaterFilm Energy Inc.** Medford, NY. (631) 291-5147, gfxi@optonline.net gfxtechnology.com *Makers of a greywater heat exchanger. It likes ≥ 24" fall to do its job, and works best with extensive shower use.*

s23 **Valterra Products, LLC.** Mission Hills, CA. (818) 898-1671 valterra.com *Makers of RV dump valves. Check website for distributors in your area.*

s24 **Hydro-Rain** Salt Lake City, UT. (888) HYDRORAIN, hydrorain.com *Manufacturer of Blu-Lock HDPE irrigation fittings and pipe. Visit website to find a distributor in your area.*

Index

About the Author

Optimal, integrated design has been Art Ludwig's day job for 35 years. His specialty is complex, deep green, integrated "systems of systems" for water, wastewater, energy, shelter, and transportation. Designing these systems requires coordinating multiple specialties and coming up with original innovations to fill gaps.

Art created his own program in ecological systems design at SBCC and UC Berkeley, and through extensive independent study. His curriculum included calculus, chemistry, physics, cell biology, soil science, field botany, systems ecology, physiology, structural analysis, mechanical drafting, welding, and metal working. Art has studied and worked in 27 different countries, attaining fluency in five languages.

At UC Berkeley, his research led to the development of the first laundry detergent biocompatible with plants and soil. He went on to found a successful manufacturing business to distribute it, which he sold in 1996.

Decades after their first publication, Art's books *Create an Oasis with Greywater* and *Water Storage* still top Amazon's list of best-selling plumbing books. His 500-page website, oasisdesign.net, is top-ranked by Google for topics ranging from search engine optimization to integrated design for fire to understanding water quality measurements.

Art developed numerous original innovations that he has published, unpatented, into the public domain for the common good. These include the Branched Drain and Laundry to Landscape greywater systems. The latter, a best practice that has qualified for rebates and federal job training stimulus funds in California, has propagated worldwide.

He has contributed to building codes in three states. His quantitative analysis of the health risks of greywater cleared the way for more rational regulation of greywater in California, where he played a major role in the crafting of new greywater standards. Art also spearheaded the introduction of a bill legalizing research on sustainable building in California.

In 2012, Art hosted a landmark sustainability policy colloquium bringing together leaders in natural building, permaculture, and public interest activism with heads of building and health departments. He was a keynote speaker at the California Association of Building Officials' annual conference later that year. His quantitative analysis of historical and emerging hazards attributable to the built environment helps regulators and policymakers address the dramatic rise in emerging hazards.

Art has done hundreds of presentations and workshops on diverse topics from structural engineering of natural buildings to financial management to understanding water. His consulting clients include city agencies, state governments, ecovillages, retreat centers, etc. Over a nine-year period, he assisted an indigenous community in Mexico with all aspects of sustainable development. Over the past several years, Art has dedicated approximately a thousand hours a year to public interest research and sustainability policy activism.

Art lives with his family by a creek in the mountains behind Santa Barbara, California. The house exemplifies Art's goal of living better with less use of resources: the home utilizes about $5 a month of electricity and gas per person and 14 gallons of water a day per person indoors. Rainwater, reused water, and only 20 gallons of metered water a day for irrigation outdoors produces 150 pounds of fresh fruit per year per person—at least four different kinds any day of the year. The quarter-acre property infiltrates more water to the underlying aquifer than it consumes.

Working on the formula for the first plant and soil biocompatible laundry detergent.

Testing ingredients on plants at the UC Berkeley Gill Tract greenhouse.

House Features After Water Makeover

General
- Seven people on a quarter-acre in Santa Barbara, California
- About 250 ft² of house per person

Efficient fixtures
- Eco-Luxury Bathing Chamber—*save half the water and energy of a regular shower*
- Low-flow showerheads, faucet aerators
- Bathroom faucets—*turned down to 0.5 gpm*
- UHE toilets—*use 0.8 gal/ flush*

Water reuse
- Laundry to Landscape greywater
- Branched Drain greywater—*for all fixtures except washer*
- Green Septic—*subsoil infiltration chambers provide sanitary subsoil irrigation and purification of toilet water*

Alternate water supply
- 100% of site rainfall infiltrated—*into storage in the root zone (about 35,000 gal capacity)*
- Run-on diverted onto site and infiltrated into soil—*100,000–500,000 gal/ year for plants and aquifer recharge*
- Rooftop rainwater—*3,500 gal cistern provides fire emergency water in summer, laundry and toilet supply in winter*

Energy
- Electricity, propane—*about $30/ month total for both*
- Passive solar space and water heating—*about 90%*
- Solar clothes dryer—*aka laundry line*
- Firewood—*oaks on site provide the tiny additional bit of heating needed*

Materials
- Yard clippings—*all transformed into soil fertility on site by mulch basins*
- Toxic products—*not purchased*

Complete home water budget, *before and after water makeover; visual summary in graph at right.*

Main variables for you to input					
Input numbers in green highlight below. For help, see links and calculators at right					
Before	**After**	Units		Change	% change
6	6		Average population	0	0%
27.0		hcf/mo	Average metered water usage		
$10.00	$5.00	$/hcf	Marginal (highest) water rate	-$5.00	-50%
15.6		hcf/mo	Indoor usage (metered or estimate)		
14,191	14,191	ft2	Area of lot	0	0%
1,939	1,939	ft2	Area of roof	0	0%
100	100	ft2	Area of hardscape	0	0%
0	0	ft2	Lawn area	0	~
5,928	5,928	ft2	Irrigated landscape area	0	0%
0	4,000	ft2	Area developed for infiltration	4,000	~
6	6	ft2	Open water surface	0	0%
6,218	1,918	ft2	Other area		
87,000	87,000	ft2	Run-on catchment area to infiltration	0	0%
70	60	Min/in	Saturated soil perk rate	-10	-14%
20		in/yr	Average yearly rainfall		
7		in/yr	Reference drought year rainfall		
1		in/hr	Reference peak rainfall event		
51		in/yr	Potential evapotranspiration		
55		in/yr	Evaporation from water surface		
180		days	Average length of dry season		

SUMMARY					
before	after	units	item	Change	% change
Water supply					
175,968	175,968	gpy	Water from sky on lot	0	0%
0	539,400	gpy	Run on water captured	539,400	~
239,760	79,571	gpy	Metered water use	-160,189	-67%
50,188	65,331	gpy	Rainfall from sky utilized by plants	15,143	30%
0	38,984	gpy	Run-on utilized by plants	38,984	~
0	17,252	gpy	Effective water reuse	17,252	~
0	5,173	gpy	Indoor rainwater use	5,173	~
50,188	126,739	gpy	Alternate water source use	76,551	153%
289,948	206,310	gpy	Total private water	-83,638	-29%
Metered water use					
239,760	59,655	gpy	Total metered water use	-180,105	-75%
109	27	gpdc	Per person metered water use	-82	-75%
63	39	gpdc	Indoor estimate from billing of metered	-25	-39%
44	16	gpdc	Indoor estimate from measurements o	-28	-64%
101,045	44,250	gpy	Outdoor metered water use est. from	-56,795	-56%
Food production				lbs/yr change	
100	2,244	lbs/yr	Produce from site eaten	2,144	2144%
Water commons effects					
-157,182	526,906	gpy	Runoff net absorption (runon-runoff)	684,088	435%
-57,774	566,172	gpy	Groundwater recharge total	623,946	-1080%
-297,534	486,600	gpy	Net community water use (recharge	784,135	-264%
-24%	712%	gpy	Recharge/ metered water ratio	7	-3053%
-97,424	0	gpy	Sewer flow avoided	97,424	-100%
7,500	105,530	gpy	Irrigation saved off site due on site fo	98,030	1307%
Landfill effect					
2,400	9,602	lbs/yr	Plant matter diverted from landfill	7,201	300%
Carbon effects					
-8,310	305	lbs/yr	Reduction in carbon footprint of wa	8,615	-104%
0	16,695	lbs/yr	Carbon offset from on site energy pro	16,695	~